THE MIDDLE EAST

World Political Theories

World Political Theories will change the way we think about non-Western political ideas. Each book in the series looks at a particular political region, and how thinking about politics has developed there. In doing so, the books will ask how universal political theory actually is, and to what extent place makes a difference. Through looking at the historical development of political thinking, and at the ways in which it is being used and changing today, the books provide important context for understanding contemporary politics in Africa, the Middle East, East Asia and Latin America, and introduce new ideas and challenges to conventional political theory.

THE MIDDLE EAST

The politics of the sacred and secular

SHAHROUGH AKHAVI

Zed Books
LONDON & NEW YORK

The Middle East: The Politics of the Sacred and Secular was first published
in 2009 by Zed Books Ltd, 7 Cynthia Street, London N1 9JF, UK
and Room 400, 175 Fifth Avenue, New York, NY 10010, USA

www.zedbooks.co.uk

Copyright © Shahrough Akhavi 2009

Deewani calligraphy on the cover translates as
"Those who teach me have my everlasting respect."

The right of Shahrough Akhavi to be identified as the
author of this work has been asserted by him in accordance
with the Copyright, Designs and Patents Act, 1988

Designed and typeset in Monotype Joanna
by illuminati, Grosmont, www.illuminatibooks.co.uk
Cover design by Lucy Morton @ illuminati
Printed and bound in Great Britain
by CPI Antony Rowe, Chippenham and Eastbourne

Distributed in the USA exclusively by Palgrave Macmillan,
a division of St Martin's Press, LLC, 175 Fifth Avenue, New York, NY 10010

All rights reserved. No part of this publication may be reproduced,
stored in a retrieval system or transmitted in any form or by
any means, electronic, mechanical, photocopying or otherwise,
without the prior permission of Zed Books Ltd.

A catalogue record for this book is available from the British Library
Library of Congress Cataloging in Publication Data available

ISBN 978 1 84277 896 8 hb
ISBN 978 1 84277 897 5 pb

Contents

	Acknowledgments	vii
ONE	Introduction	1
TWO	The sacred and the secular	51
THREE	History and social change	74
FOUR	The individual	119
FIVE	Society	149
SIX	The state	195
SEVEN	Conclusions	234
	Notes	250
	Bibliography	274
	Index	283

For Soraya, Nur Hayati

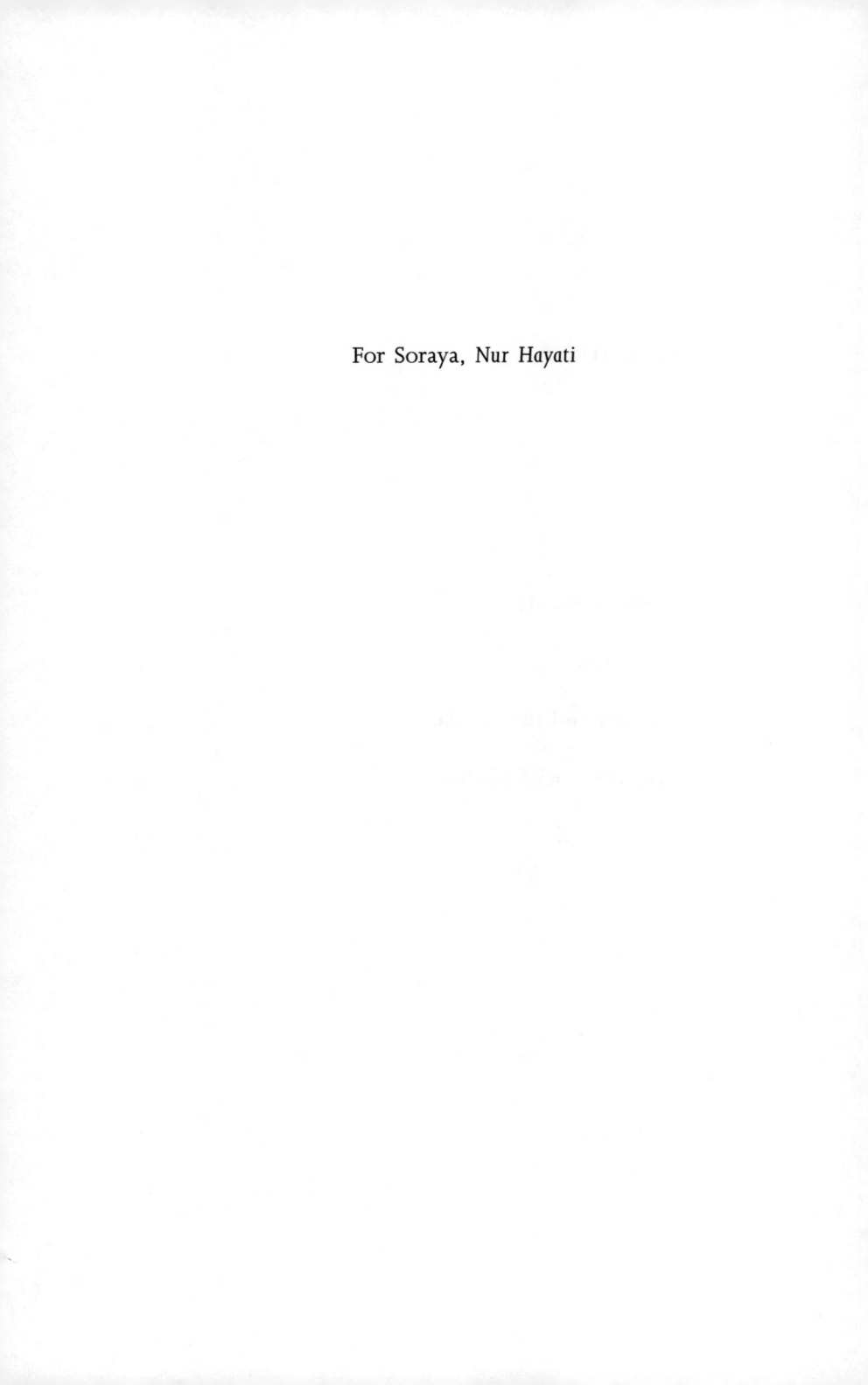

Acknowledgments

I would like to thank the following organizations for their financial support at various points in the last several years as I have worked on different parts of this work: the Ford Foundation, the National Endowment for the Humanities, the American Research Center in Cairo, the Fulbright Senior Scholar Research Program, and the Social Science Research Council.

Some material has appeared earlier in the following outlets, and I thank the publishers for allowing me to draw upon material from those sources. They are as follows: "Shariati's Social Thought," in *Religion and Politics in Iran: From Quietism to Revolution*, ed. Nikki R. Keddie (New Haven: Yale University Press, 1983), pp. 125–44; "Sunni Modernist Theories of Social Contract in Contemporary Egypt," *International Journal of Middle East Studies* 35:1 (February 2003), pp. 23–49; "Shi'i Theories of Social Contract," in *Shari'a: Islamic Law in the Contemporary Context*, ed. Abbas Amanat and Frank Griffel (Stanford: Stanford University Press, 2007), pp. 137–55.

A note on the use of the masculine pronoun: In earlier drafts of this work, I utilized such formulations as "s/he" or "him or her" or "his or her" at those points in the manuscript when the antecedent noun was gender-neutral (as with human being, or individual).

However, I often found that sentence construction became overly complex or convoluted in those sentences containing numerous clauses or phrases for which these qualifying terms had to be utilized. Reluctantly, I have decided to use the masculine pronoun throughout. However, I do so purely as a matter of style and not gender preference.

ONE

Introduction

This book, as part of the World Political Theories series, examines the intellectual debates in contemporary Middle Eastern political theories on such issues as the nature of society, the role of the individual, and the conceptualization of the state. At the same time, it is also my purpose to critique aspects of these theories, in the hope of contributing to the dialogue that their authors deserve in writing them in the first place. This book is not meant to be a sustained engagement with the secondary literature on Middle Eastern political theories.

There is a rich store of such literature, beginning in a sustained manner since the early 1960s. Perhaps among the first publications were Albert Hourani's magisterial *Arabic Thought in the Liberal Age* (1962), Serif Mardin's seminal *The Genesis of Young Ottoman Thought* (1962), and Malcolm Kerr's innovative *Islamic Reform* (1966). Some works have been in the nature of edited volumes, such as Kamal Karpat's *Political and Social Thought in the Contemporary Middle East* (1968, 1982) or Sylvia Haim's more narrowly based collection, *Arab Nationalism: A Compendium* (1962, 1976). Other works have focused on single societies, such as Anouar Abdel-Malek's *Egypt: Military Society* (1968). Yet other efforts have been in the tradition of single-authored works influenced by the literature on modernization and development, either in the form of various essays written at different times, such as Leonard Binder's *The Ideological Revolution in the Middle East* (1964), or a sustained argument presented in the form of a monograph, such as the same author's *Islamic Liberalism: A Critique of Development Ideologies* (1988). Somewhat different from the latter was Hamid Enayat's *Modern Islamic Political Thought* (1982), and Issa J. Boullata's *Trends and Issues in Contemporary Arab Thought* (1990), both written more from the perspective of the history of ideas. Many works have more recently been published with a focus on Arab nationalism, political Islam (Islamism), and democratization and civil society, such as, respectively, Adeed Dawisha's *Arab Nationalism in the Twentieth Century* (2005), Basam Tibi's *The Challenge of Fundamentalism: Political Islam and the New Disorder* (2002), and Michaelle Browers, *Democracy and Civil Society in Arab Political Thought: Transcultural Possibilities* (2006) As a result of all these efforts, the overlap of Middle Eastern studies and social and political theory has become a fascinating and exciting area of research. I hope that the present work will make a small contribution to this steadily growing library of research.

The region is, of course, much too large and the period of time too extensive to do more than provide representative coverage. Entire monographs may be devoted to many of these topics or many of the thinkers that I have chosen to focus upon. I have also had to be selective. Thus, I do not discuss the role of women in contemporary political theory; nor do I assess writings on international relations. It is not that these matters are not important. Clearly, they are. But giving them proper consideration would have made an already lengthy manuscript even longer, and one has finally to make choices of inclusion and exclusion. This does not mean that these choices may not themselves be criticized, but that is another matter.

Reverting to my initial comment that this volume is part of a series entitled World Political Theories, two factors need to be discussed. First, one must conceptualize political theory itself. Second, one needs to identify and define a newly emerging field that scholars call comparative political theory, since this is the field that best can make sense of the subject matter suggested by the general rubric of the series.

What is political theory?

Theory is "a form of systematic knowledge systematically pursued."[1] Political theory, then, is systematic knowledge about politics systematically pursued. Western political theory started with the ancient Greeks. But it has also had a long tradition in non-Western societies. The kinds of questions systematically posed and systematically addressed in the various cultures that have possessed a tradition of political theory have varied with their mutually diverse material and cultural experiences. But just as Socrates (470–399 BC), Plato (428–348 BC), and Aristotle (384–322 BC) are often invoked as pioneers of Western political theory, other civilizations also have had their founding fathers in this realm. Thus political theory in Egypt reverts to the *Maxims* of Ptahhotep (lived c. 2400 BC), in Mesopotamia to the *Code* of Hammurabi (d. c. 1750 BC), in China to the *Analects* of Confucius (d. 479 BC) and the *Mencius* of Mencius (d. 289 BC), in India to the *Arthashastra* of Kautilya (lived c. 300 BC), and in Islam to *al-Ahkam al-Sultaniyya* of al-Mawardi (d. 1058 AD) and the *Siyasatnama* of Nizam al-Mulk (d. 1092 AD).

Politics pertain to the dynamics of cooperation and contention among people seeking to promote their interests in public arenas. Thus, political theory is the study of what human beings think are the key issues of politics and of how people have tried to solve the questions germane to those issues. Political theory is not to be equated with ideology, nationalism, or policy. Instead, it consists of conceptualizations of such values as justice, authority, responsibility, obedience, and freedom and how these values are related to such purposes as well-being, the common good, happiness, and a virtuous life. Ideology, nationalism, and policy all bear on these values and purposes. They provide the context for a society's orientation to public life. Political theory, by contrast, is the study of how these three factors impact the expectations and the conduct of the people who advance such ideologies, nationalist sentiments, and policy preferences.

In his 1969 article, "Political Theory as a Vocation," Sheldon Wolin writes that political theory deals with "'wholes' made up of interrelated and interpenetrating provinces of human activity," and the task of the political theorist is "to locate 'divisions' in the human world and embody them in theoretical form. For example, what aspects of that division which [sic] we call 'religion' have a significant bearing on the activity called 'economic?'"[2] In dealing with these "wholes," political theorists seek to provide explanations, evaluations, and, at times, prescriptions.

Comparative political theory

Middle Eastern political theories have long been influenced by theories about politics that they have encountered from outside the region. In the "era of recording" (*'asr al-tadwin*), as the period of scholarly activity in early Islam has been called, bodies of knowledge from Greek, Persian, and Hindu civilizations were transmitted to, translated and debated by Muslim scholars, who integrated important concepts from those discourses into their own understandings of Islamic theology and law. This trend may also be seen since the French Revolution.

The interactions between autochthonous Middle Eastern political theories and political theories from other regions bring us into the realm of comparative political theory, a fledgling sub-field of political theory that is closely associated with the pronounced trends of globalization in international relations identified especially in the decades of the 1990s and 2000s. In Dallmayr's words, comparative political theory refers to "inquiry which, in a sustained fashion, reflects upon the status and meaning of political life no longer in a restricted geographical setting but in the global arena."[3] It suggests that theory is by its nature comparative, and so its practitioners advocate bridge-building between "comparative politics" and "political theory" as these traditional sub-fields of political science have been historically understood. As Dallmyr puts it, comparative political theory stresses "mutual interrogation, contestation, and engagement" across cultures.[4] In that process, comparative political theorists acknowledge that scholars working within specific civilizational traditions may differ in the degree of emphasis they accord to particular concepts and theoretical frameworks. But they also maintain that the immanent critiques of those frameworks can show that alternative understandings of common concepts can shed light on the strengths and weaknesses of those same frameworks.

Middle Eastern political theories are neither regionally specific nor are they converging with Western political theories. Instead, the emphasis is upon how the modern and post-modern experiences of societies in the contemporary world impact upon the understandings Middle Easterners have about their own politics. Because those experiences have in great measure involved interactions with Western cultural traditions and Western imperialism, Middle Eastern political theorists have long been both deeply influenced and highly critical of Western political theories and political practices. At the same time, the historical heritage of Middle Eastern culture provides a storehouse of concepts and contingencies upon which Middle Easterners have drawn in the effort to construe the contemporary world.

Middle Eastern political theories

It is advisable to utilize the plural, "theories," since no monolithic body of knowledge exists that one can apply to politics of the entire region over different historical periods. This would be true even were one to discuss narrower periods since the French Revolution, World War II, or the period since the collapse of the Communist political systems in 1989–91.

Moreover, as already mentioned, these theories are not *sui generis*. Critical dimensions of a theory or theories include (1) the sorts of questions that they pose, (2) the analytical processes involved in trying to answer those questions, and (3) the responses generated by those processes. Considered in this light, many questions that seem relevant for Middle Eastern political theories are also relevant for the political theories of other world regions. To select just one, what forms of rule and representation of interests are best suited to achieve the maximum benefit for the people as a whole?

Furthermore, analytical approaches seem equally available to Middle Easterners as to non-Middle Easterners, whether these be hermeneutical (i.e. interpretative) or positivistic methods, whether one applies class analysis (focusing on the impact on politics of social stratification) or elite analysis (emphasizing the role of the circulation of power brokers on the political system). Finally, the answers given to particular questions, employing particular methods of analysis, can be as relevant to Middle Eastern political theories as to non-Middle Eastern political theories. After all, the answers to questions about the best form of rule and model of representation of interests could be secular republican, authoritarian, liberal pluralist, Marxist, corporatist, or some combination of several of these.

Returning to the question of what is particularly Middle Eastern about Middle Eastern political theories, the only logical reply is that these theories relate to such generic building blocks of political theory as justice, equality, freedom, reason, obligation, representation, and the like, as these are relevant for people living in the Middle East region. One can establish frameworks for an understanding of how these concepts "play out" for Middle Easterners from either a religious or a non-religious perspective.

But things are not so simple as that. For one thing, the very notion of a religious perspective is itself divisible into at least two dimensions: (1) a doctrinally religious perspective; (2) a culturally religious perspective. Moreover, secular orientations could be deistic, meaning that they could leave some scope for transcendental factors. On this argument, God created the universe but, having done so, did not thereafter interfere in its workings, including decisions made by people bearing on social, cultural, political or economic matters.

Additionally, it is difficult to separate religion from the secular. The first amendment of the American Constitution bars Congress from enacting laws regarding "an establishment of religion or prohibiting the free exercise thereof," but it does not restrict Congress from passing laws that authorize public expenditures on parochial schools, whose purposes include transmitting values on behalf of the religion with which they are associated.

The sociology-of-knowledge approach

Whether through engagement with the outside world or with Middle Eastern thought and experiences, Middle Eastern political theories have emerged as a result of the actual realities through which Middle Easterners themselves have passed. In other words, those theories do not take shape in some "natural" way, full-blown from the head of Zeus. Consequently, the best approach for the understanding of Middle Eastern political theories is that of the sociology of knowledge, an orientation that stresses the social sources and social consequences of contemporary Middle Eastern political theories. It is also an approach that interests itself in turn with how knowledge, once produced, is utilized by individuals and groups to shape social processes, organizations and movements.

This approach emerged in the nineteenth century as a way of suggesting that the pursuit of objective truths will likely be fruitless, because all knowledge is socially generated. That being the case, purely scientific truth was unattainable. The approach originated mainly under the influence of Marxism, and particularly the concept that one's beliefs and actions need to be understood in terms of the actor's class position, or educational and social background, or political affiliations and interests. In the twentieth century, refinements to the arguments were made, particularly by those who felt that it was too simplistic to maintain that beliefs and actions based on those beliefs were essentially determined by monocausal variables such as class affiliation.

In the late twentieth and early twenty-first centuries, political theorists such as Hans-Georg Gadamer and Charles Taylor have refined such ideas by emphasizing that our moral preferences and judgments are a product of the interaction of ideas and material conditions that, as it were, we process through frames of language and cultural interpretation. Such thinkers often cast their thought within a critique of atomistic liberalism (or libertarianism). They do hold on to the assumptions of earlier sociology of knowledge writing that human actions are bounded by the roles that they occupy, that there is no telos driving human behavior, that history is the product of international and unintentional behavior of human beings located in concrete temporal and spatial circumstances, and that it does not unfold in some disembodied way, abstracted from the actual people who alone make it. These later writings, in short, refine certain earlier assumptions that seemed to be causally overdeterministic about the impact of background factors on behavior but continue to emphasize the social construction of knowledge and reality.

If we apply some sociology-of-knowledge assumptions to Middle East or Islamic history, therefore, it is difficult to conceive that Shi'ism could have emerged apart from the historical legacy and role of the South Arabian (as opposed to Central and Northern Arabian) tribes at the time of the rise of Islam. We know that for the former leadership ought to be vested in charismatic leaders. As these tribes embraced the new religion of Islam, they could not be unmindful of their own traditions. Accordingly, Shi'ism, which stresses the rule of imams who are direct descendents of the Prophet's family through his daughter Fatima, became a doctrine and set of practices that were particularly associated with these South Arabian tribes. As Weber might say, such tribes had an "elective affinity" for a form of rule that stresses the charisma of the leader of the household, whose authority would be passed to the next in the dynastic line. It took a century or so after the Prophet's death in 632 AD before the major principles of Shi'ism became crystallized, but the basics were in embryo already at the time of the succession crisis faced by the members of the Islamic community upon their Prophet's departure.[5]

By contrast, the Central and Northern Arabian tribes lacked a monarchical tradition. For them, leaders were "first among equals," rather than privileged and entitled rulers. Instead of conceiving of leadership along dynastic lines, their historical experiences had taught them that leaders should be identified through consensus. In this way, the choice of leader would occur by taking into account the person best able to lead the community under the then prevailing circumstances.

In both cases, social and historical conditions shaped the political theories of Shi'i and Sunni Islam. At the same time, those theories also had important impacts on the relations and institutions of the Muslims in that and later periods. At its best, the tradition of the sociology of knowledge recognizes the importance of historical factors upon ideas but also the significance of ideas for the evolution of historical trends. In the earlier example of Shi'ism, the sixth Imam, Ja'far al-Sadiq (d. 765), maintained that it was acceptable, even mandatory, for Shi'a to disguise the fact of their faith (a doctrine termed *taqiya*) because to reveal that information would have subjected them to harm. This encouraged believers to quietism rather than social protest, a perspective that prevailed until the 1960s, when Ayatollah Ruhollah Khomeini (d. 1989) and Dr. 'Ali Shari'ati (d. 1977) began to stress that the time had come, because of changed historical circumstances, to abandon the doctrine of *taqiya*. Instead, people should openly proclaim their fidelity to Shi'ism, which would hasten the return of the Hidden Imam. This shift in doctrinal perspective, itself tied to changed historical circumstances (namely, that Shi'ites were no longer a vulnerable community under threat of extinction), led to dramatic oppositional activity that eventually became the Iranian revolution of 1978–79. Ideas had become powerful stimuli for drastic action to alter the existing power arrangements in Iran and, possibly, beyond.

As will be seen, the dialectical interplay between social realities and ideas is helpful in understanding why Middle Eastern political theories have taken the forms they have over the many centuries since the early Islamic period. The history of the region, if seen through the prism of Islamic civilization, is one of contention but also non-contentious interaction between two identifiable perspectives. Lapidus has called these perspectives, respectively, the "courtly cosmopolitan" version and the "urban religious" version.[6]

The courtly cosmopolitan perspective arose as a consequence of the evolution away from Arab tribalism and limited kingship in the earlier years of Islam into an imperial realm with the symbols, narratives, and discourses appropriate to such a system. Its characteristic features were court ceremony and etiquette, art, architecture, literature, philosophy, poetry, and statecraft. By contrast, the urban religious perspective evolved within its own sphere (not entirely disconnected, of course, from the courtly cosmopolitan perspective). Here, the key is the rise of the clergy due to the need of urban populations for guidance on religious matters. These matters, in turn, were channeled through the clergy's institutions, including their seminaries. Varying interpretations of scripture by various schools of jurisprudence arose to a large extent out of the rivalries and competition among religious social forces contending for influence. Coordinate with this was the rise of sects and religious brotherhoods. All of these developments could be explained in large measure by the need of urban populations for popular religious guides who could explain to rank-and-file Muslims what Islam law and theology were all about and required of them as believers.

The way individuals thought about political issues from either of these two perspectives was greatly influenced by the actual historical circumstances of the times in which they lived. Simultaneously, however, conceptualizing politics could not but shape the actions of the social groups animated by those ideas, actions that in turn affected the course of the historical evolution of Middle Eastern societies.

The purpose of the remainder of this chapter is to provide a summary of historical developments in the Middle East since the rise of Islam[7] and also to introduce the central concepts of Middle Eastern political theories, as expressed by classical, medieval, early modern, and modern writers.[8] I will classify these developments since the rise of Islam under the following broad categories: (1) the classical period, 610–750; (2) the medieval period, 750–1450; (3) the early modern period, 1450–1800; (4) the modern period, 1800 to the present.

Although there is no agreement on the origins and endpoints of the classical, medieval or other historical eras identified above, these terms do appear to have a general meaning that is accepted by most analysts. In the historical summary below, I will only endeavor to highlight the major developments. Readers who seek greater detail and elaboration are encouraged to consult works by scholars such as Marshall Hodgson and Ira Lapidus.[9]

The classical period, 610–750

Max Weber's study of world religions underscored the importance of societies that were experiencing great pressures as a result of internal and external developments. Under such circumstances, religious leaders may emerge whose stated purpose is to bring a new transcendental message, their actions also offering the society an opportunity for new directions. He additionally argued that such leaders arise at times of existential crises, and he analyzed their conduct in the context of charismatic situations in which the community's rituals of existence are breaking down, causing its members to seek salvation from such danger. The rise of Islam has been explained variously by scholars. Broadly, though, there are four key trends in these explanations. First, some attribute importance to the person of the Prophet, Muhammad (570–632).[10] Second, others have emphasized people's increasing dissatisfaction with paganism, yet their sense that Judaism and Christianity had also fallen short. Third, others underline a growing unhappiness over the erosion of egalitarian values by a growing pride of wealth on the part of the wealthy.[11] Finally, some maintain that Islam was a later product of an earlier effort led by Muhammad to fuse Arab norms of valor and Jewish ethical values to defeat and recover the holy land from the Byzantine Empire.[12] My own understanding incorporates aspects of the second and third arguments, but this debate will not likely be resolved for a long time to come.

Muhammad is said to have begun receiving revelations in the year 610. Islam as a political phenomenon, however, is associated with the period following Muhammad's flight from persecution in 622 from his native town of Mecca to Medina. In fact, that city's leaders had already been urging him to come to resolve local disputes. Medina thus became the critical base of his activities on behalf of spreading the faith. During this period, 622–632, certain embryonic social, political, and economic institutions of the new community were established there. The purpose of this proto-state was to make it possible for the members of the Islamic community to obey God's commands and thus to prosper in accordance with God's design for human beings receiving His word.

The social structure of rural and urban Arabia at this time was tribally based. Hence, the proto-state that arose in Medina was very different from the modern nation state. Crone notes that the Medinan state did not conform to the modern concept of state, which entails sovereign governmental institutions with jurisdiction over an extent of territory. The new political community did, however, possess features we could associate with an embryonic state, such as an executive that executes policies, a mechanism for arbitrating disputes, and the wherewithal for extracting resources and conducting offensive and defensive operations in war. Yet its offices were associated with incumbent rulers rather than depersonalized institutions and processes endowed with their own rules and operating procedures.[13]

The rudimentary political institutions established in the Prophet's lifetime and in the period of his early successors – collectively known as the "Rightly Guided Caliphs" (632–661) – were meant to meet the limited requirements of tribal Arabia. Interestingly, they were also somewhat influenced by trends in the neighboring Persian and Byzantine Empires. Among such institutions were the tribal armed forces, the treasury, the organization of tax collection, and the mechanisms for the administration of justice.

Gibb suggests that a crisis beset the young Islamic community with the onset of the rule of the Umayyad Caliph Hisham ibn 'Abd al-Malik (ruled 724–743), a crisis centered on the operation of the political institutions in the context of a greatly expanded realm. His rule represented the period when "the political organization of Islam was confronted with the problem which every expanding organism must meet when it reaches the limits of its expansion."[14] He maintains that the political system established upon the Prophet's death "was essentially a military organization for the purposes of expansion and enjoyment of the fruits of conquest ... with no administrative organs for other purposes."[15] This seems somewhat exaggerated, since if it indeed were true, how would one account for the ability of the caliphate – the institution of rule established by the Prophet's successors – to sustain its economic functions? But Gibb's focus on the failure to institutionalize state offices in organizations structured by impersonal rules is crucial.

At any rate, by the time of Hisham, the recalcitrance of the Muslim community's tribal forces mandated their integration into something resembling a rationalized chain of command. But this did not happen. The motivations of the rebels in the eastern realms of the caliphate who brought an end to the Umayyad caliphate in the mid-eighth century included anger over the personalized rule of the Umayyads, which was biased in favor of Arab Muslims as against the non-Arabs. An opportunity seemed at hand to solve the problem of institutionalizing rule to prevent such personalism in the future, but the caliphs of the new 'Abbasid house (749/50–1258) continued the old model of personalized leadership.

Meanwhile, the idealized model of community, including its politics, was rapidly receding into the past, and it was proving increasingly difficult to recapture it. That model stressed the overarching role of Islamic values as the integral means by which the Prophet and his earliest successors unified the community. By the time the caliphate reached its apogee (in the mid-ninth century) the model had mutated into what Lapidus calls "the imperial Islamic society." The characteristics of this new model were as follows:

> Tribal armies were displaced by newly recruited client forces who were expected to be more dependent upon, loyal to, and obedient to their rulers; and tribal chiefs were replaced by administrative cadres drawn from the conquered populations ... the caliphate was transformed from the charismatic succession to the religious authority of the Prophet into an imperial institution and a regime governed not by religious norms but by the laws of political survival. As the caliphate took an increasingly secularized political identity, the religious heritage of the Prophet came to be embodied in his companions and their disciples and successors, scholars, and holy men. Eventually, the caliphs retained only a nominal role as the official representatives of Islam and the official fount of state and religious authority, while the Muslim populace came to be organized into schools of law, theological sects, Shi'ite communities, Sufi lineages, and brotherhoods representing the legacy of the Prophet.[16]

In making this distinction between the earlier idealized model of the community and "the imperial Islamic society," Lapidus suggests that religion became separated from politics early on. This is worth stressing, in view of the inveterate insistence by many Muslim writers that religion and politics are integrated, and that Islam is simultaneously "religion and state" (din wa dawla) or "religion and secular worldly affairs" (din wa dunya). While one might theoretically argue this integration of religion and politics (though not without challenge), one could not make a convincing empirical case for it.

The theoretical argument would be as follows. Islam's doctrine of salvation requires the creation of the community of believers, the *umma*, membership of which is mandatory. Although individual Muslims may err in their efforts to follow God's commands, the *umma* – as the Prophet himself is said to have professed – "shall never agree upon error." The community, once created, cannot be left to its own devices. Its members must work on its behalf to promote and defend its interests. Yet, this cannot be done in a vacuum and always involves politics, economics, and social organizations and processes. The community's interests include not simply the ethical behavior of its members, but the means by which the collectivity can prosper. This requires mechanisms that, for example, permit the raising of taxes, the allocation of resources, the elaboration of public policies, the arbitration of disputes, the mobilization of assets to guard against external attack, and the like. The *umma* could not survive if its members did not organize themselves in ways to facilitate these activities. In a word, they had to establish government. So politics is intimately bound up with the religious injunctions.

This theoretical argument may be challenged as follows. It may be true that the doctrine of salvation requires political, economic and social organization and activity in order to promote and defend the interests of the community, but that does not mean that one is bound to the model of rule identified with the time of the Prophet and of the Rightly Guided Caliphs (i.e. 622–661). In fact, the Prophet himself enjoined the Muslims to establish their own patterns of worldly affairs (including government) in the famous "date palms Hadith."[17] In that tradition, the Prophet's reluctantly provided advice on how to improve the yield of date palm trees actually led to the opposite. His reaction to the people was: "As for matters of religion, come to me; but as for matters of your world, you know better about it than I do." The lesson of the Hadith is that each generation of Muslims is free to establish its model of political, economic, and social system as they best see fit in the context of the actual circumstances in which they are living. Moreover, those advocating separation of religion and politics reject their rivals' argument that since Muhammad had been both Prophet and statesman, this proves their integration. They admit that he had served in both capacities, but they insist that Muslims chose him as a statesman insofar as they considered him to be the best qualified to rule, not insofar as he was the Prophet of Islam. In short, they did not choose him to lead by virtue of his religious office, *ex officio*, but by virtue of their consideration of him as best qualified to be the political leader.

Empirically, there is even less support for the notion of the integration of religion and politics in Islam. The reality of Islamic history abundantly shows that politics has long been a matter of realpolitik, according to which the ideals of Islamic virtue, morality, and piety had been superseded by practical calculation and the interests of state, party, and faction. The state, as represented by the caliph himself – in later centuries, the *sultan*, the *malik* (king) and the *shah* (king, emperor) – and his administrative and military staffs, became a separate arena of rule and patronage. Society, on the other hand, composed of religious groups, guilds, brotherhoods, clans, and lineages, remained apart. The state left to these groups considerable latitude and autonomy to conduct their own affairs, while, for their part, the groups extended legitimacy (often reluctantly) to the secular rulers.

Of course, this did not mean that the state refused to patronize Islamic thought and practices. On the contrary, such states were

> officially committed to the defense and patronage of Muslim worship, education, law and *jihad* [literally, exertion for the sake of the faith], but they [i.e., the states] were not inherently Islamic institutions... By the cultivation of local languages, poetic traditions, architectural motifs, musical themes, and cultic practices, Middle Eastern states ... identified themselves as cosmopolitan, imperial, and patrimonial regimes.[18]

Historical developments in the medieval period, 750–1258

The Umayyad dynasty fell because of (1) growing dissatisfaction with its pro-Arab favoritism, which generated a great deal of opposition, particularly in the eastern territories;[19] (2) destabilizing dynastic conflicts; (3) the costs of the leaders' military campaigns, especially those of the caliph Hisham. Military campaigns in earlier times (such as the conquests of Egypt, Syria and Iran in the era of the Rightly Guided Caliphs) had largely been financed with assets seized by the armies in the course of fighting. But the later wars, fought simultaneously on several fronts, led to disastrous defeats and to the diffusion of the Syrian forces that were the backbone of the Umayyad military over large swathes of territory.[20]

The 'Abbasids altered their predecessors' secular limited kingship to a broader model of universal empire after the fashion of Alexander the Great (d. 323 BC). They did, however, continue the secularizing trends. Concomitantly, the identity of the umma came to be defined pluralistically, rather than giving primacy to the ethnic Arabs. Jurists and the propagandists of the new order stressed a paradigm of patrimonial imperium. Whereas the Umayyad leaders had not refrained from claiming monarchical privileges and legitimation, the 'Abbasids went much further to embellish their powers with the emblems of a vast and complex imperial order.

This change also was reflected in the nature and scope of the institutions underpinning 'Abbasid rule, marking a dramatic shift from the far simpler political system of the Umayyads. That system essentially had depended upon garrisoned tribal warriors, an elemental taxation system, and an inchoate system for the administration of justice. Taking the place of these underdeveloped institutional forms stood a system of "typical staff arrangements" – to quote Guenther Roth[21] – that are endemic to patrimonial systems. The ruler mediates these staff arrangements through a clientage system in which officials receive patronage in exchange for service. Failure in these duties may lead to the reappropriation of their offices and their reassignment to other subordinates. As rule extends over progressively wider areas, the leader has to rely in his appointments upon individuals from outside his family. The state's growing size and complexity can be seen in the growth of new institutions, such as the exchequer (*bayt al-mal*), ministerial system (*wizara*), the land tax bureau (*diwan al-kharaj*) and numerous judicial bodies, including the tribunals authorized to hear complaints against derelict officials (*diwan al-mazalim*). The following passage captures the essence of leadership and the state in the mature 'Abbasid state:

> From an Arab super-shaykh governing by the intermittent consent of the Arab aristocracy, the caliph became an autocrat, claiming a divine origin for his authority, resting it on his armed forces, and exercising it through a vast and growing bureaucratic organisation.[22]

As we have seen, the state operated as a separate institution from the Islamic order, even though its *raison d'être* was to uphold that order. Reasons of state trumped religious considerations. In other words, the state – the caliphate – took initiatives or responded to constraints not on the basis of Islamic norms and values but on grounds of expediency. It was "transformed from the charismatic succession to the religious authority of the Prophet into an imperial institution and a regime governed not by religious norms but by the laws of political survival."[23]

Because of the increasing secularization of the state, it is to societal groups that one must look to locate the articulation and defense of Islamic norms and values. Among such groups were the professional men of religion, the leaders of the schools of law, Sufi mystics, and community leaders of neighborhood associations. In general these elements did not play official roles in the state administration. They did not see it as their business to oppose the state, except in the most extreme cases of dereliction.[24] The government viewed their role positively and encouraged followers to provide the regime with at least passive support as long as the rulers implemented "what God has allowed" and banned "what God has prohibited." These groups played a critical role in providing and implementing the regime's "political formula," in Mosca's terms, that was needed for community integration.

In the second half of the 'Abbasid era (roughly coinciding with the seizure of power in Baghdad by the Buyid [Buwayhid] amirs in 945 until the collapse of the caliphate at the hands of the Mongols in 1258) the caliphate entered into a long period of decline. Though the Buyids were themselves Shi'a of Iranian provenance, they prudently did not depose the Sunni caliph nor seek to make Shi'ism the official religion, a step that would have generated profound resistance. Buyid rule lasted for approximately a century. With their departure from the scene, another group, this time Sunni in persuasion, came to the fore: the Saljuqs. Saljuq leaders were from a prominent military family of Turkomen who had entered the Middle East proper from Central Asia and converted to Sunni Islam. Their peak period of rule over the Fertile Crescent, Palestine, and Iran was that of Alp Arslan (1063–72) and Malik Shah (1072–92). Another powerful Turkic dynasty was the Ghaznavids (977–1186), whose sway extended over Khurasan, Afghanistan, and northern India.

The Buyids, Saljuqids, and Ghaznavids represented the most prominent – though not the only – groups that challenged the rule of the 'Abbasid house. By this time, the stature of the 'Abbasid caliphs had been eroded by repeated seizures of power at the hands of these warlords, whose ranks also included the Saffarids (866–900), Samanids (819–999), Hamdanids (905–1004), and Fatimids (909–1171). These military coups came to be known as "the amirate by seizure," in contrast to the legitimate form of "amirate by investiture." Because the caliphs were too weak to oppose such seizures of power, they were advised to make a virtue out of necessity by accepting and retroactively sanctioning them, on the grounds that system stability was more important then preserving the integrity of the caliph's theoretical authority.

Intellectual developments in historical context: the jurists, political philosophers, and theologians of Islam

In the face of the growing discrepancy between Islamic norms and actual developments, jurists such as al-Baqillani (d. 1013), al-Baghdadi (d. 1037), al-Mawardi (d. 1058), al-Ghazali (d. 1111), ibn Taymiyya (d. 1328), and ibn Jama'a (d. 1333) saw it necessary to develop a theory of the caliphate. These were not works in political theory in the usual sense of that phrase. They did not address key questions such as the causes and consequences of *coups d'état* by tribal leaders; nor the mechanisms of governmental decision-making; nor the relationship between groups in civil society and the state. There were some exceptions to this, such as the writings of the North African jurist ibn Khaldun (d. 1406). But, for the most part, Muslim constitutional theory concentrated upon idealistic descriptive discussions regarding the moral attributes of would-be caliphs, qualifications for office, a detailing of their functions, and summary statements concerning how the caliphate was supposed to operate according to the divine plan.

However, alongside the idealistic strain in the writing of these jurists may be seen their pragmatic coming to terms with the realities of power politics on the ground. By the time of the later constitutional theorists, such as al-Ghazali and ibn Jama'a, these writers basically held that the duly constituted authority of the caliph lay in the hands of that leader who effectively held the power of rulership. Such a position dramatically differs from the earlier insistence that the caliph have the full range of moral virtues possessed by the "Rightly Guided" initial four successors of the Prophet.

Philosophers, dissatisfied with the Sunni jurists' approach to politics, assumed the task of raising questions that the jurists were loath to pose. These philosophers were strongly influenced by the ancient Greek authors, including Plato (d. 347 BC), the neo-Platonists, Aristotle (d. 322 BC), and Galen (d. 216). Exactly why these scholars turned away from jurisprudence or theology to political philosophy at the time that they did, beginning with al-Kindi (d. 873), is a matter of some conjecture. But a critical factor was the translation movement that was already in process, under the aegis of the 'Abbasid caliphs. Al-Kindi himself showed how important these writers considered Greek philosophy to have been when he wrote:

> We must not be ashamed to admire the truth or to acquire it, from wherever it comes. Even if it should come from far-flung nations and foreign peoples, there is for the student of truth nothing more important than the truth, nor is the truth demeaned or diminished by the one who states or conveys it; no one is demeaned by the truth, rather all are ennobled by it.[25]

Philosophical tendencies proved stronger among the sects, and especially Shi'ism, since the mainstream Sunni tradition vigorously opposed anthropocentric analysis and critiqued methods of inquiry that, to the Sunni jurists, seemed to reject dogma. By contrast, sectarian movements in Islam proved more hospitable to Gnostic currents of thought, which emphasized redemptive knowledge of God and attaining knowledge of the human being's origins and destiny.

Ironically, however, the philosophers ultimately refrained from empirical analysis of the political system(s) of Islam. Instead, their writings contain a strongly utopian bent. They introduced expressions such as *siyasa madaniya* to betoken civic polity or political regime. They focused on how a city ought to be administered, as contrasted to how it actually is governed. However, it is nevertheless the case that the philosophers, through the use of reason, deduced propositions relating to the governance of the city independently of the holy law, something that the jurists would never do. The "Virtuous City" (*al-madina al-fadila*) of philosophers such as al-Farabi (d. 950) and ibn Rushd (d. 1198) provided guidance about how the human being might attain terrestrial happiness, but also laid the basis for the individual's place in the afterlife.

We have seen how the jurists and the philosophers construed their subject matters largely in response to historical contingencies. The jurists responded to power politics. The philosophers reacted to the growing tendency, encouraged by the 'Abbasid caliphs, to translate the great works of Greek (and also Indian and Persian) philosophy into Arabic. Yet this tendency was not a purely intellectual exercise; no doubt it was in response to these rulers' search for solutions to the pressing problems of statecraft, government, and politics.

Now, another group of thinkers, the specialists in Islamic theology, also had contributed their share to the intellectual trends in the Middle East in the Umayyad and 'Abbasid periods. We can again ask what had led these theologians to turn to their specialized subject matter, namely the characteristics, qualities, and attributes of God. As with the jurists and the philosophers, the theologians launched their enterprise in great measure in response to historical developments that were taking place on the ground.

The major movements of Muslim theology, chronologically, include the Khawarij, the Murji'a, the Qadariyya, the Mu'tazila, the Ash'ariyya, and the Maturidiyya. The Khawarij were the earliest of these movements. They originally supported the claim to the caliphate advanced by the adherents of the Prophet's cousin and son-in-law, 'Ali ibn Abi Talib (d. 661), not because of his being the Prophet's cousin and son-in-law but because they believed he was the most pious candidate. However, when 'Ali agreed to arbitration over a challenge to his title, they rebelled against him and killed him for putting his divinely ordained appointment into question. Their theological position held that the only thing that mattered was the faith of the believer and his righteous behavior. As long as these were "true," nothing else mattered. However, if they believed that a Muslim was not a true believer, they advocated killing him, since unbelief was a manifest affront to God, as they saw it. Although the Khawarij played a minor role in the development of Islamic theology, contemporary violence-prone advocates of the immediate application of religious law (*shari'a*) in all public and private arenas of life are labeled modern-day Khawarij by state officials. The Grand Mufti of Egypt so termed the assassins of Egyptian President Anwar Sadat in 1981, for example.

The Murji'a (literally, those who postpone) arose in reaction to the Khawarij, but belatedly so, some generations later. The founders of the Murji'a included a certain Hasan, son of Muhammad ibn-Hanafiyya (d. 700). Hasan adopted this creed following his father's somewhat reluctant rebellion against the Umayyad caliphate in the period 685–687. Hasan's father was himself a son of the fourth caliph, 'Ali, by a wife other than Fatima. Hasan, by contrast, adopted a conciliatory position in the aftermath of this second 'Alid revolt (the first being that of Muhammad al-Hanafiyya's famous step-brother, Husayn b. 'Ali in 680). This recapitulation of events once again shows that social movements are the progenitors of ideas, which do not suddenly emerge out of thin air.

At any rate, the Murji'a believed in postponing judgment on whether a believer who committed a major sin was a Muslim or not, implying that the matter was up to God. They downplayed themes of God's wrath and punishment in favor of emphasizing His mercy and promises of reward. Because of their willingness to suspend judgment regarding the culpability of putative sinners, they concluded that Muslims ought to obey their rulers, even if they disagreed with them. In their view, belief (in Islam) was based on inner faith more than the acts of the believer. If the individual's intent was considered to be true to Islam, then one ought not to contend against him, and this included rulers. Such ideas, of course, rendered service, no matter how inadvertently, to the actual rulers of the time.

The Qadariyya, established by Ma'bad al-Juhani (d. 699) and Marwan al-Dimashqi al-Qubti (d. 730), took a different tack. Their name referred to the capacity (*qudra*) of the individual to act, which in turn entrained his responsibility for actions undertaken. The issue of human choice and responsibility in the context of God's omnipotence could hardly be avoided in theological discussions that were increasingly occurring at that time between Muslims and the Christians. For the Qadariyya, if the human being was not the effective agent of his actions, then God's punishment for wrongful acts or rewards for righteous ones would be meaningless. In short, the human being has the freedom to choose his actions and is aware of this trait. Once God bestows this ability upon someone, He has no responsibility for that individual's choices. Note that the original source for the human being's power to act is God, whereas the responsibility for the action is the human being's.

The practical effect of this position is that the caliphs, being human, were responsible for their actions, which, as we have seen, amounted to the growing secularization of rule. If one believed that such secularization amounted to wrongdoing, then one could contest the authority of these leaders. The implications of the Qadariyya position, in other words, were grave for the legitimacy of the rulers of the Muslim community. It is therefore not surprising that some Qadari thinkers were executed. According to Van Ess, the Qadariyya arose as a political movement in Syria that stressed the accountability of rulers, and in Basra, where emphasis was placed on avoiding the ascription of evil to God.[26]

For its part, the theology of the Mu'tazila has been considered the rationalist Muslim theology par excellence. The founders of this school included Wasil ibn 'Ata' (d. 748), 'Amr b. 'Ubayd (d. 761) and Abu al-Hudhayl al-'Allaf (d. 849/50). The reasons for the rise of the Mu'tazila are not clear. They do not appear to have emerged as a political protest movement. Moreover, considerable variation characterized their thought. However, irrespective of divergences, they generally held that one can convincingly demonstrate the existence of God only through rational means, for otherwise the mere assertion of it invites questioning and doubt. They did not see anything remarkable in this requirement, since they believed it could be readily met. Reason requires one to believe that effects have causes. The cause of the creation of the cosmos must be some primary force. For if it were due to a series of parallel causes, then which among those was the initiator of all the rest?

The Mu'tazila cleaved to the doctrine of God's absolute unity. While acknowledging His omnipotence, they emphasized His justice.

On the issue of whether a grave sinner is nevertheless a Muslim, the members of this movement "stood apart" or "isolated themselves." In this, their position resembled that of the Murji'a, who believed it best to postpone judgment. They also uncompromisingly refused to anthropomorphize God, considering Him to be a unique essence. The Qur'an's attribution of characteristics such as sight and speech to God they interpreted as simply aspects of His essence. They considered the Qur'an itself as created in historical space and time, and not something eternal and timeless, a view that provoked the hostility of other groups, who believed that this questioned God's omnipotence. They held that the human being is fully responsible for the choices he makes, based on his possession of free will and reason, this latter quality permitting him to distinguish between good and evil.

It was in reaction to these Mu'tazili doctrines that Abu Hasan al-Ash'ari (d. 935), who himself originally had belonged to this movement, broke with them. He insisted that God had eternal attributes, such as speech, sight, and hearing, in contrast to the Mu'tazila's imputation of these traits to His essence. He did not abandon rationalism, but he believed that the Mu'tazili tendency took it too far. In the view of the Ash'ariyya, the structure of the cosmos consisted of entelechies or monads "in the process of being or becoming." True to this vision, such monads were independent of one another, except in their relationship to the Supreme Being. In this system, no arrangement of cause and effect existed, as the monads themselves were constantly in transition into being and into non-being. The basis for such a world-view among the Ash'ariyya is that this is the only way one can make sense of God's power. Only by holding that things are in a continuous state of flux from being to non-being and back again to being can one maintain God's supervention over all developments. Causation in the normal sense cannot exist, because that would place limits on God. Human action is "acquired" from God at the instant before the individual acts. This seems to suggest that God is responsible for the choices that human beings make. However, a doctrine of secondary causality was evolved, whereby God is the source of all human acts, but the individual nevertheless acts through intentions that are presumably based on non-rational factors, such as feelings or instincts.

These considerations also apply to natural phenomena. For example, if volcanic activity occurs, this is not the result of geological laws involving the movement of the earth's tectonic plates. Instead, it occurs because God wills it to occur at that instant and to stop at a different instant. God's willingness to bring things about and to nullify them could only be defended through this kind of occasionalistic ontology.

The world, then, comprised a series of episodes or occasions that are infinitely unstable and result from God's will. The good and the evil that happen in the world, in this highly constricted setting, are things that only God, not human beings, can comprehend. The Qur'an, too, comes into being in this sense. To argue, as the Mu'tazila do, that the Qur'an is created is to place limits on God. In fact, the doctrine of the created/uncreated Qur'an became the subject of the famous trial and tribulation of jurists in the caliphate of al-Ma'mun (d. 833), who made Mu'tazilism the official doctrine of the caliphate, against the Ash'ari position. But after a brief interregnum of Mu'tazili ascendancy, Ash'arism replaced it in the caliphate of al-Mutawakkil (d. 861). This action did not immediately settle the issue, as it took several generations afterwards for Ash'ari occasionalism to become the dominant theological position in Sunni Islam, the position it holds today.[27]

The last theological school to be summarized here is the Maturidiyya, established by Abu Mansur Muhammad al-Maturidi (d. 944). This school is second only to the Ash'ariyya in importance in Sunni Islam. Al-Maturidi argued against Mu'tazili and Ash'ari positions, but he also developed his doctrines in disputations with Jews, Christians, Zoroastrians, and Manichaeans. In his perspective, God's interest in human beings stresses justice, a major theme of the Qur'an. The Maturidiyya believed God endows human beings with an understanding of propriety and morality, a fund of intellect, and self-awareness, which allows the individual the freedom to choose between options. The believer should use his reason and knowledge in order to gain as much understanding of God as possible. The heavenly design in sending Prophets is motivated by the desire to provide guidance, but whether or not human beings accept the advice of these messengers is an open question. Unlike the Ash'ari notion that people "acquire" their action from God at the instant before they act, the Maturidiyya held that individuals act out of their own intent. God's role, in this context, is to materialize these actions. In other words, if God did not exist, the actions would not take place. Since He exists, they happen. But at the same time, the individual is the intender of his actions. It is not as though God or the Prophets are responsible for them. In this manner, the Maturidiyya hold the human being to account for his choices and actions. They believe God is the force that materializes these actions, and yet they absolve God from the evil consequences of misdeeds by errant individuals.

The alignment of the two dominant Sunni theological schools, the Ash'ariyya and the Maturidiyya, with the juristic schools of al-Shafi'i (d. 820) and Abu Hanifa (d. 767), respectively, provides insight into the continuing influence of conservative thought in Middle Eastern political theory in regard to human freedom and choice. Both the Ash'ari and Maturidi ontology and epistemology are conservative, but the Maturidi school is more liberal in that it gives greater scope to the individual as the agent of his actions. But even the Maturidi perspective is hesitant on this issue, lest the matter devolve into an anthropocentric view in which the conception of God is deistic. Deism is certainly not the Maturidi view. The Maturidiyya maintained, as we have seen, that the intention of the believer is critical in the outcome of his action. On this view, God will permit errant behavior by an individual whom He knows in advance *intends* to engage in wrongful behavior; or will permit righteous behavior by an individual whom He knows in advance *intends* to engage in upright conduct. Individual action, then, is not, as with the Mu'tazila, the result of unrestricted freedom of choice based on reason.

The conservative juristic influence of the Shafi'i school, which stressed Qur'an and Hadith as sources of law and sharply restricted the application of human reason to determine a legal ruling, has compounded the conservative orientation of Ash'arite theology. Al-Shafi'i systematized the science of Hadith (the sayings and actions of the Prophet) by eliminating large numbers of traditions that had acquired local currency but that he identified as spurious. These included traditions accepted as sound by the Muslims of Medina on the mere grounds that the Prophet had made the city his home for several years. Al-Shafi'i maintained that the Qur'an and the sound traditions of the Prophet constituted the acceptable sources of Islamic law. He also permitted the use of independent judgment, but under highly constrained conditions: namely, the use of analogical reasoning and this only if based on the existence of a legal proof. In this, he rejected the Hanafi school's more liberal allowance of either the jurist's opinion or his discretionary preference to determine a legal rule. These he deemed arbitrary and so a threat to the integrity of the religious law.

The Hanafi juristic school is more "liberal" than the Shafi'i in the scope it allows for human reason in the search for a legal norm. But it, too, as with its ally, the Maturidi ontology and epistemology, sets fairly strict limits upon the autonomy of human reason in regard to God's nature, His attributes, and the room available for human rationality. The Hanafi school upholds an Islam of the "middle way," as captured by the Qur'anic expression (2:143) of *umma wasat* (middle, i.e. upright, community). Textual proof supersedes rational proof in this system, but his rivals still criticized Abu Hanifa for his alleged willingness to substitute his own personal opinion and discretional preferences for the Hadith of the Prophet. This seems much exaggerated, however, and Abu Hanifa, who himself did not compose legal texts, cannot be credibly understood to have advocated unfettered human judgment in the search for a legal norm.

The Ottoman period

The Ottoman Empire (1312–1923) was the most powerful political system in the pre-twentieth-century Muslim Middle East. This political system differed from the early Islamic state and from the Umayyad and 'Abbasid dynasties in that the state exhibited a higher degree of organizational coherence. The gradual and continuous expansion of the Ottoman Empire occurred in pursuit of conquests in Europe, North Africa, and Asia through a dynamic that emphasized the role of the *ghazi* (warrior) ethic. At the Empire's zenith, Ottoman forces were at the gates of Vienna on two separate occasions, 1529 and 1683. So formidable did Ottoman power appear to the Europeans that they feared its armies would eventually invade and occupy their capitals. Hodgson calls the Ottoman political system a "military patronage state."[28] The key to this concept is the bureaucratization of power, central supervision over the periphery, and "a monolithic and all-inclusive army." While such a characterization of the army seems hyperbolic, the point is that the coherence of the Ottoman military machine, at least in the Empire's heyday, stood head and shoulders above the military under 'Abbasid rule, both before and after the onset of the "amirate by seizure." The importance of the army in state consolidation during the Ottoman period is captured by the following characterization:

> In its absolutism, the Ottoman state had a military character ... built upon the tradition of looking upon the central power, including all its administrative branches, as one great army and ... regarding this army as at the personal service of the monarch.[29]

The Ottoman state was initially a small frontier enclave that grew to become a powerful empire. Even in the period of decline the original warrior ethic was not suppressed, as sultans of the empire would invoke this tradition as an exemplary model in the service of the faith. This ethic "influenced the state's historical existence for six centuries: its dynamic conquest policy, its basic military structure, and the predominance of the military class within an empire that successfully accommodated disparate religious, cultural, and ethnic elements."[30] Rapid expansion into the Balkans, followed by consolidation of gains in Anatolia, and then victories over the Mamluks in Egypt, Syria and Iraq made the Ottoman Empire a formidable force in the eyes of its Christian foes.

The Ottoman conqueror of Egypt, Selim I (ruled 1512–20), did not claim the title of caliph but rather "servant of Mecca and Medina." Although his successor, Sulayman the Magnificent (ruled 1520–66) did appropriate the title of caliph, he justified this by stressing his duty of protecting the Muslims, and not the caliph's function of interpreting, defending and implementing the *shari'a*. In the eighteenth century, by which time the Ottoman state was in decline, the myth arose that the last of the 'Abbasids, resident in Cairo at the time of Selim's conquest of Egypt, devolved the title of caliph upon him.

Earlier, it was stated that in the Umayyad and 'Abbasid periods, writings on government stressed that it was divinely ordained, and its purpose therefore was to facilitate the Muslim's ability to be faithful to God's commands and thereby to prosper. Only in this way could the individual prosper. Generally speaking Ottoman constitutional jurists maintained this view without much modification. Partly, this was due to the Ottoman officials' preference for the warrior tradition and the values that it bespoke. As one source has put it, the state's relationship to the Ottoman *'ulama'* evolved gradually, over time, from "the original indifference of the *ghazis* to the bookish *'ulama'*" to "a profound respect for them as the mainstays of communal solidarity. Yet, the central ideals of the *ghazis* continued to dominate the Ottoman Muslim imagination."[31]

However, after failing again to take Vienna in 1683, the Empire entered a long period of decline, marked by large-scale territorial losses. Those who wrote on political questions at this time were the Ottoman scribes, whose main purpose was to focus on the practice of statecraft, rather than to theorize about politics. In a way, this was a reprise of the pattern in an earlier period, when, under the Saljuqs a "mirror for princes" tradition had arisen, the leading thinker of whom had been Nizam al-Mulk (d. 1092). The main characteristic of that literature, centuries before Machiavelli, was advice to rulers on how best to conduct their rule. As Lewis puts it, discussing the Ottoman scribes six centuries later,

> Their concern was practical rather than theoretical, with statecraft rather than political philosophy. Their writings include whole books, or chapters in larger books, devoted to the arts of government, and variously addressed to rulers, ministers, or secretaries of state. These writings reflect very clearly the professional skills, aims, and outlook of medieval Islamic bureaucracies.[32]

The Ottoman state had officially adopted the Hanafi legal system, and the jurists were content to emulate the writings of their Arab predecessors in regard to the constitutional theory of the caliphate. The Ottoman legists provided minor embellishments and emendations to the earlier writings in the form of *hashiya/hawashi* (marginal notations). Thus, as late as the mid-nineteenth century, according to Mardin, "The political theory by which the rule of the Ottoman sultans was justified... identified political power with the vicarage of God."[33] This was what the great medieval Arab jurists – none of them Hanafis, incidentally – such as al-Baghdadi, al-Mawardi, al-Ghazali, ibn Taymiyya, and ibn Jama'a had maintained.[34]

The medieval Arab jurists' conception of political theory, which was accepted by the Ottoman Hanafi jurists, assumed that matters of state stemmed from the law. Khadduri has described the model that arises from such a system with the neologism of "nomocracy," according to which the law thus qualified is divine.[35] Following from this are all the concepts normally associated with political theory: natural law, obligation, responsibility, representation, interest, authority, and many others besides. The full implications of the dependence of these concepts on the divine mandate will be examined in a later chapter. For the moment, however, it is important to note that modern Muslim political theorists in the nineteenth through the early twenty-first centuries needed either to accommodate the nomocratic model to their own perspectives, which gave rise to an uneasy synthesis in which many of the central propositions acquired an ad hoc quality, or to break radically with that model, either on behalf of lay systems of belief in which anthropocentric concerns prevail, or in the service of a "pure" Islam that insisted upon the literal application of the *shari'a* (Islamic law) in all spheres of life, public as well as private.

European imperialism and Middle Eastern reaction

At the height of the Ottoman Empire's power in the sixteenth century the European system was characterized by multi-state rivalries. Embassies representing the interests of these states were established, and diplomacy rationalized. The Ottomans constituted a threat to Austria, the Balkans and Venice, but the Papal States also considered them a menace and tried to engineer coalitions of European states to prevent further Ottoman advances, which went as far as Vienna in 1529. However, Vienna's defenders held, and the Ottomans were unable to take the city, despite another try in 1683. Meanwhile, a naval loss to Venice in 1571 at the Battle of Lepanto marked a turning point, after which Ottoman territorial losses came in succession, with only a few periods of reinvigoration.

These losses greatly increased toward the end of the seventeenth and into the eighteenth centuries. By the end of the eighteenth century, Russia had not only become a Black Sea power but had wrested the Crimea from Ottoman control. On the eve of World War I, the Ottoman Empire had lost approximately 40 per cent of its land mass at the height of its power. The long period of decline from the late seventeenth to the early twentieth century had been marked by four trends: (1) military defeats at the hands of the Europeans, followed by punitive peace treaties and annexation of lands; (2) European occupation of Ottoman territories in the outlying areas – especially the Arab provinces in North Africa, Egypt, Syria, and Iraq; (3) European sponsorship of secessionist movements among the various nationalities of the Empire (such as Greeks, Serbs, Bulgars, Jews, and Arabs); (4) reduction of the Ottoman Empire, through the capitulations, to the status of a virtual tributary state. Ultimately, these disasters generated efforts to reform the Empire in various fields.

These reform efforts followed a certain dialectic. After the initial shock over the wartime defeats, the government sought to introduce military reforms to defend the Empire against its European enemies. But military reforms require reforms in education, as the use of siege artillery in theater warfare, for example, necessitated knowledge of trigonometry. These educational reforms themselves required curtailing the 'ulama''s control over the schools and academies. But this in turn necessitated training administrators and scribes in new legal codes and administrative processes. To proceed with such training entailed legal reforms. Meanwhile, the state had to rationalize public finance administration and commerce in order to strengthen the economy. Political reforms were also deemed essential, as the morale of the population could no longer be upheld by the traditional patrimonialism that characterized the rule of the Empire's leaders for so many centuries.

The French Revolution had a major impact on the Middle East, not only because in the years following it France became a formidable imperial power in Middle Eastern lands (North Africa and the Levant), but also because that great upheaval introduced an entirely new vocabulary to the French themselves. This, in turn, had consequences for the development of political theory in the Middle East because of the travel of Muslim intellectuals from the region to Europe, as well as the translation of books on politics in the Ottoman Empire. The printing press had been introduced into the Empire in 1721 and thus was already well established by the time of the French Revolution. By the mid- to late nineteenth century, Middle Easterners were being introduced to writings in

European nationalism, liberal democracy, and market economics. Still later, socialist, Marxist, and corporatist ideas began to filter into the region. All of this represented an enormous intellectual challenge for Middle Easterners interested in developing a political theory that could serve to bring about the kinds of cultural, political, social, and economic advances that were deemed necessary for any society in the contemporary age. The big question was whether or not the Middle Eastern response would be accommodationist in its orientation to these external ideas, imitative, or rejectionist.

The familiar story of "The Eastern Question," an expression referring to the competition by the European states to dominate the Ottoman Empire and project their power into the "Near East," as the region was called at that time, is too well known to be recapitulated in any great detail here. Their success culminated in a series of protectorates, colonies and mandates from the 1830s through the 1950s, and even into the early 1970s. The table opposite provides information on colonial control of the various states of the Middle East, independence dates, and trajectories of independence from the European states.

Western imperialism spawned reactions other than Ottoman (and Egyptian and Tunisian) reform movements. Ultimately, as the political, economic, social, and cultural influence of the Europeans infiltrated into the Middle East region, efforts arose to contest such domination from within society. The trajectories toward independence taken by the people of the various territories of the area differed. In some cases, an internal war proved to be the pattern, as occurred in Turkey (1919–23), Algeria (1954–62), and South Yemen (1965–69). In other cases, a militant nationalist movement, characterized by significant violence, was the response, as in Morocco (1920–56), Tunisia (1934–56), Egypt (1919–52), Palestine (1920–49), Syria (1920–46), Iraq (1920–58), and Sudan (1898–1956). Elsewhere, a retreating colonial power decided it was too costly to maintain its hold, as in the shaykhdoms of the Arabian Peninsula (1961–71). Some regions, such as Iran, although militarily occupied, politically

State	Colonial control	European state	Independent	Trajectory of independence
Morocco	1912	France	1956	Militant nationalism
Algeria	1830	France	1962	Internal war
Tunisia	1881	France	1956	Militant nationalism
Libya	1911	Italy	1951	Transition from UN
Egypt	1882	UK	1952*	Militant nationalism
Sudan	1898	UK	1956	Militant nationalism
Somalia	1884	UK, France, Italy	1960	Devolution
Djibouti	1880s	France	1977	Devolution
Palestine	1917	UK	1949	Militant nationalism
Syria	1920	France	1944	Militant nationalism
Lebanon	1920	France	1944	Devolution
Jordan	1921	UK	1946†	Devolution
Iraq	1920	UK	1958‡	Militant nationalism
Saudi Arabia			1932	Indigenous establishment
Kuwait	1899	UK	1963	Devolution
Qatar	1868	UK	1971	Devolution
UAE	1892	UK	1971	Devolution
Bahrain	1861	UK	1971	Devolution
Oman	1798	UK		
South Yemen	1839		1967	Internal war
Yemen			1918	Collapse of Ottoman Empire
Turkey			1923	Internal war
Afghanistan	Semi-colony	UK, Russia	1919	Indigenous
Iran	Semi-colony	UK, Russia	1921	Indigenous

* The British supposedly granted Egypt independence in 1923, but this was only nominal.
† The British supposedly granted Transjordan independence in 1946, but it (later, Jordan) remained a British semi-colony for many years under King Hussein (ruled 1951–1999).
‡ The British supposedly granted Iraq independence in 1932, but this was only nominal.

dominated, and economically penetrated, had not experienced any formal colonial status – Lenin reserved for these territories the epithet "semi-colonies." Other areas had not been subject to outside control, as for example the interior of the Arabian peninsula and Yemen. Finally, Libya, which had been a colony of Italy, made the transition from Italian rule in 1943 to trusteeship status in the United Nations in 1945, and independence in 1951.

Albert Hourani has called the period from the French Revolution in 1789 to 1939 as "the liberal age" in the development of social thought in the region. Scholars refer to the stirrings of intellectual engagement in the Middle East region with the challenges of European civilization and European state power as "the awakening" – *al-nahda*. The general thrust of this *nahda* was to explore both the historical development of modernization outside the region, in Europe, and the possibilities of Middle Eastern societies applying the supposed benefits of such modernization. Most of the participants in the "awakening" were motivated by two objectives: utilizing new ideas in order to rid their societies of outside domination, and using them to achieve greater prosperity. In general, three categories of thinkers were involved in the effort: (1) the 'ulama', or professional men of religion; (2) the scribes, who were state officials; (3) the intellectuals – men of letters, memoirists, travelers, journalists, and educators (whether in the traditional schools and universities, such as al-Azhar (est. 969), or the newer institutions, such as the Dar al-'Ulum (est. 1871) and Cairo University (est. 1925). These categories are not necessarily mutually exclusive. For instance, scribes in earlier historical periods were also members of the 'ulama' stratum. This also applies in later periods.

During the period from the end of World War I to the mid- to late 1960s, several intellectual approaches rivaled each other in the political theories that advocates were proposing for the societies of the Middle East. These included Islamic theories of politics, liberal pluralism, socialism, Marxism, and corporatism. Nationalism, which is not so much a form of political theory per se but rather an overarching body of sentiments and ideas that one may associate with any of these theories, arose in at least two variants: (1) territorial patriotism, such as Turkish nationalism, Iranian nationalism, or Egyptian nationalism; (2) pan-nationalist movements, such as pan-Arabism. These pan-nationalist movements have historically emphasized integral nationalism, which, in addition to stressing the common characteristics of a people that serve as the basis for their coming together, may harbor the more radical ideas of exclusiveness, militant expansionism, and, perhaps, racism.[36] Many intellectuals adopted an eclectic mix of some of these; and, of course, even in the case of those who identified more specifically with one of these approaches as against the others, the formulation of the major questions that they wanted to solve, not to mention the methods for solving them and hence the particular solutions themselves, varied.

Although it is impossible to discuss in detail the actual developments in the Middle East region in the post-World War I period through the achievement of independence by many of the territories of the Middle East in the 1940s and 1950s, a brief survey of these developments in three states helps to demonstrate the linkage between them and the rise of the dominant political theories of the region over the last half century.

TURKEY

After the collapse of the Ottoman Empire, contention arose within the ranks of the political and military elites on how to proceed. The Ottoman Sultan and his royalist supporters believed it would still somehow be possible for him to rule on the basis of the traditional Ottoman legitimacy formulas of monarchy and the caliphate. The group known as the Young Turks, who had led a military coup in 1908 and removed the then sitting ruler, and who were in charge of the Ottoman war effort in World War I, seemingly wavered between a constitutional monarchy (1908–13) and a military dictatorship (1913–1918), overlain by a pan-Turkish integral nationalism. Their major rivals, the supporters of Mustafa Kemal (1881–38), an Ottoman general who had distinguished himself for his valor in the war, rejected both tendencies in favor of a civilian republican model that turned out to emphasize corporatist values and Turkish territorial patriotism.

The defeat of the Central Powers in World War I meant, for Turkey, the occupation of Istanbul, the loss of the remaining non-Turkish areas of the Ottoman Empire, and the partition of Anatolia itself, leaving only a small rump Turkish state. However, Mustafa Kemal and his supporters nullified the partition of Anatolia in a series of historic battles against the Greeks, who had occupied large areas of Anatolia under the aegis of the Entente powers. Italian and French occupying forces allied with the Greeks withdrew upon Greece's defeat at the Battle of Sakarya River in August and September 1921. British contingents in the area of Istanbul almost engaged Turkish forces but a compromise was arranged instead. At the Lausanne Conference in 1923, Kemal secured international recognition of the independence of the new Turkish Republic. An admirer of Western-style modernization, he embarked on a series of reforms that, by his death in 1938, had formally disestablished the Islamic institution from the public sphere and made the state the major actor in that arena. Many changes were introduced in the legal, educational, military, administrative, and economic fields. The political system was formally presidential with a parliament and a cabinet, although the model was authoritarian, rule being exercised by a single political party, the Republic People's Party (RPP). Emblematic of this authoritarianism was the decision by the Grand National Assembly (parliament) to vest Kemal in 1938, his last year, with the title of Atatürk, Father of the Turks.

This authoritarian model began to evolve into a quasi-democratic one when the RPP began to fragment into two factions in 1946–48, and eventually one of these became the Democrat Party. The 1950 elections proved a watershed, as the Democrats won, and the ruling RPP voluntarily relinquished power.

A decade later, however, the army intervened in the effort to prevent what its leaders perceived to be an effort by the Democrats to dismantle the Atatürk legacy of secularism. Military intervention recurred in 1971, 1983, and 1997 (although in that case its action was more of what may be called a "veto coup," meaning the army achieved its purpose, by threatening praetorian intervention). If the army coup of 1960 sought to prevent the undoing of Atatürk's legacy, the coups of 1971 and 1983 had more to do with civil unrest in Turkish society as a consequence of worrisome economic trends and consequent labor and student actions. The "veto coup" of 1997 targeted the Prime Minister, Necmettin Erbakan, whose Islamist party, Refa, had received a slim plurality (21 per cent) of the votes in the parliamentary elections of 1995. Even without these military interventions, significant political turnover has characterized Turkish politics since 1950. The 1950s saw five governments, the 1960s nine, the 1970s twelve, the 1980s four, the 1990s ten, and the 2000s, three (to mid-2008). The dominant issues in Turkish politics in the last generation include: (1) what part should religion play in public life; (2) what does citizenship mean in relationship to ethnic differences in Turkish society; (3) what is the proper model for the state; (4) what is the appropriate role of women in Turkish society; (5) what is Turkey's relationship to Europe; (6) what should be Turkey's regional role; (7) what is the best way to resolve sharpening class cleavages in Turkish society.

EGYPT

In 1914, the British rationalized their colonial domination of Egypt, which began in 1882, by declaring the country a UK protectorate. Ostensibly, the reason was that Egypt was part of the Ottoman Empire, which had become belligerent towards Britain in World War I. However, Egypt's ties to the Ottoman Empire were purely nominal at that time, so it is apparent that the British wished to strengthen their colonial control there, and not to "protect" Egypt from the ravages of conflict. In 1919, the country erupted in a general uprising that led, in 1922, to the abolition of the protectorate and the establishment of a kingdom to which the British granted "independence." However, the country did not become independent, as the British never intended to permit it to shake off British rule. In 1923, the masquerade of an independent Egypt was continued with the promulgation of a constitution. In 1936 the British again granted "independence" to Egypt, but such independence was mostly illusory, even though by its terms the hated capitulations (extraterritorial privileges for the Europeans) were abolished and Egypt became a member of the League of Nations. The British, however, continued to control the Suez Canal, military matters, the economy, and foreign policy. However, the move gave greater coherence to Egyptian territorial patriotism. Unlike Turkey, which gained its independence in 1923, Egypt's independence did not come until 1952. The independence movement itself consisted of various social forces. The supporters of the Wafd Party (a reference to the Egyptian delegation that tried to attend the Versailles Peace Conference in a vain attempt to gain Egyptian independence from Britain) might be characterized as favoring liberal democracy at least in principle. Another trend was represented by the Muslim Brotherhood, established in the Suez Canal city of Ismailiyya in 1928. Smaller groups represented fascist and Marxist tendencies. What united them all, however, was a deep desire to evict the British.

In 1952, middle-ranking military officers seized power in a *coup d'état*, exiled the pro-British monarch, and inaugurated a republic. These men did not have any coherent policy beyond expelling the British and espousing general economic reforms. Seven weeks after seizing power, they did pass a land law limiting holdings to 200 feddans (one feddan is slightly more than an acre). Because the new leaders were the first truly native rulers of Egypt in nearly two thousand years, they gained instant legitimacy among the masses.

When the regime negotiated the withdrawal of the British, which was announced in June 1954 and completed in June 1956, its leaders became even more popular. Their crowning achievement, however, was the nationalization of the Suez Canal in July 1956, the news of which was greeted with enormous and widespread acclaim. By now, Gamal Abdel Nasser (Jamal 'Abd al-Nasir) (1918–1970) had emerged as regime leader. His espousal of Arab nationalism, non-alignment in the Cold War, domestic welfare policies, strong state intervention in markets, and central planning, became the hallmarks of the political system. Politically, the regime was authoritarian, having abolished all political parties and relied for the mobilization of the population on the device of the mass rally, instead. In this way it mobilized support from above while denying opportunities for mobilization from below. For example, trade unions, the press, and professional syndicates were licensed but integrated into the state apparatus.

The regime was unable to solve the pressing economic problems of the country, which were compounded by a series of wars with Israel. Defeat in the June 1967 war set the stage for a transition from the system under Nasser to an economic privatization model under Anwar Sadat (1918–1981) and Sadat's successor Hosni Mubarak. The trauma of the June war has continued to impact on Egyptian society fifty years later. After Nasser's death, regime legitimacy was eroded among the masses because his successors dismantled a good deal of the previous social welfare programs. While popular unrest generally did not become so serious as to threaten the regime, the bread riots in January 1977 showed how narrow had become the base of its support.

The phrase "crisis of the intellectuals" entered the Egyptian vocabulary in the aftermath of the June war.[37] Although the pietistic intellectuals had been critical of the regime almost from its earliest days, because of its repression of their most important movement, the Muslim Brotherhood, the non-pietistic intellectuals had steadily supported it within the framework of leftist anti-imperialism and a deep antipathy toward the West's support for the State of Israel. However, many of these intellectuals did resent the regime's efforts to politicize the universities and make the higher educational institutions serve the interests of the state. Yet anti-Western and anti-imperialist sentiment was widespread, and that antipathy cut across a number of faultlines or cleavages that otherwise separated these secularists, bringing together Marxists, liberals, non-Marxist socialists, and corporatists. After the June war, the secular intellectuals on the whole continued to support Nasser, but when he died in 1970 they became highly critical of his successor and the privatization model known as *infitah* that he established. Marxist intellectuals focused upon the sharpening of class contradictions internally and the decapitalization that they perceived to be accompanying Egypt's growing incorporation into the world capitalist economy. Non-Marxist intellectuals condemned the praxis of the Sadat and Mubarak regimes, pointing out their hypocrisy in advocating economic liberalism but in fact encouraging speculation and corruption that undermined those markets. The Islamists joined in the criticism, but from their own particular perspectives, which emphasized the failure to give priority to *shari'a* in the operation of the country's laws.

Unlike Turkey, Egypt has not witnessed a series of overt military interventions. But the regimes from 1952 to 1973 were run by the military, and since the early 1970s have depended upon the support of the military. The rulers even today still rely upon the old state-of-emergency law that the British had introduced during their occupation of the country. Violence-prone groups among the general Islamist tendencies engaged in bitter conflicts with the state in the early to mid-1990s in particular, although their violence went further back in time to around 1974. The state has harshly repressed these groups, but it has also applied coercive measures against its non-violent critics. Leaders of the professional syndicates, such as the lawyers, journalists, and engineers, have themselves taken on the central state institutions, including not just the cabinet and the parliament but also various official religious bodies, such as al-Azhar, the office of the Mufti, and the Supreme Council for Islamic Affairs. A number of writers have both analyzed and advocated the development of civil society in Egypt. Others have insisted that it, and the democratic theory upon which this concept rests, are "Western" in origin and nature and have no place in a Muslim society such as Egypt. Instead, they believe that traditional concepts exist in the Islamic tradition, such as *shura* (consultation), *ijma'* (consensus), and *maslaha mursala* (public interest), that can serve as the basis of Egyptian democracy. Still others have fiercely attacked secular-minded (but not anti-religious) intellectuals by pronouncing unbelief upon them on the putative grounds that the latter desire to destroy the true faith.[38]

IRAN

The consequences of World War I for Iran (then Persia) were mainly indirect but still highly disruptive. Due to financial mismanagement by the previous rulers, the economy had deteriorated to such a degree that when the war broke out, even though Iran was not a theater of battle, shortages became a dire problem, and inflation skyrocketed. British and Russian intervention in the country's affairs in the nineteenth and early twentieth centuries had paralleled European intervention in the affairs of the Ottoman Empire. The Russian Revolutions of 1905 and 1917 had repercussions in Iran. The former influenced the course of Iranian events of 1905–09 known as the Constitutional Revolution, during which Iran gained a constitution and parliament; the latter led to border incursions into Iran from the Russian Caucasus, skirmishes between White and Red military forces, and efforts by the Bolsheviks to create soviets in northern Iran. When the Soviets supported an effort to create one of these in Gilan province, a young colonel Reza Khan (1878–1944) of the tsarist militia in Iran known as the Cossack Brigade led the effort to suppress that movement. Meanwhile, in 1919, the British tried to persuade the Iranian parliament to ratify an agreement that would have converted the country into a British protectorate. Although this plan eventually failed, and the British withdrew their military forces from Iran, they retained their oil concession, the Anglo-Persian (later Anglo-Iranian) Oil Company.

Reza Khan, with some support by the British, mounted a coup and named himself war minister in 1921, prime minister in 1923, and king in December–January 1925–26. His plans were similar to those of Mustafa Kemal Atatürk, but, as just noted, he did not establish a republic but rather retained the monarchy by creating a new dynasty. Meanwhile, prior to his rise to power, intellectuals from the ranks of state bureaucrats (the scribes mentioned earlier in relation to the Ottoman Empire), elements of the 'ulama', pietistic laypersons, and men of letters and the free professions had been analyzing and seeking to resolve the problems of nineteenth- and twentieth-century Iranian society from their various perspectives.

Just as Atatürk found support among some intellectuals for his efforts, and Nasser for his, Reza Shah also attracted significant support from the Iranian intelligentsia, a number of whom his regime had sent to European universities and who had returned to Iran to support enthusiastically his modernization policies. They especially endorsed his efforts to create a modern state through military, administrative, economic, and educational reforms under the aegis of a vigorous campaign of territorial patriotism. However, the 'ulama', notwithstanding early endorsements, did not lend their support; quite the contrary – they opposed Reza Shah since they were the targets of his hostility. Moreover, many of those intellectuals who did support Reza Shah were critical of his authoritarian rule.

With the onset of World War II, Iran declared its neutrality. The British, however, regarded Reza Shah with great suspicion, believing him to be pro-German. When Germany invaded the Soviet Union in June 1941, the Soviets joined the British in exerting enormous pressure on Iran and eventually invaded the country, exiled the monarch and militarily occupied the country. The war proved devastating to Iran economically. But the forced abdication of Reza Shah opened the political system to a form of political pluralism, even though his son, Muhammad Reza Pahlavi (1919–1980), was placed on the throne in his place.

During the 1941–53 period, two major developments unfolded: (1) the political system opened up, and many different currents and orientations emerged, ranging from proto-fascist tendencies to liberal pluralist, socialist, and Marxist trends; (2) the clergy, who had been repressed by Reza Shah, now emerged as important actors, although by no means acting as a unified group. A nationalist movement that blended ideas of Iranian territorial patriotism with Shi'ite cultural themes took hold of the country. The leader of the secular wing of this nationalist movement was Muhammad Musaddiq (1880–1967), a wealthy aristocrat who, however, did not identify with his class but rather with the Iranian people as a whole. He had served in various governments in the late Qajar period and also in the nation's parliament before he was banned from that body and exiled to his estate to the northwest of Tehran. With Reza Shah's fall from power, Musaddiq again ran for parliament and eventually became chairman of that body's Oil Commission. By 1949, he had determined to sponsor legislation to nationalize the Anglo-Iranian Oil Company (AIOC). As a result of domestic developments, the Shah, who bitterly opposed him, saw it as necessary to bow to public pressure and to nominate Musaddiq to become prime minister in April 1951. He had already shepherded the bill to nationalize AIOC before this event, and now as prime minister he sponsored enabling legislation to implement this action.

The British refused to recognize this move and tried to prevail upon the United States to join in an effort to remove Musaddiq from power. In a clandestine operation mounted by British MI6 and the CIA, Musaddiq was in fact overthrown, and the pro-British Shah, who had fled to Rome in panic at the onset of the coup when events seemed to be going against the plotters, was restored to the throne. From that time until his own removal in 1979, the Shah became increasingly authoritarian and corrupted by power and money. The intellectuals after 1953, with very few exceptions, were outraged at the imperialist policies and behavior of the Western powers and refused to lend their stature and support to the monarchy. The clergy, ironically, had largely abandoned Musaddiq at the critical moment and by and large supported the monarchy, fearing Musaddiq's secularism. But within a matter of seven or eight years, they, too, began to adopt a critical posture toward the dynasty as the regime began supporting policies that were inimical to their interests: land seizures, nominally enfranchising women, and appropriating the resources of the clergy. Although the secular and the religious opposition did not unite during the disturbances of 1960–63, those disturbances might be considered in retrospect as an accelerator for the Iranian revolution of 1978–79. During the period 1953–79, Iranian intellectuals articulated a variety of political ideas. Some avowed one or another variant of liberal thought; others opted for socialism; yet others endorsed Marxism. It is probably true that all of them embraced some form of Iranian nationalism, although some subscribed to a pan-Iranian ideology that suggested that all the inhabitants of lands that had been directly influenced by Persianate civilization deserved to be united under a common government. Among the intellectuals, quite a few embraced some aspect of Shi'ite political theory, stressing the juristic theory of the Imamate as a reformist or even a revolutionary doctrine.

When it came, the Iranian revolution of 1978–79 resulted from complex developments that were animated by both internal and external causes. Although it would be misleading to call the revolution an "Islamic revolution," in view of the participation of many social groups, not all of them religiously based, it is nonetheless worth noting that without the participation of the 'ulama' it is not likely to have succeeded (or at least not so quickly).

Since 1979, the dominant narrative in Iranian political theory has been the "guardianship of the jurist" (Arabic, *wilayat al-faqih*; Persian, *velayat-i faqih*). This concept will be discussed later, but for now it may be said that it is identified with the thought of Ayatollah Ruhollah Khomeini, who advanced it to vindicate the right of the clergy to rule. This argument went beyond that proposed by some 'ulama' at the time of the Iranian Constitutional Revolution in the early twentieth century, which advocated the right of the clergy to represent the nation in a parliament. Because it is the official state ideology, this doctrine has monopolized political theoretical discourse over the more than thirty years since it was officially adopted. If anything, it became further elaborated in 1987–88 as a result of a ruling by Khomeini that made the guardianship of the jurist into the absolute mandate of the jurist. It is fair to say that many Iranian intellectuals reject the thesis of the guardianship of the jurist, either in its relatively more flexible, pre-1987/88 version or the rigid, post-1987/88 interpretation. Since Khomeini's death, the doctrine has remained in place, despite a brief eight years of the "liberal" presidency of Muhammad Khatami (1997–2005). Meanwhile, however, the gap between state and society has widened significantly as a consequence of the regime's culturally repressive policies.

The interrelationship of social and intellectual trends reprised

Beginning shortly after the June war of 1967, considered a calamity among Arab and most Muslim populations of the Middle East, a number of intellectuals who had formerly been identified with the secular approaches of liberal pluralism, Marxism, socialism, and corporatism found themselves gravitating either to Islamism – a neologism from the French that refers to a movement whose members reaffirm the unity of religion and politics and who seek the rapid (if not immediate) application of Islamic law in all arenas of life – or to a greater appreciation of the importance of Islamic principles in explaining the political process. Of course, this has not meant the disappearance of secularists[39] among the intellectuals of the Middle East. For good or ill, the debates that have been occurring between the Islamist intellectuals and secularists have not only failed to achieve a synthesis but have even fallen short of patient engagement. Although some observers suggest that one should at least take note of the various occasions, beginning with the early 1970s, during which Arab thinkers have congregated to discuss especially the themes of "authenticity" and "renewal," the general consensus seems to be that the interlocutors seem not to be listening to each other. Matters have reached such a pass that many articulators of a conservative perspective that is highly suspicious of "alien" ideas have cleaved ardently to an "Islamization of knowledge" position. The hallmark of this perspective is that knowledge in the human and social sciences must be made thoroughly consonant with scriptural understandings of Islamic belief. Opposed to this perspective are secularists (by which is meant those who are committed to ontological and epistemological perspectives that uphold scientific explanations and causal analysis).

These theoretical approaches arose as a result of the particular economic, political, and social circumstances of the Middle East region over that time period. However, one cannot be dogmatic on this point. If those circumstances were indeed the source for the particular theoretical perspectives that have been identified, then why were the latter so varied? After all, if the economic, political, and social circumstances of the Middle East during this period can be distilled into European colonial domination, why did that domination not produce a single political theory? The answer is that local variations throughout the region shaped the specific political theories that emerged. And those political theories, in turn, have consisted both of the official state narratives in the individual political systems of the region for the period under review, and of the narratives of the non-state intellectuals, whether pietistic or secular or both.

Let us look at the cases of Egypt and Iran, for instance. As we have seen, both were monarchies during the late 1940s and early 1950s, and in each strong nationalist feeling against Great Britain crystallized into a nationalist movement to eliminate the British presence. In the one case, Egypt, the movement succeeded (despite a British, French, and Israeli invasion); in the other, Iran, it failed. In both countries, the British resisted, but in Egypt they lacked American support, whereas in Iran they received it.

The outcomes in the 1950s and 1960s, so far as the official state narrative was concerned, was non-Marxist socialism in Egypt and royal dictatorship in Iran. So far as the intellectuals' narratives in each country were concerned, whether pietistic or secular, a range of these may be identified. In Egypt, because of the state's success against the British, at least the non-pietistic intellectuals generally adopted some variant of its socialist ideology, with a minority critical of socialism and instead cleaving to either corporatist or pluralist positions. In Iran, social democracy became the theoretical position of the remnants of the nationalist movement. Interestingly, some pietistic intellectuals placed themselves in this category because they were strong supporters of the National Front, which was the organization most closely associated with the nationalists' hero, Muhammad Musaddiq. But other pietistic intellectuals, suspicious of socialism, opted for "Islamic" positions in their theoretical perspectives, even though tacitly and implicitly some of these perspectives were not uncongenial to certain elements of social democratic thought, such as concern for the welfare of the disenfranchised. What appears not to have happened in the Iranian case is the abandonment of Marxist positions by Iranian intellectuals in favor of Islamist ones. Thus in Egypt individuals such as Tariq al-Bishri, 'Adil Husayn (d. 2001), and Muhammad 'Imara, who had all been attracted to Marxist ideas or even had embraced Marxism, changed their perspectives in favor of Islamist positions. This does not appear to have occurred in Iran – although one might add that leading thinkers of organizations such as the People's Mujahidin of Iran (PMOI) had for several years tried to combine Marxism and Shi'ism; and independent thinkers, such as 'Ali Shari'ati (d. 1977), had adopted some Marxist vocabulary and conceptualizations but were critical of Marxist "materialism."

Conclusion

This chapter has discussed the purpose of this volume, conceptualized both political theory and comparative political theory, summarized the sociology-of-knowledge approach, and reviewed various eras of Middle Eastern history from the rise of Islam in the seventh century to the twentieth century. I have tried to characterize the nature of politics in these historical periods while also trying to make the case that ideas, concepts, and theories about politics over this stretch of time were generated by thinkers in response to concrete historical developments that occurred during those periods. I also have argued that such ideas and theories, once they enter history, in turn make significant impacts on the latter's course.

Thus, the changes brought about as a consequence of the early Islamic conquests transformed a city state (Medina) into a limited form of patrimonial kingship radiating out from that city state until it in turn became transformed into a large imperial system. Theories to legitimize rule that arose in the earlier period could not easily explain the new circumstances, thus necessitating the rise of novel explanations for why a religiously inspired ruler ought to accept seizures of power that apparently violated the religious injunctions. In later times, Ottoman reformers, faced with the daunting task of dealing with European imperialism, sought to deploy concepts of constitutionalism that rested on citizenship and representation as a way of restoring vitality to their society's political order. And in the twentieth century, similar efforts were expended by advocates of change throughout the Middle East region. In each of these periods – early Islam, Umayyad Kingship, 'Abbasid imperial rule, the late Ottoman period, and the twentieth-century Middle East, vigorous debates occurred among the intellectuals about the proper course of action. But no matter how they differed, their theoretical perspectives and proposed solutions were driven by the need to respond to concrete historical developments that, in turn, were themselves to some degree shaped by the ideal interests of the actors.

TWO

The sacred and the secular

The *Oxford English Dictionary* defines the term "sacred" as "things, places, or persons and their offices that are set apart for or dedicated to some religious purpose and hence entitled to veneration ... made holy by association with a god." Islam, which is a faith based on submission by human beings to God and carrying out His commands as fully as possible, is, as it were, a "sacred religion." The reason it seems necessary to resort to this apparently redundant usage is, as we will see, that there is something called a "civil religion," according to which the venerated founding myths of a political community function as a substitute for divine faith to promote communal solidarity.[1]

In the preceding chapter, emphasis was placed on the sacred dimension in the history of Middle Eastern political theory since the rise of Islam. Politics and the state historically have been mainly considered as divine gifts, which followed God's plan, rather than artifacts created by human beings. As shown in the previous chapter, with the rise of Islamic philosophy (as opposed to Islamic jurisprudence and theology), some thinkers tried to articulate a separate sphere for the political, but these efforts were quickly marginalized.

Despite their interest in establishing and maintaining this separation, the Muslim philosophers were not secularists in the sense of conceiving of politics as "belonging to the world and its affairs, as distinguished from ... religion; civil, lay, temporal. Chiefly used as a negative term, with the meaning ... non-religious or non-sacred." Accordingly, secular and secularism are not meaningful concepts to apply even to thinkers significantly influenced by Plato and Aristotle, whose concerns were to expound on the man-made law – the nomos – so as to allow the human being to achieve the goal of complete fulfillment. The Muslim philosophers firmly kept in mind the coexistence of the divine law, which was God-centered, and the nomos, which was anthropocentric. They believed the two could be reconciled, but they never believed that reliance on nomos would lead to human happiness, since such a goal could not be attained in some asoteriological manner.

In this chapter, I pay attention to the Sunni theory of the caliphate by Abu al-Hasan al-Mawardi and by Taqi al-Din ibn Taymiyya. Some additional analysis will be provided for the writings of three other Sunni writers on the caliphate, Abu al-Mansur al-Baghdadi, Abu Hamid al-Ghazali, and ibn Jama'a. An inquiry will be made into the Shi'i juristic theory of the imamate, which significantly differs from Sunni perspectives in regard to the theoretical qualities of the ruler, if not in the practical accommodation to the actual power holders. Also, discussion will highlight the central themes in the theory of politics and the state by two Muslim philosophers, al-Farabi and ibn Rushd, to generate a "de-sacralized" model of politics, as it were, although, as mentioned in the previous paragraph, it would be wrong to suggest that they wished to remove God from consideration of politics. Following this, focus will be placed on ibn Khaldun's sociology of the state.

The Sunni juristic theory of the caliphate

We start with the constitutional theory of the caliphate by al-Mawardi, who was born at a time when the 'Abbasid caliphate in Baghdad had lost much of its power and authority in the face of (1) the rise of

Shi'ite dynasties in Egypt (the Fatimids), and in the heartland of the caliphate itself (the Buyids, 945–1055); and (2) encroachments by Turkic tribes into the lands of the caliphate and seizures of power by their leaders, such as Mahmud of Ghazna (ruled 998–1030) in Afghanistan, Iran, and India, and the Seljuq monarchs in Transoxiana and Iran (1038–1157).

Al-Mawardi was a towering figure in Islamic jurisprudence, an exponent of the Shafi'i school who was widely admired for his great erudition and modesty. He felt it his duty to vindicate the actual caliphate as the legitimate Islamic institution of rule. As all jurists did, he held that the primary goal of the Islamic state was to uphold the faith of Islam and to promote its interests. Yet, the legitimacy of this state was being severely tested by usurpers. If matters were to continue, the situation would become dire, as Islam itself then would be in danger. In other words, given the apparent undermining of the power and the authority of the caliphs, who after all were deemed the legatees of the Prophet's mantle and his successors as leaders of the umma, al-Mawardi believed he had to show that the society, the state, and the political leaders were legitimate in Islamic terms, despite the clear gap between Islamic ideals and reality.

Al-Mawardi was forced to make a virtue of necessity, and so he was willing to countenance clear violations of the caliphs' authority as acceptable if challengers to that authority did not explicitly act against doctrinal injunctions.[2] This "doctrine of necessity, is exemplified by the following passage from his major work, *Al-Ahkam al-Sultaniyya*: "When someone from [the caliph's] retinue gains authority over him and rules autocratically over affairs without appearing to commit any act of disobedience and without any manifest sign of opposition ... this does not exclude him from the Imamate and does not impair the validity of his governance."[3] Mawardi deduced the divine ordainment of the caliphate in the Qur'an (4:59: "O ye who believe, obey God, obey the Prophet, and those in authority among you."). He discussed ten functions performed by the caliph, including enforcing the *shari'a*, such as defending the umma, collecting taxes, distributing booty won in wars, allocating *zakat* (alms), and leading the congregational prayer.

Because, for al-Mawardi, the source of the authority of the caliph was God, who ordained the institution of the caliphate, there can be no doubt that he viewed the latter as a sacred institution, and not a civil one. The task of its leader, the caliph, was to protect that other divinely ordained institution, the *umma*. In fact, the Hanafi jurist Abu Yusuf Ya'qub bin Ibrahim al-Ansari al-Kufi (d. 798), who lived about a century and a half before al-Mawardi, stressed "God's choice, by which the caliph became a vicegerent of God on earth." In doing so, according to Lambton, Abu Yusuf "opens the way ... to the theory of the ruler as God's shadow on earth, which was later to be transferred to the temporal ruler once the caliph had ceased to be the effective and immediate source of power."[4]

Al-Mawardi also discussed the manner by which an individual becomes caliph, granted that the primordial investiture is divine in nature: (1) by designation, as exemplified by the successful insistence of the first caliph, Abu Bakr (d. 634), that his successor should be 'Umar ibn al-Khattab (d. 644); (2) by "election," as shown by the choice of Abu Bakr by five of the Prophet's companions, and of 'Uthman (d. 656) by six companions. Once the caliph acceded to his position, it was left up to an undefined body described in the sources as "the people of loosing and binding" (*ahl al-hall wa al-'aqd*) to ratify the investiture. Presumably, these are individuals of stature in the community. Their approval constitutes, in Mawardi's judgment, a contract (*'ahd*) between the leader and the *umma*, although we should be careful to note the extremely narrow basis of "representation" by the people of loosing and binding. Indeed, Kerr equates them not with a representative body but with a semi-closed caste of self-appointed commissioners whose membership in the group is based on elitist principles unrelated to the express wishes of the people.[5]

Al-Ghazali also contributed to this discussion. He, too, was pragmatic about the low fortunes of the caliphate as a result of power seizures by tribal chieftains. Ghazali held that "power belonged to the caliph, but the exercise of it could be divided between more than one person."[6] It was important to retain the caliph as the symbolic spiritual head of the community, but the *sultan* — or temporal ruler — could legitimately be considered the wielder of temporal power. The critical matter for al-Ghazali, as indeed for all the theorists of the Caliphate, was to establish the origins of the institution in God's commands. As he put it, "the Imama [i.e. the caliphate] is not required by reason, but by the divine law [Shar']."[7] Not only did the "authority verse" of the Qur'an (4:59) make this connection, but at least two other verses do so as well. The first of these is Qur'an 2:30, which alludes to God's preference for Adam over the angels as his representative: "I have placed on earth a vicegerent [*khalifa* — caliph]." And the second is 38:26, in a reference to David: "O David, we have made of thee a vicegerent on earth, so judge thou truthfully between men."

If the caliphate is a divinely mandated institution, as argued by these constitutional theorists, one would not expect them to try to establish an independent sphere for politics, in which human beings were expected to generate a theory of the state. And, in fact, they did not. As Rosenthal puts it,

> an independent political philosophy is not to be expected. The existence of the state in the political organization of ... the Muslim community is taken for granted. The jurists do not ask whether and why there must be a state. They are only concerned with the [interpretation and] application of the *shari'a*... the state ... is to guarantee the maintenance of pure Islam, in conformity with its law... Prayer, fasting, the giving of alms ... all combine to make up the life of the members of the *umma* bound to Allah.[8]

Indeed, by the time of Badr al-Din ibn Jama'a — writing roughly around the time of the collapse of the caliphate as a result of the Mongol invasions — any power holder who claimed the caliphate was acknowledged to be the rightful caliph,[9] so anxious were the jurists to maintain the theoretical principle that the *umma* required a caliph, and that, lacking the latter, the community would not be able to carry out God's commands. For their part, the caliphs acted as though their power came directly from God. The following citation is instructive on this point:

> Whatever may have been the basis of 'Abbasid legitimism, it was the priority of the ruling caliphs to reinforce the theocratic nature of their power. The same expressions were employed in their case as in that of the Umayyad caliphs. Al-Mansur declared himself, it is said, "the power of God on earth."[10]

Reacting to these historical and doctrinal events on the caliphate was the jurist Taqi al-Din ibn Taymiyya, a contemporary of ibn Jama'a. Interestingly, twentieth- and twenty-first-century Islamist groups claim him as a foundational inspiration, despite the fact that he maintained that the caliphate – an institution they wish to restore – was not an obligatory institution.[11] In his writings, he in fact ignored the caliphate. It is not that he believed that the state was irrelevant. But, rather, it had the essential function of "bringing about in reality the reign of unity [of God], and to prepare for the coming of a society devoted to the service of God."[12] For ibn Taymiyya, then, the ruler should be obeyed because the application of the shari'a is in the religious community's interest in serving God. God designates the leader of the community through that body, whose infallible consensus is somehow suffused independently of the individual members who comprise it. For ibn Taymiyya there is no caliph, no theoretical foundation exists for the caliph or the institution of the caliphate, and there is no election or designation of the leader by the people. "The exercise of authority is a religious function and a good work which brings one near to God, and drawing near to God means obeying God and his Prophet."[13]

The Shi'ite theory of the Imamate

Upon the death of the Prophet in 632 AD, the early Islamic community was left without a leader. The Prophet had not made provisions for the leadership of the umma, although his companions improvised solutions. Two general tendencies arose: the first stressed the selection of the leader based on certain qualifications, provided that he belonged to the Prophet's tribe; the second stressed the entitlement to lead by the Prophet's closest male relative. The first tendency prevailed, and its adherents came to be known as *ahl al-sunna wa al-jama'a* – or Sunnis/Sunnites. The second tendency came to be known as the view of the *ahl al-bayt*, literally "the people of the house" – referring to the household of the Prophet – whose leader in their view was the Prophet's paternal first cousin and son-in-law, 'Ali b. Abi Talib (d. 661). Although the appellation of *ahl al-shi'a* – or Shi'is/Shi'ites – was not used to qualify this second tendency until several decades after the Prophet's death, we will apply it anachronistically to cover the earlier period as well.

For the Sunnis, not only must the successor to the leadership of the *umma* come from the Prophet's tribe, but he must embody to the highest degree (at least theoretically) the qualities of knowledge, justice, and piety. The candidate had to be the most versed in the religious doctrines and principles, but also have the qualities of discernment, perspicacity, and wisdom. Shi'ites believed that 'Ali was the exemplary embodiment of these qualities. And specifically as to knowledge, they felt that it was both sapient and prescient in nature, meaning that 'Ali could foretell future events.

The Shi'ite leaders came to be known as Imams. This word originally referred to 'Ali but then also to 'Ali's offspring, through one of his wives, Fatima, who was a daughter of the Prophet. Shi'ism historically developed into several branches, depending upon the importance that believers attributed to various of these offspring. Those who believed that the line of Imams stopped with Zayd (one of the offspring of the fourth Imam) came to be known as Zaydi (or Fiver) Shi'ites. By contrast, those who held that it stopped with Isma'il (one of the offspring of the sixth Imam, Ja'far), came to be known as Isma'ili (or Sevener) Shi'ites. Finally, those who believed there were twelve Imams in all, with the last disappearing in 873/874, came to be known as Ithna'ashari (or Twelver) Shi'ites.

In the modern era the Twelvers are the most politically significant. The Fivers, historically concentrated mainly in Yemen, have been the least politically influential, which is not, of course, to discount their importance in their locale.

The Seveners, or Isma'ilis, were once politically powerful as the founders of dynasties – for example, the Fatimid dynasty in Egypt. A number of scholars in Islamic history were Isma'ili Shi'ites, including some of great erudition, such as Abu Ya'qub al-Sijistani (d. c. 980?) and Hamid al-Din al-Kirmani (d. 1021) But their political significance in the modern period has ebbed, and their contemporary significance in the main is in the form of Sufi mystical movements, as manifested in brotherhoods such as the Naqshbandi order, stretching across vast stretches of the Middle East, Central Asia, and the Indian subcontinent.

Twelver Shi'ism (also known variously as Ja'fari Shi'ism, Ithna 'Ashari Shi'ism, and Imami or Imamite Shi'ism) remained limited territorially for centuries, but its political significance evolved in the early modern period, with the rise of the Safavid dynasty in Iran (1501–1722), and also in areas of present-day Iraq and Lebanon, as well as regions of the Persian Gulf. In this volume the term "Shi'ism," when otherwise unqualified, will refer to twelver Shi'ism.

The first principle of the Shi'ite doctrine of the Imamate was that the world cannot exist for a moment without the proof of God's existence. Such proof was manifested in the Imams, from 'Ali, who was the first, to al-Mahdi, the twelfth and last. Shi'ites believe the Qur'an refers many times to their Imams, usually in verses specifying God's light. The Muslim community must be led by the Imam. No other rule is recognized as legitimate. The persecution of Shi'ites historically does not mean that Shi'ism is inherently revolutionary. One might logically think that because only one Imam – 'Ali – out of the twelve actually ruled, with the others murdered or persecuted by the Sunni caliphs, Shi'ites would naturally be inclined to revolution. But, in fact, the Imams counseled their supporters to political quietism and to practice pious dissimulation of their beliefs in order to protect the Shi'ite community from destruction. They believe that the twelfth Imam disappeared as a youngster in 873/4 on God's command in order to prevent the extinction of the line of Imams. His going into occultation appears to contradict the theoretical tenet that the presence of the Imam is required to prove God's existence, but Shi'ites believe there is no contradiction because the Imam's vanishing was on God's own command. The others were persecuted by the Sunni leaders, most of them being killed. The last Imam to escape such a fate is believed to have entered into hiding on command of God, despite the religious injunction that the absence of the Imam even for a moment means that evidence of God's existence is not at hand. As for pious dissimulation, it seemed essential to protect the faithful from repression and death, but, as we shall see, Ayatollah Khomeini called for its end in the 1970s on grounds that the very existence of the Shi'ites was no longer threatened.

Shi'ites believe that the Hidden Imam, al-Mahdi, will return to inaugurate the Day of Judgment. In the 1970s, some Shi'ites believed that Khomeini was, if not himself the Hidden Imam, then the "gate" to him. In Islamic tradition, the term "gate" has powerful allegorical symbolism and can refer to a forerunner of a more powerful figure to come.

The Qur'anic mandate for the rule of the Imams is believed to be located in that scripture's "authority verse," 4:59: "O ye who believe, obey God, obey the Prophet, and those in authority among you." Until Khomeini introduced his novel argument that the clergy should rule, according to his doctrine of *vilayat-i faqih* (Arabic, *wilayat al-faqih*), the phrase "those in authority among you" had been interpreted by the Shi'ite *'ulama'* to refer to the twelve Imams.

Upon the occultation of the twelfth Imam, the Shi'ites were said to remain in contact with him through a series of four agents who were imputed to be most knowledgeable about the faith. But with the death of the fourth of these agents, the Imam was considered to have left the state of the "shorter occultation" and entered that of the "greater occultation." The latter will last until the end of time, with the apocalyptic return to earth of the Hidden Imam.

Gradually, the Shi'ite theory of the Imamate evolved a role for the 'ulama'. Originally, they were considered almost exclusively as the guardians and the interpreters of the religious law. Eventually, by the late thirteenth century and into the fourteenth, Shi'ite jurists had taken the position that the 'ulama', being the "fortresses of Islam" and the "secondary legatees of the prophets" – as represented by Hadiths attributed to the Prophet regarding the "relators" [sing. rawi; pl. ruwat] of scripture and scriptural traditions – possessed some of the Imams' authority. Just as the four agents during the period between 873/874 and 940 comprised the "special agency," so the clergy as a whole after 940 and until the return of the Hidden Imam constituted the "general agency." What was the nature of the authority devolved from the Imams upon the clergy? It was not their substantive authority, but rather the authority to tend to the needs of the disadvantaged, such as widows, orphans, minors, the mentally infirm, and any believer who was not competent to make decisions on his or her own, that was required by the faith. As can be seen, these basically relate to matters of ritual and are not pertinent to substantive power, whether related to religious or political power.

Until 1905, the 'ulama''s authority in Shi'ism was mainly moral, although that did not prevent them from participating in politics. During the Constitutional Revolution in Iran, the clergy gained the power to represent the electorate in that country's parliament, having taken the trouble to vindicate the concept of a legislature in the first place. But the argument for executive rule by the clergy in Shi'ite Islam only emerged from a series of lectures given by Khomeini in January 1970 entitled "Islamic Government" – Hukumat-i Islami – and the concept of vilayat-i faqih (mandate of the jurist). Finally, in a fatwa issued by Khomeini in January 1988, executive rule by the clergy was transformed into the absolute mandate of the jurist (vilayat-i faqih-yi mutlaqa). Khomeini, as with the jurists in earlier centuries, embedded his theory of the state in divine will. Ironically, "Khomeinism" came to accept secular concepts, such as the separation of powers and popular sovereignty (no matter that this latter was undercut by elitist provisions privileging the 'ulama').

Hence, the Shi'i juristic theory of authority clearly and uncompromisingly founds rule upon divine ordainment. While the Sunni constitutional theorists maintained the divine foundation of the institution of the caliphate or, in ibn Taymiyya's case, the ruler's sovereignty, the Shi'ite theorists argued that the Imams were both endowed with the divine grace and possessed qualities that made them nearly divine themselves. In neither case, of course, was secularism a legitimating factor for rule.

A final point is that the Sunni and Shi'i juristic theories of rule evidently emerged in response to actual historical developments. Sunni theory tried to respond to the amirate by seizure. Shi'i theory arose in the aftermath of 'Ali's and his descendants' failure to be recognized as the legitimate rulers.

The classical philosophers and political theory

Philosophy entered into Islamic thought by way of Muslim jurists reading translations of the political works of Plato, the analyses of neo-Platonist thinkers who sought to amend the master's ideas, and those Muslim jurists' understandings of Aristotle's commentaries on Plato. The likely reason why these jurists read the Greek sources, albeit in Arabic translations, is because weak rulers in Baghdad encouraged the translation movement as a way of seeking answers to why their fortunes had sunk so low, even answers from outside the Muslim world.

In *The Republic* Socrates asks what is justice and considers various possibilities in discussion with his listeners. One replies that justice is defined by the rulers: "might makes right." Another replies that justice lies in giving to a person his legal due. A third responds that it consists of granting to someone that which is "fitting" or "good" for him, which implies others must decide what that is. These others are philosophers, who deserve to rule because of their wisdom, the quality par excellence that they embody. Other versions of justice appear: we all have vocations, so justice consists in our discharging our various functions, such as a bricklayer laying bricks (but not a carpenter doing so); or, alternatively, justice has to do with the human psyche and his or her soul, which, when put in order, brings the individual to the full materialization of justice. If this is done singly by each of us, does it mean that justice will have been served for the entire community? At least theoretically the process of each of us putting our psyches and souls in order (by which is meant, one supposes, in some semblance of harmony with one's environment) can lead to harm being done to the community on grounds that what benefits the individual does not necessarily advantage the group. In considering these versions, Socrates noted that justice will not be attainable unless the *polis* reaches its ideal state.

Muslim philosophers were fascinated by these issues. Because all considered themselves committed Muslims, they needed to work their understandings of justice into the revelation. The key was to reconcile the revelation, in the arena of which knowledge is transmitted (*naql*) with science, whose domain is knowledge based on reason (*'aql*) and hence a matter of mental construction based on the initiative of the thinker.

Both realms were based on law: revelation on divine law, and science on the laws of nature. Rosenthal argues that for the Muslim philosophers, divine law and natural law could be reconciled:

> they saw the problem of revelation and reason as a contrast between the divinely revealed law, mediated by a prophet, and the human laws devised by reason... in their attempt to reconcile revelation with philosophy they insisted that, since truth was one and indivisible, the intention of revelation and philosophy must be identical... Accepting the concept of the twofold meaning of scripture, they taught that religion speaks in metaphors and parables for the masses, who are capable of understanding them only literally.

The inner, hidden meaning is accessible only to the philosopher, and by demonstrative argument. Truth thus arrived at is the same as that taught by philosophy.[14]

Not only did these Muslim philosophers believe in the reconcilability of divine and natural laws, but they considered it important to ask "how laws and institutions might shape moral conduct."[15] The jurists were mainly interested in strengthening the morals and ethics of the believers, and so they saw political rule in that context. Their unit of analysis was not organizations, structures, and institutions so much as the community of believers, considered in the context of God's commands enjoining ethical conduct. The philosophers, however, were interested in constructing a science of politics as that domain in which human behavior is the subject of interest. The issues include causes, processes, and consequences of human action. Because of their close reading of Greek philosophy, with its stress upon the individual as a "political animal," the Muslim philosophers presumed that it was advantageous for human beings to live in association with one another. And as with the Greeks, especially Aristotle, the Muslim philosophers paid attention to patterns, generalization, and extrapolation.

The philosophers drew parallels between the political ruler and the prophets, specifically the Prophet of Islam. They perceived rule as crucial for unifying the community, and they investigated rulership in terms of those qualities best suited to motivate a ruler in the wisest course to materialize the happiness and prosperity of his people. The philosophers also were interested in the political dimensions of prophecy, such as the nature of power and authority vested in prophets and the exercise of these in the service of the common good.

Depending on which philosopher one is speaking about, an examination of the subjects of interest to them yields an eclectic mix. Ibn Sina (Avicenna, d. 1037), as Butterworth shows, is not interested in regimes, their variety, the causes of their rise and decline. Nevertheless, the topics for which he evinced concern covered a broad range, including:

> questions fundamental to politics: the nature of law, the purpose of political community, the need for sound moral life among the citizens, the importance of providing for divorce as well as for marriage, the conditions for just war, the considerations that lie behind penal laws, and the goal of human life. Avicenna's description of the way the political community arises and the provisions made for it by a ruler as wise as a prophet shows why traditional Islamic political rule is praiseworthy and alludes to what is wrong with regimes that prize freedom, the pursuit of wealth, or conquest rather than adherence to moral virtue.[16]

Ibn Rushd, on the other hand, was fond of the analogy of the mendicant, whose treatment to cure physical ailments is likened to the recipes that the wise ruler makes available for the perfection of the body politic, which is considered to be centered on the soul. He urged the understanding that the Prophet's leadership was based on a grasp of the people's needs and on a rhetoric and language that, because it was based on allusion and metaphor, had to be explained as such, rather than taken literally.

Ibn Rushd was a jurist of great erudition in Islamic law, and this made it more difficult (though not impossible) to criticize him for being overly influenced by Greek philosophy. He also was careful to accept that the human intellect was too limited to be able to construe God's meaning in certain elements of the revelation and so had simply to accept God's word regarding these. But he refused to concede the larger point that the human being was so limited in his or her understanding that reason must be laid aside. In fact, he argued that it was the duty of the human being, insofar as he was able, to use reason to understand as much about the revelation as possible. Ibn Rushd's illustrious predecessor, Abu Hamid al-Ghazali, had maintained in his famous book *The Incoherence of the Philosophers* that what the philosophers had written was "incoherent." Ibn Rushd's rejoinder, in his own well-known work, *The Incoherence* of the *Incoherence*, was that al-Ghazali's philosophical understanding was itself incoherent, and hence, when he provided an exposition of the thought of the Muslim philosophers, that exposition was beset with diffuseness and opacity.

To ibn Rushd the revelation was divine law, revealed by the Prophet. This law was inerrant because divine. Man-made law did not share this quality, as it was subject to the fallibility of the human being. However, that did not prevent ibn Rushd from seeing a similarity between the revelation and philosophy, namely that both were grounded in law:

> the law ... has a central place in the political thought of Plato and Aristotle as well as in that of Al-Fārābī, Ibn Sīnā and Ibn Rushd. This means that the study of the *Republic*, the *Laws* and the *Nicomachean Ethics* led the Muslim philosophers to grasp more fully the political character implied in the *Shari'a* of Islam (as in the *Torah* of Judaism). Hence revelation is for them not simply a direct communication between God and man, not only a transmission of right beliefs and convictions, a dialogue between a personal God of love, of justice and of mercy and man whom he has created in his image; it is also and above all a valid and binding code for man, who must live in society and be politically organized in a state in order to fulfill his destiny. In short, it is the law of the ideal state. As such it includes regulations about worship and charity just as Greek law dealt with temple sacrifices. It provides for man's welfare in this world and prepares him for the hereafter, and thus alone guarantees his perfection and happiness as a religious being. In so doing it goes beyond the *nomos*, the man-made law of Greek philosophy, which knew of no twofold happiness, though it was equally designed to enable man to reach his goal, intellectual perfection.[17]

Even though the Muslim philosophers were keen to show that they were not advocating the secularization of the religious law, the 'ulama' came to see them as doing precisely that. The 'ulama' could not forgive the philosophers' interest in the pursuit of "true knowledge of the nature of the good regime,"[18] because that seemed to deflect one from the paramount task of worshipping God by unquestionably accepting His commandments This is ironic, because the philosophers fully wished to integrate philosophy and revelation without diluting either the content or the significance of the latter. Indeed, they recognized the superiority of the religious law.

At any rate, none of the works of the major Muslim philosophers has received much attention in the Muslim seminaries. For a span of about three centuries, five Muslim philosophers, al-Kindi (d. 873), al-Farabi, ibn Sina (Avicenna) (d. 1038), ibn Bajja (Avempace) (d. 1138), and ibn Rushd sought to construct the edifice of a Muslim political philosophy that would move the discussion about politics beyond the dry books of jurisprudence. But despite their highly creative minds and writings, they were unable to do so, and knowledge of their thought has always been limited to an elite group of scholars who explicitly wish to understand what they wanted to say. Hence, Islamic political thought remained for centuries what the jurists were prepared to say about the caliphate as a divine institution, the qualifications of the ruler, the various functions of the caliph and his officials that had to do with the collection of religious taxes, the conduct of *jihad*, and the nature of commercial contracts.

It would take the great sociologist ibn Khaldun to bring attention back to some of the broad theoretical questions about politics that the philosophers were wont to ask. He was dissatisfied with Muslim political thought and his intellectual project sought to vitalize this field. Born two hundred years after ibn Rushd, and like that master an outstanding jurist, it was his contribution to provide a theoretical understanding of social change. Although he stressed that the best form of rule was – like that of the Prophet and the rightly guided caliphs who succeeded him – religious in nature, ibn Khaldun had no patience with those who wished to idealize the subsequent caliphate. Instead, he sought to understand what forces accounted for the rise of political communities in the first place, explain the sources of their strength and power, and articulate the reasons for their decline. Because ibn Khaldun himself was involved in many political plans and even intrigues, a number of which backfired,

Mohamed Talbi's judgment is probably accurate when he states: "The flowering of his genius took place... as the result of the fusion of the traditional disciplines in which he had been educated with the rich harvest of political experience which, through a bitter series of failures and impasses, had made him aware of the meaning and deep significance ('ibar) of history."[19]

Ibn Khaldun's intention in writing his masterpiece, *The Prolegomenon*, was to elaborate the science of history. Until his generation, Muslim historians tended to follow a linear narrative, based on chronological accounts. Ibn Khaldun's contribution was to provide a theoretical framework for the understanding of historical materials. Methodology and critical inquiry were of central importance, and recourse to rule-based methods for the conduct of inquiry was, in his view, the only path to the understanding of human history. Not that he rejected received wisdom from the early Islamic historians and jurists regarding the evolution of the *umma*, but he was as much interested in the patterns of that development as he was in earlier writers' conclusions about what happened. Laws, criteria, patterns, models, paradigms – all of these were important for a full understanding of social change. What caused a once vibrant community, based on tribal relations and values, blended with the unifying element provided by revelatory belief, to lose its vigor? This was not the kind of question that the jurists asked. But the Muslim philosophers would have understood the need to ask such questions, since they themselves were interested in discovering the rules that make a truly good system of rule arise and maintain itself.

The Prolegomenon is a work with a truly modern imprimatur. How does the environment influence human beings? What are the anthropological dimensions of communal life (of course, he does not use the word, "anthropological")? What is the nature of tribal association and the civilization based upon it? Where do states and their governments come from, and how may one best study them in terms of their functions and structures? What accounts for the rise of urban civilization, and why does it give way to effeteness and collapse? What are the key elements of political economy? What is the relationship between cultural norms and values and institutional structures? These are questions that a contemporary social scientist would certainly ask, and this is why ibn Khaldun is considered by so many observers as the forerunner of the social science disciplines. As Talbi states:

> He could not in fact penetrate to the heart of reality, describe the struggles and conflicts, the tensions and the successive failures of states and civilizations produced by their internal dissensions without encountering, and calling attention to, the process of dialectic, especially since he had encountered logic in his earlier years and since the ideas of contradiction, antithesis, opposition, the complementariness of opposites, of ambiguity, of complexity and of confusion had long been familiar to the Muslim thinking in which he had been educated. They are thus often evoked as operative concepts permitting understanding and explanation.[20]

In the same way that the Muslim philosophers were prepared to deal with political systems in their own right, ibn Khaldun was prepared to expound on methodological and theoretical questions relevant to an understanding of social change. The difference, however, was that whereas the philosophers sought to integrate their understandings of how states ought to be properly constructed, for example, with the divine revelation, ibn Khaldun did not seek to integrate his theory of social change with God's divine purpose. He spent most of his intellectual energies studying tribal society and trying to understand why the government of the *umma* (which was tribal in structure, even though the unifying element was now religious) became perverted under the caliphate into kingship (*mulk*). For the first time, then, a secular theory of society and the state, social solidarity and mobility, was introduced. To be sure, it was introduced by a thinker who felt himself to be a believer to the core. But for all of that, ibn Khaldun was much more important for his theory of development than he was for his interpretation and application of Maliki jurisprudence.

Ibn Khaldun was the founder of the sciences of sociology, historiography, and perhaps economics as well. He made unparalleled contributions to the development of these fields. He considered the development of human civilizations to be a product of social and economic structures. He introduced a methodology for the study of human history that was dialectical in nature, stressing that the process of historical development is not incremental and linear but a matter of contradictions and conflict. He had little use for the chronological narrative histories of his predecessors except as sources of raw data. An inductivist and empiricist, he set great store by observation as the path to understanding. In comparison to the Muslim philosophers, he did not believe that speculative thought could furnish true understanding of how human beings established their communities, flourished, and, most importantly, declined.

As most commentators have specified, the dynamic that he believed underlay social change was 'asabiya, a word not easily translatable into English. It is frequently translated as "solidarity," but its meaning in Arabic is broader because it denotes the ethos of collective solidarity, zealousness, partisanship, even clannishness, and in its extreme form, prejudice and chauvinism. Its central meaning, for ibn Khaldun, was a spirit perhaps captured by the French phrase *esprit de corps*, with the key notion of enthusiasm. Ibn Khaldun believed that tribal communities have this quality almost by definition of their existential condition. Not only that, but they ride this characteristic forward as the community grows and becomes consolidated. But while this quality is highly necessary for the growth of the happiness and prosperity of the tribal members, as tribes become sedentarized and urban-based it erodes.

While urban civilization, which ibn Khaldun called 'umran (a concept that entails the prosperity that comes with settled living), has many advantages, including the development of culture and refinements, the problem of the loss of 'asabiya is a serious one. It is the cause of the decline of the system because urban living spoils the hardy spirit. Although this cyclical theory of the rise and decline of systems was not new (the Romans, such as Polybius and Cicero, had similar notions), ibn Khaldun was the first among the Muslim thinkers to reflect along these lines. He lived at a time of shifting fortunes of amirates in Spain and North Africa, shifts caused by disunity and seemingly atavistic tribal rivalries that could hardly escape his notice. So, despite the positive aspects of tribal life and the key tribal value of 'asabiya, he did not advocate a renunciation of urban Islam in favor of a return to some "pure" Islam of the early period. All he knew was that this 'asabiya had somehow to be restored, failing which Islamic civilization faced a calamity. Lacking a solution to this decline, perhaps he thought he could at least make a major contribution by showing how it had come about.

Conclusion

In this chapter, I have sought to provide an exposition of the Sunni theory of the caliphate from the pen of al-Mawardi and ibn Taymiyya, the Shi'i juristic theory of authority, the work of the Muslim philosophers, and the thought of ibn Khaldun. When al-Mawardi began to write on the constitutional theory of the state, the 'Abbasid caliphate was in serious trouble. A Shi'ite dynasty, the Buyids (ruled 945–1055), held power, although it permitted the caliphate to remain in Sunni hands. Such circumstances moved al-Mawardi to uphold an accommodationist theory – that is, one that maintained the necessity to accept the realities of power politics as the only way to retain the office of the caliph. A man of vast erudition, he nevertheless did not minimize the pragmatic need to accept the reality that the caliphate must accept the diminution of its authority. Since he and his colleagues believed the caliphate was a divinely ordained institution, this was no small matter. By the time of ibn Jama'a, Sunni constitutional theory had essentially been reduced to the principle that whoever demonstrated superior power in the community was entitled to the office of caliph. It is clear that these juristic theories arose in response to actual developments on the ground. It is likewise clear that shattering historical events, such as the Mongol destruction of the caliphate, influenced ibn Taymiyya in his denial of the necessity of the caliphate altogether.

The Sunni suppression of Shi'ism led to the marginality of both Shi'i thinkers and their thought. As early as the sixth Imam, Shi'a were counseled to piously dissimulate their faith because not to do so would subject them to harm and potentially even the extinction of their numbers. The juristic theory of the Imamate that Shi'i *'ulama'* constructed remained highly idealized, as it had to be, given the adverse historical circumstances in which the Shi'a found themselves.

Still, both the Sunni and Shi'i theories survived the very negative circumstances of seizures of power, rebellions, and the destruction of the caliphate itself. The concepts endemic to these theories were wielded by later groups in ways that helped their cause as against that of their rivals. Thus, the Ottomans and the Iranian Safavids in the fifteenth and sixteenth centuries worked out their understandings of the earlier writings in ways that enabled them to advance their dynastic interests for an extended period of time. In this way, we can see that ideas about authority do not remain abstracted from the historical playing field but rather influence that history in important ways.

Attention was also given in this chapter to certain aspects of the thought of two Muslim philosophers, al-Farabi and ibn Rushd. They sought in their own way to generate a "de-sacralized" model of politics, so to speak, but such a model was not intended to displace the role of God from their theories of politics. Influenced especially by Plato and the neo-Platonists but also by Aristotle, their concern was motivated by the desire to reconcile revelatory and philosophical truth. They, too, lived in unsettled times, especially al-Farabi. No doubt he felt that military seizures of power in the Middle East heartland needed to be placed within the framework of a political theory that championed the beliefs of Muslims in their faith but that also showed that philosophical ethics and aesthetics could combine with scriptural verities to produce superior outcomes. Ibn Rushd, who lived in less tumultuous times in Spain, no less than al-Farabi, felt strongly that the political philosopher's task was to provide a model that fully integrated religious faith with political virtue. But, as we have seen, their efforts did not have lasting impacts, and, ironically, their thought was perhaps more appreciated by non-Muslims than by the Muslims themselves.

Finally, the chapter turned attention to Islam's peerless pioneer in the realm of social theory, ibn Khaldun. He was much less interested in how the caliphate should operate but instead sought to understand how politics work, how social groups maintain their unity, and what causes the rise and decline of civilizations. In short, ibn Khaldun was interested in matters central to the concern of contemporary social theorists and was centuries ahead of his time.

Ibn Khaldun was not a secularist if by that term one means a believer in institutional differentiation brought about by social change to the point that religion becomes less relevant in the public sphere and also in individual consciousness. In fact, he would vehemently reject such a thesis. Instead, his "secularism" lies in his interest in long-term trends, existing within time – as opposed to the transcending of temporality. In that context, what interested him was relationships, among human beings and between them and social structures, economic trends, social patterns. For him, the state was an artifact, its dynamics were subject to causal propositions, and the explanation of its behavior was in itself a major topic of concern. He took great pride in explaining history through empirical inquiry. But, at the same time, he was rooted securely in his beliefs as a Muslim and as a practitioner of Maliki jurisprudence. From that perspective, he was familiar with the classical Sunni theory of the caliphate, but his own explanation of that institution derived from his pragmatic understanding of politics as an arena of power and struggle.

As ibn Khaldun surveyed the turbulent landscape of the region in which he grew up, he integrated his experiences – which included falling in and out of favor with the powers that be – into his matter-of-fact model of the "power state," as Rosenthal terms it.[21] In him, also, we find that concrete conditions were central in the shaping of his ideas, although in his case the further impact of those ideas on historical developments is less clear. This is no doubt due to the fact that following his death, his contributions seem to have been forgotten for centuries until they were invoked by generations of writers in the twentieth century, especially those interested in the ideas of Arab nationalism.

THREE

History and social change

The sociologist Robert Nisbet once wrote: "Change is a succession of differences in time in a persisting identity."[1] In order to know if change is occurring, one must be able to see differences occurring over time affecting an identifiable entity. No change occurs if one arrays models of "the Chinese family" in the era of the Ming Dynasty (1368–1644), "the Inuit Eskimo family" in nineteenth-century Alaska, "the Mesopotamian family" in the epoch of Ur of the Chaldees, and "the Soviet family." This is a mere juxtaposition of models. Difference does not equal change.

Nisbet then supposes that a field researcher has visited a community at a certain time and reported these observations: (1) first-cousin marriage was allowed; (2) divorce was prohibited; (3) marriage occurred only under ecclesiastical auspices. Decades pass, and the field researcher returns to the site of his earlier visit and now finds that: (1) marriage within six degrees of kinship is forbidden; (2) divorce is allowed; and (3) civil marriages are permitted. Change has definitely occurred.

These comments bear stressing because many contemporary Middle Eastern political theories – and virtually all of those that are grounded in the premiss that Islam is both religion and state fail to meet this historicity test. Writers who seek to demonstrate that "Islam" is "the only solution" (al-hall al-wahid), for example, may discuss the early Islamic community (622–661) as a golden age; the era of the 'Abbasid caliphate under the caliph Harun al-Rashid (ruled 786–809), as another such period; the epoch of the Cordoba caliphate in Spain under 'Abd al-Rahman III (ruled 929–961) as yet another such time; and so on. They believe that a reified "Islam" was able to provide the best of what there was to offer the Muslims in these periods, but they ignore the actual historical record that alone can provide the evidence on the emergence of particular social forces that acted in particular ways under particular circumstances to bring about model solutions to their needs in the different historical periods through which they lived. Instead, what is offered is a series of ideal types of what the thinker in question believes ought to have existed. These ideal types are in fact ahistorical cross-sectional descriptive depictions of the normative preferences of the writer in question. What is needed, instead, is a dynamic analysis of how things got to be the way they became, which can only be established if one pays attention to the historical record, not by skipping it.

Some Algerian, Moroccan, Syrian, and Egyptian thinkers on historicization

The writers discussed in this section have a reputation of impatience with the standard fare of political theory in the Arab world. They use terms such as "crisis" or the "murder of thought" or the "unsaid" in Arab writings on political matters. Some try to champion the pioneering path blazed by an earlier thinker, such as al-Miskawayh (d. 1030) or ibn Khaldun, while others lament the marginalization of a movement – such as the Mu'tazila – and wonder how things might have been different had they remained at the center of intellectual activity.

The contemporary Algerian thinker 'Abd al-Ilah Balqaziz has concluded that modern Arab thought has not produced a theory of politics, understanding by theory "a conceptual system that enjoys a modicum of theoretical semantic coherence and stability." He attributes this partly to conceptual diffuseness (as for example the failure to distinguish among concepts such as power and authority or class and group. But he also faults the ahistorical nature of Arab thought, or, as he puts it, its preoccupation with texts rather than with historical reality.[2] As the Syrian academic Basam Tibi puts it, Islamic fundamentalists (defined as those urgently desiring to implement the *shari'a*, or Islamic law, in all walks of life) "dismiss these historical facts ... to them, all that matters is the scripture, not history itself.... Islam as a pure principle expressed in the scripture is immutable, regardless of history, time, culture, location, or whatever."[3]

If Balqaziz and Tibi are correct, the question is why these Islamist theorists disregard history. The answer seems to be that the reification of Islam is the only way to ensure that one not question how Muslims have actually behaved over the course of history on matters such as social justice, liberty, authority, equality, social justice, obligation, and many other values at the core of political theory. The reason for the desire not to question how Muslims have actually conducted their affairs is that they have not done very well in this realm. It is safer to say that "Islam maintains that..." or "Islam supports..." or "Islam says..." or "Islam views that..." But "Islam" is not an actor. Instead, it is Muslims who act. Islamist theorists do not acknowledge this clear fact. They merely state that Islam should be judged not according to the empirical record of more than fourteen centuries of history but rather by the prescriptions found in the sacred texts and in the normative consensus of the jurists over that period of time about what Islam stands for.

This is the line of argument taken in the following excerpt from the work of Muhammad Salim al-'Awwa, who is one of the more sophisticated contemporary Arabo/Muslim political theorists, and an articulate member of the Egyptian Muslim Brotherhood:

in some eras and in some instances implementation deviated from these basic principles that Islam had laid down, but implementation is not to be taken as the norm for the principles themselves in this connection – or in connection with any [other] matter. Islam is [to be] understood and appraised according to its principles and its regulations, and not according to the deviations of some who explain these principles or deviations of some who have implemented these regulations.[4]

'Awwa is in fact telling us to consult the scriptures (the Qur'an and the Sunna of the Prophet) and the normative rulings of jurists over the ages in order to explain politics in Muslim political systems. Yet if we follow this procedure, we would find, for example, that the 1936 Soviet Constitution was among the most enlightened organic laws in history. Clearly, it would be wrong to conclude from this that that document explained how politics worked in the Soviet Union.

The need to historicize explanations of politics and of social change is critical. An early advocate of this was the Moroccan theorist 'Abdallah Laroui ('Abdallah al-'Arwi), in a work that he wrote originally in French in 1974 entitled *The Crisis of the Arab Intellectual*.[5] In this work, he is interested in the cultural bases – including politics – of Islamic civilization's traditions, and he does not shy away from advocating historicization ("historicism" is his word) as a way of overcoming what he believes has been a long period of stagnation in Muslim thought. In disapproving terms, Laroui lamented "philosophy's perennial temptation ever since Plato to escape from history, from dialectic, and from the event."[6] How does one overcome this bias? "Yet, it has long been demonstrated (in different cultural contexts) that the renewal of philosophy rarely comes from any source other than reflection on contemporary politics."[7] Although Laroui, who until 2000 taught at Muhammad V University in Rabat, was also critical of the eclectic thinking of Arab intellectuals whom he saw as "Westernizers," he considered an escape into traditionalism to be just as alienating as emulating the West.

Now there are two types of alienation: the one is visible and openly criticized, the other all the more insidious as it is denied on principle. Westernization indeed signifies an alienation, a way of becoming other, an avenue to self-division (though one's estimation of this transformation may be positive or negative, according to one's ideology). But there exists another form of alienation in modern Arab society, one that is prevalent but veiled: this is the exaggerated medievalization obtained through quasi-magical identification with the great period of classical Arabian culture.[8]

The problem of traditionalism, as he calls it, is that it is built upon absolutes, "the absolutes of language, culture, and the sagas of the past." What is to be done? Laroui believes that nothing less than historical consciousness will do. By this, he does not mean simply being aware of the historical record, but the intellectual rigor of analysis and synthesis grounded in historical facts. Only through this means will the Arab be able to experience and thus be able to explain reality, as opposed to resting content with a series of hypostatizations of that reality. "Then he will see reality perhaps for the first time. He will see that the absolutes he worships are alien to him, for they may be interiorized only through intellectual analysis and synthesis, that is, through voluntary effort – never through inward understanding and intuition."[9]

Laroui's insistence upon dealing with reality, rather than with scriptural norms, as the only means by which contemporary Arabs and Muslims can explain how they have arrived at their present condition is ironic, because his historicist position requires him to hold that historical development is teleological, that the historical trajectory of a people moves to a certain goal or end point. In other words, although he urges the historicization of theories of social change, which should mean that outcomes and explanations of those outcomes are open-ended, his historicism appears to undercut that salutary prescription by encouraging disregard for the concrete and the contingent in favor of the teleological, with its overtones of determinism. It is true that he emphasizes (Arab) nationalism rather than class as the motor force of historical change, but the dynamic is still directional. Marxist historicism sees the ultimate triumph, in Western society, of the working class. Laroui's Marxist-influenced historicism emphasizes the triumph of Arab nationalists. The historical trajectory is toward a goal that is inherent in the dynamics of the class or of the ethnic group, rather than conditioned by actual historical contingencies that are external to that class or ethnic group.

But we should not allow this shortcoming to obscure Laroui's larger point, which is that understanding social change requires historical concretization, not abstraction. Other social and political theorists have picked up on Laroui's initiative to place history in the center of explanations of social change: for example, the Algerian Mohamed Arkoun (Muhammad Arkun), the Syrian Burhan Ghalyun, and the Egyptian Nasr Hamid Abu Zayd. But most of these thinkers reside in Europe or, if they have not settled there, they have been strongly influenced by Marxist and other types of leftist thought.

Mohamed Arkoun is a Berber from the Kabyle region of Algeria. Since 2002 he has been an emeritus professor at the Sorbonne in Paris. He has been an expatriate for many decades, teaching, as well as at the Sorbonne, at various universities, including Lyon, Paris, the Institute for Advanced Studies at Princeton, and UCLA. The French government awarded him the Légion d'Honneur in 1996. He was also the winner in 2002 of the seventeenth Giorgio Levi Della Vida Award for his lifetime of scholarship on Islam.

Arkoun argues on behalf of historicization of social change in a work he published in 1996. At one point, he writes that it is important for Arabs and Muslims to explain the contemporary situation in which their co-religionists find themselves. Admitting a sense of urgency, Arkoun declares forthrightly the need to introduce the concept of "historicity" (*al-ta'rikhiyya*) to Muslims. Militant Muslim public opinion not only rejects the concept itself but even rejects thinking about it, he holds. Yet this is perverse. Why? For one thing, all the Qur'anic verses and *ahadith* (sayings of the Prophet) came forth in circumstances that greatly varied from each other and contributed to what Arkoun calls the "epistemological framework" of Islam. Despite such variation, however, an ideal (i.e. idealized) Islam emerged out of this ebb and flow and became a reified entity, namely "the true religion." It nullifies all other Islams (meaning interpretations of their faith by well-meaning Muslims who do not necessarily accept the template of the "true religion" offered by the militant Islamists). It itself cannot be nullified. Thus, it is supreme (muta'al) and beyond history. To their way of thinking, one can surmount all the difficulties that will be produced by an "Islam" such as this, on the one hand, and historicity, on the other.[10] Arkoun thus adds his voice to the growing, but still very small, chorus of Arab and Muslim intellectuals calling for a halt to the domination of hypostatic discourse in contemporary Arabo-Muslim political theory.

Burhan Ghalyun's support for the effort at historicization is filtered through language that is more recondite and abstract, but the point still comes over. He, too, is an expatriate, a Syrian national who is Professor of Sociology and Political Science at the Sorbonne in Paris. He has joined the cause of the many intellectuals whom the state has arrested, detained, and incarcerated and generally finds himself on the side of those who wish to give optimum rein to the human capacity for reason. In one of his most important works, published originally in 1986 with the dramatic title *The Assassination of Reason: The Trials and Tribulations of Arab Culture between the Salafiyya Movement and Subjection*, he laments the marginalization of reason across the epochs of Arab civilization. How did this come to pass? He defines reason as a cluster of interlocking concepts that are systematized and ordered according to axioms and premises through which humans seek to grasp and to represent objective reality. Reason had been an important factor in Arab culture for generations. Ghalyun believes that reason is a central theme of the Qur'an and a major tool in the early debates among the jurists. God endowed humans with reason because He wished to enlighten them, but Muslims eventually came to abandon reason in favor of following the traditions of their forebears.

Reason is a constituted and acquired system that is linked to culture. Being part of that culture, it reflects the social and historical circumstances that produce it. In other words, reason is a contingent, not a timeless, product. When a new civilization appears, a transformation occurs in the concept of rationalism associated with the old one that is replaced. A change occurs in the connection between the principles of the operation of human reason, on the one hand, and the particular cultural experiences of the community represented by the new civilization, on the other. With the success of the new civilization, the rationalism with which it is associated envelopes the former rationalism of the lapsed civilization in a kind of dialectical supersession or overcoming.

Because rationalism is produced in historical contexts, it cannot be universal or absolute. Rationalism from one civilization to the next produces a restructuring in the minds of human beings as those minds consider major issues and problems that can be solved within the range of existing historical circumstances. The function of a system of reason in any civilization, argues Ghalyun, is to order the reality that encompasses that civilization. The strategy that system of reason utilizes for that purpose differs with different realities. By this, he suggests that a system of reason for creating order out of the flux of events and occurrences that happen within the reality of one civilization will not be the same with respect to that process in another civilization.

Ultimately, his point is that rational systems do not travel well across civilizations without significant modifications in their premisses, definition, and operationalization of concepts, and the means for the attainment of normative ends. Such modifications must occur in reference to the experiences of the people. Moreover, sometimes within an existing civilization or culture the rational system begins to lose its ability to order that culture's reality. If it is not to end up in conceptual muddles, the system of reason must restructure its concepts through trial and error, based on experimentation and pragmatism. Ghalyun thus stands for an epistemology of praxis, in which knowledge arises through action, rather than speculation.

In Ghalyun's opinion, Arab thought is currently facing a crisis and is in dire need of experimentation and pragmatism for the sake of reconstructing rational systems appropriate for it. Of course, he does not advocate undisciplined pragmatism, whereby matters are brought forward that have nothing to do with the historical record of the society or culture or civilization of the Arabs themselves. Quite the contrary, awareness of that historical record is a *sine qua non* for the successful construction of the new system of reason that is needed. And that is exactly his problem with scripturalists, who appear to believe in the timelessness and ahistorical nature of one epoch in Middle Eastern history and want somehow to materialize it in the late twentieth/early twenty-first century. Accordingly, Ghalyun holds, the struggle in modern Arab thought for the sake of reconstructing the rational system – that is, the sum of the basic dynamic concepts that propel and guide consciousness – is connected to the struggle between the new and the old. This struggle continues up to now, and he hopes that it will renew the concepts of history, politics, society – indeed, reconstruct their structures.[11]

From the historian Burhan Ghalyun we consider the semiotician Nasr Hamid Abu Zayd. Abu Zayd is an expatriate Egyptian who teaches currently at the University of Utrecht. He was forced to leave Cairo University, where he was a professor of Arabic literature, as a consequence of accusations against him of unbelief at the time of his promotion case (the processing of which took three years, from 1992 to 1995) on grounds that his writings were blasphemous. His intellectual position on the Qur'an as a work of literature that can be studied through contemporary methodologies, including semiotics, caused his critics to condemn him for apostasy. A court eventually found him guilty, and it additionally ruled that his marriage to his wife was null and void because a Muslim woman may not be married to an apostate. Under these circumstances, both he and his wife emigrated to Holland, where they now live.

In a work published in 1997, he criticizes what Abu Zayd calls "the historicism of the religious text." By this concept, he seems to mean that religious texts become historically fixed in time and space and hence are rendered timeless, whereas they should be, as with all texts, deconstructed according to changing conditions and the circumstances of those for whom such texts were intended to be meaningful. In Abu Zayd's view, this situation produces "a discursive mode as absolute truth," and the defenders of this believe that critique and analysis are tantamount to unbelief, atheism, and heresy. He notes that these charges were made against the Mu'tazila, who tried to show the temporality of the Qur'an, rather than accepting its eternality assumptions.[12] And, of course, he believes that he himself, as one sympathetic to Mu'tazilite positions, has been treated the same way by the Islamists.

The issue of ahistorical analysis, the need to concretize discussions about social change in the historical record, and the inadequacy of appealing to texts to explain empirical realities are joined in a work by Fu'ad Zakariya entitled *Reality and Fantasy in Regard to the Contemporary Islamic Movement*. Zakariya is among the most outspoken Egyptian critics of political Islam (Islamism). A philosopher and social critic, Zakariya has written works on Spinoza, rationalist philosophy, contemporary Arab philosophy, aesthetics, cultural criticism, theories of art and music. He has taken to task facile solutions proposed by those who argue that the immediate application of Islamic law is the only way for Muslims to prosper, by pointing out the contradictions in such a position.

Zakariya does this with telling effect in the following discussion about his reactions to an article written by Shaykh Khalid Muhammad Khalid in the Egyptian daily newspaper *al-Ahram*, on 24 June 1985. In that article, Khalid discussed the concept of *shura* (consultation). The term appears twice in the Qur'an, once as a noun in 42:38 (*wa amruhum shura baynahum* – "for their affairs are a matter of counsel"), and once as a verb in the imperative form in 3:159 (*wa shawirhum fi al-amr* – "so, consult them in affairs"). Khalid, following the pioneering path of Muhammad 'Abduh, the great reformer and Grand Mufti of Egypt (d. 1905), reads into the concept of *shura* a full-blown model of democracy. Before turning to Zakariya's analysis of Khalid's conclusion about *shura*, it is worth making the following points, which Zakariya does not himself raise.

The verses in question appear in contexts that make it difficult to materialize democracy from them. In 42:38, the context is that God is telling the Prophet, through the archangel Gabriel, to relate to those who choose to believe that their material possessions are transitory, whereas God has in store for them benefits that are eternal. There follows a series of descriptive phrases, that believers should show aversion to sin, readiness to forgive, obedience to God, and organize their affairs as a matter of counsel. The counsel to be taken in regard to their affairs, however, is religious, not political, having to do with moral belief and devotional duties, as can be seen both from the overall context of the preceding and succeeding verses, and also from the fact that this chapter is one of the Meccan suras, meaning it was revealed before the Prophet's flight to Medina. Such suras are characterized by abstraction and appeals to ethical pieties, not concrete social and economic matters.

The context for Qur'an 3:159 is God saying to the Prophet through the archangel Gabriel and also, via the Prophet, to potential believers that He is the giver of life and death, that death in His cause will be met with His mercy. God specifically addresses the Prophet to remind him of His command that he treat the people gently, lest they turn away from the message of Islam, and adds: "So pardon them and pray that forgiveness may be theirs and consult them in matters." This verse was revealed in Medina, whence the Prophet had fled to escape his enemies and had established the Muslim community. The verses of the Qur'an that deal with social and economic matters (about 10 per cent of the entire scripture) were revealed in Medina. But what is the nature of the consultation commanded by God of the Prophet? The context of the previous and succeeding verses seems to indicate that it would be for the purpose of eliciting questions from the people in case they needed clarifications on issues relating to belief, the devotional duties, the nature of rituals (such as prayer, fasting, and the like), the Day of Judgment, and so on. Even if one were to concede that the consultation mandated by God was in the nature of political consultation, one would still have to show that the Prophet would take the advice offered in the consultation, as opposed to considering such advice without having to take it. And in neither of these alternatives do we have a full-blown conceptualization of the concept of democracy.

At any rate, Zakariya quotes Khalid as having written in his article in *al-Ahram* that democracy

> is the democracy that we see today in the democratic countries, and its pillars are: (1) the nation is the source of authority; (2) the necessity for the separation of powers; (3) the nation has the absolute right to select its leader; (4) the nation has the absolute right to select its representatives; (5) the establishment of a free and bold [shuja'a] parliamentary opposition that can cause the fall of the government when it deviates; (6) a multi-party system; (7) a free press, whose cause must be promoted. This, my brother, is the system of rule in Islam, without perversion or distortion.

In reply to this characterization of *shura* Zakariya says that Khalid has provided nothing more than an ideal type of democracy, but the concept of *shura* is far narrower in scope than Khalid has stated. In any case, would Khalid have arrived at this definition if his thinking operated with reference solely to general principles embodied in the sacred scriptures of Islam? Would he have defined *shura* in terms of all these points if he had not himself been influenced by the writings of John Locke, Charles de Montesquieu, Jean-Jacques Rousseau and Thomas Jefferson? Would he have defined it this way had not the experiences of the modern states, which preceded the Arab and Islamic worlds by many decades in the domain of democracy, not supported the ideas of these philosophers through their implementation? Could Khalid have explained *shura* in this manner had he himself not been a person who had acquired his democratic leanings and orientation through his own reading and learning about the experiences of Western societies and their political systems? If it is rejoindered that Khalid indeed could have arrived at such a definition by consulting the Islamic heritage alone, then, says Zakariya, one must ask why these principles had never been adumbrated or implemented throughout the entire history of Islam?[13]

Zakariya thus pleads for awareness of the historical record. As soon as one does this, one must focus upon human agency as the key factor in any explanation of change. History, in short, does not somehow automatically unfold. Rather, it is people – to be sure, acting in groups, classes, and/or movements – who engage in actions that comprise the totality of the historical record.

Hasan Hanafi and Muhammad 'Imara in the light of ahistorical analysis

Let us look at the explicit call by two contemporary Egyptian writers, Muhammad 'Imara and Hasan Hanafi, to ground social and political theory in historical analysis so as to avoid falling into the usual scripturalist reifications. There can be little doubt that they were motivated and influenced by 'Abdallah Laroui's demand for historicization in 1974. But, unfortunately, not only did they not elaborate such a project themselves (saying that this was a job for many hands and themselves resting content with glossing a set of principles); but they themselves have not carried out their own recommendations in their subsequent research.

Hasan Hanafi received his Ph.D. in philosophy from the Sorbonne in 1966. His dissertation is entitled "The Methods of Exegesis: An Essay on the Science of the Foundations of Islamic Jurisprudence." He has dedicated himself to the cause of Islamic renewal, with its corollary of abandoning the method of imitation or emulation of early Islamic models of knowledge and practice. He has made use of both

Marxist and phenomenological concepts. He has also written articles for the media, including a long series of articles for the Kuwaiti newpaper *al-Watan* in 1981 and 1982 on the Islamic movement in Egypt against the backdrop of the assassination of Anwar al-Sadat. He is currently Professor of Philosophy at Cairo University. Hanafi founded an intellectual movement that he called "the Islamic left," hoping that it might find resonance among the broader masses, but it has remained a highly esoteric effort limited to a small number of the Egyptian intelligentsia. He is a controversial figure, both for his politics and for the inconsistencies in his writings. But the volume of his output is very large, and there is no denying his visibility as an active academic. After the Iranian Revolution, Hanafi abandoned his erstwhile model of the revolutionary leader, whom he typically had seen as an anti-imperialist socialist and nationalist, and came to see the religious jurists in this role instead.

Hanafi sounds the theme of historical consciousness more than once in his writings. In 1990, against the backdrop of the collapse of the Soviet-type systems in Eastern Europe, he participated in a number of discussions with the Moroccan philosopher Muhammad 'Abid al-Jabiri on issues of the day. In typical equivocating fashion, he entitled one of his presentations "Liberalism: Ash'arism Has Not Succeeded in Egypt" but then went on to show Ash'arism's enduring impact in that country! In this piece he praised liberalism's positive points, including its dedication to the rights of the individual against the tyranny of the state and government, but he noted that it was difficult to transplant the liberal model from its home in the UK and the USA to other societies. His solution was to desist from citing Western liberals and instead attribute to the Islamic scriptures verses or ideas that were suited to the liberal temperament, such as "there is no coercion in matters of religion" (Qur'an 2:256) or "Let him who wishes to believe do so, and him who wishes to disbelieve do so" (Qur'an 18:29).

However, more was needed than attribution to appropriate texts, since, as we have seen, the invoking of texts is no warrant for the implementation of the ideas in those texts. Accordingly, Hanafi appeals for "historical consciousness" (al-waʻy bi al-taʼrikh). At the time that he was writing, he believed that four political movements were afoot in Egypt: liberalism, Islamism, Marxism, and nationalism. In his view, the historical roots of the crisis of freedom and democracy could be seen in all of them. The only way for liberalism and democracy to succeed, he maintained, was to extirpate the roots of domination by rulers and submissiveness by the people. How? By "reconstructing the cultural treasure that is still alive in our national culture on a new foundation that makes the human being effective as the agent of history." Hanafi lamented the error of his generation in separating political awareness from historical consciousness and appealed for their integration.[14]

It seems very likely that Hanafi was influenced to think along these lines by at least three sources: French leftist philosophers whom he encountered and read when he was studying in France; Egyptian Marxists such as Anwar ʻAbd al-Malik (Anouar Abdel-Malek), Samir Amin and Mahmud Amin al-ʻAlim; and Antonio Gramsci, including his notion of the role to be played by "organic intellectuals" as a force mediating between the working masses and the professional revolutionaries of the vanguard party. To Gramsci, the ideological hegemony exercised by these intellectuals and party professionals upon the workers would eventually bear fruit in the larger society, but the process would itself take a long time. Meanwhile, these intellectuals, in forming a "hegemonic bloc," would respect cultural values and norms that animate the broad masses of the population. For Egypt this meant Islam. Rather than the Leninist contempt for the prevailing cultural values of the pre-revolutionary society, Gramsci insisted not only upon taking such values into account but noting their motivating power for popular action. Thus, instead of the Leninist notion of a rapid takeover by a militant cadre of revolutionaries, Gramsci proposed an evolutionary trend that ultimately would integrate the cultural values of the overall population in a general, graduated, but inexorable social movement toward a socialist society.[15]

These thoughts have their roots in two earlier essays that Hanafi published in 1979 and 1981 under the respective titles of "Why Has the Study of the Human Being Been Absent in Our Old Heritage?" and "Why Has the Study of History Been Absent in Our Old Heritage?"[16] In the former article, he noted that at a time when societies around the world were focusing increasingly on the individual in the context of his past, in the Arab-Muslim world this was not happening. Instead, "the split between ourselves and our past is increasing," and the focus is rather upon that which is alien to the individual. Hanafi conceded that traditional discussions of Islamic theology, philosophy, Sufism, and law did deal with the human being, but when this happened it was always in some larger context. The individual was never taken up as a subject in himself. Moreover, even in these discussions it was never the ordinary Muslim that received attention but rather leaders.[17]

Perhaps aware that his rivals might accuse him of trying to revise Islam by importing non-Islamic ideas into the discussion, Hanafi explicitly disclaimed that he was doing this.[18] The human being in Egypt is in crisis, he declared, and this crisis was symptomized by the fact that Egyptian universities were overcrowded, transportation systems crammed, representative assemblies stacked, political parties bereft of consciousness, and the human being subject to the oppression of the political authorities, the society, and the family.[19]

The true reason for the individual's absence from the Arab-Muslim heritage, Hanafi wrote, lay in the national consciousness, and that, in turn, was rooted in the nature of Arab-Muslim thought in all its dimensions.[20] For Hanafi how Muslim Arabs conceive the world – in a word their *Weltanschauung*, that which they have inherited from their ancestors – is the source of the present crisis. Its solution is nothing less than the reconstruction of that heritage. Central to that process, in turn, is what Hanafi enigmatically calls the "re-employment of the spiritual structures to raise up and present the human being in our contemporary consciousness."[21] Using the metaphor of the human being in the classic Islamic heritage as shrouded in hundreds of linguistic, doctrinal, theological, and canonical legal veils, Hanafi calls for the shedding of these veils to reveal finally the Muslim individual. If this is done,

> we can transpose our civilization from the old divine condition to the new human state, in which, rather than our civilization being centered upon Allah and the human being wrapped up inside veils, it will center on the human being outside the veils. This is not an easy task, because it means taking the center of civilization from Allah and placing the human being at its center, and changing its pivot from the science of Allah to the science of the human being.[22]

This extraordinary statement, calling for an anthropocentric Islam, is surely at the extreme end of the modernist call for historicization. Hanafi would likely defend his extremism by suggesting that it is no more than the logical extension of the argument that history must be placed at the center of analysis.

In the companion essay that Hanafi published two years later, with a similar title, "Why Has the Study of History Been Absent in Our Old Heritage?" he reprised this theme. He argued that "the progress of a people depends upon its discovery of its consciousness of history."[23] However, in his opinion, the Arab Muslims inherited the absence of a historical consciousness from their ancestors. The root of the problem, Hanafi maintained, lay in the fact that Arab Muslims believed that the revelation was the source of all knowledge, considered to be an *a priori* given. In other words, knowledge did not come from the investigation of natural occurrences or by dint of formal reason.[24]

Hanafi then poses the question of whether or not it is possible to establish a central role for history – in effect, a philosophy of history – in a culture rooted in revelation? To him, historicization can succeed in a civilization only if there is a conception of progress and regress, of antecedents and consequences, of linear movement and dynamics.[25] The problem as he sees it is that the model of Islamic civilization consists of a divine center ringed by an outer circular perimeter of human beings whose knowledge about the universe is fixed by the limits of the revelation. What is needed is a model of civilization in which nothing is known *a priori* and people posit hypotheses based on the realities that they observe or theoretical propositions that they deduce. "History does not arise in a divine civilization, but in a human one," he writes.[26]

In the early Islamic community, history never became an independent subject of learning. Then, the Muslims were adamant in arguing the unicity of God against Persian and Christian views that centered upon anthropomorphism and Trinitarianism. As Hanafi improbably puts it, because the Muslims were the ones who were "making history" by extending Islam to other regions, they did not see the need to "link Allah to history, to the earth, and to the lives of the people... history did not appear as a theoretical subject in view of the existence of the movement of the Arabs in history."[27]

However, when the course of history came to an end, as it were, for the Muslims as they entered a period of stagnation after the twelfth century, it was natural, Hanafi contends, for ibn Khaldun to think about history and explain the rise and fall of nations by reference to concrete historical trajectories. And after the Muslim Arabs came out of their centuries-long slumber in the nineteenth century, it is understandable that they tried to establish a philosophy of history, just as the Europeans had done in the later Middle Ages, when they turned their attention to the actual problems of the world in which they were living, as opposed to orienting themselves to matters of salvation.[28]

The preoccupation with history is central to Hanafi's outlook. In his major work to reconstruct the Islamic sciences, he writes: "What is needed is for the individual to affirm himself, apply his reason, accept responsibility, implement his mission, be aware of the masses, and grasp the dynamics of history."[29] Later, in a passage whose meaning is somewhat diffuse, he adds:

> Error cannot be changed by repentance, nor by asking God's forgiveness, but by learning, theory and action. There is no sanctuary for the human being except his action, no salvation but collective activity with others – that is, mass action, which is produced by the dynamics of history.[30]

Hanafi presumably wants to say "mass action produces history," but instead offers that "history produces mass action," as though history is an actor! Withal, he continues, saying that even the credo of the faith must be historicized. He declares boldly that the credo is not about God and the Prophet, "it is a theoretical and practical attestation about matters of the epoch and the events of history."[31]

Hanafi ties this concern with history to the lament that Muslims have either viewed the original community of believers at the time of the Prophet as the paradigmatic society or projected to the hereafter in their search for the golden age. Both looking at the past for a model to follow or looking to the future for a model to anticipate have the effect of displacing the present, he warns. This amounts to the abandonment of the human potential of the current generations of Muslims, as though the solutions to their problems lie outside of their time. "That is counter to the dynamics and course of history, its natural development."[32] And he cautions against an academic concern with ideas only. "Distinction lies not in [preoccupation with] the subject matter, as our predecessors maintained, but in effects and the ability to move people, mobilize the masses, and enter into the dynamics of history."[33]

The chronicling of events, rather than the search for patterns and laws of development, became the staple of Arab Muslim thought, in Hanafi's view. The trouble with chronicling events, as he sees it, is that it merely provides information about what happened, rather than knowledge of why. According to the tradition established by early Muslims and reinforced by the victorious Ash'arite theology, historical knowledge comes not from the search for causal explanation of variations in behavior due to variables that could be identified in some scientific way. Instead, knowledge is treated as a product of what Hanafi calls *man qala yaqulu* ("it is said that…") — that is, from a personal narration based on a chain of authority. What is produced here is not a new idea or discovered law but a statement that has been transmitted word for word.[34] Moreover, the state's appropriation of Ash'arism as the official perspective on religion and society secured that state's hegemony over everything, including people and institutions, in exactly the same way that Allah has hegemony over the world, shorn of events and history.[35]

Yet, what exactly does Hanafi suggest? His solution is that one acquires historical consciousness by gaining freedom. Sounding a strongly Hegelian theme, Hanafi boldly asserts that "history is the story of freedom." And, endorsing Benedetto Croce on this matter, he proclaims that "all history is the history of the liberation of human beings from the external tutelage of religious and political leaders."[36] Arab Muslims, he argues, need to control the course of their history through the articulation and establishment of "structures of consciousness and knowledge."[37]

Hanafi, however, fails to show analytically the nature of this connection between freedom, which he does not define, and historical consciousness. Moreover, one looks in vain through his five-volume work *Min al-'Aqida ila al-Thawrah* ('From Belief to Revolution'), to discover a historically grounded analysis of the problems of society. This project is meant to reveal how the Muslim today can find analogies to his current problems by examining his cultural heritage, using the latter as a "spiritual storehouse" from which to draw appropriate principles and concepts; and then show how that same Muslim can move from the past, armed with these principles and concepts, to the present, through the intermediary of "consciousness." But there is no systematic analysis of these "journeys" from the present to the past and from the past to the present through historical junctures of time and place in the actual developments of Arab/Muslim societies. Instead, what Hanafi does is, as Abu Zayd[38] has so well stated it, to jump from present to past and past to present, skipping over the actual historical record of centuries of time. The book, in short, is replete with a series of categorical statements about various issues such as freedom, justice, and interests, and rhetorical flourishes about how lacking mainstream Arab Muslim writing has generally been up to now (with some exceptions, such as the Muʿtazilah, ibn Rushd or ibn Hazm (d. 1064) – who nevertheless were overwhelmed by the orthodox "mass line" of Ashʿarism).

Historicization in Muhammad ʿImara's modernist Ashʿarism

Hanafi is not the only Egyptian who has recently been stressing historical context and historical consciousness. In the 1980s and 1990s, it appeared that a focus on historical grounding of analysis had a certain cachet for modernist Muslim writers. Compare Hanafi, for example, to the prolific independent scholar Muhammad ʿImara, who likewise has appealed to Muslims to pay attention to history at approximately the same time that Hanafi was doing so. In the third chapter of his misleadingly titled book *Studies in Historical Consciousness*,[39] he argued that historical consciousness is an important instrument in the construction of the Muslim community's future. Central to developing such a consciousness, he insists, is a "scientific method," enabling the writer not merely to order historical events but to analyze them so as to be able to understand the direction of developments, their relationship to social forces and national trends, in short to actual occurrences and relationships.[40]

Everybody, wrote ʿImara, seems these days to be calling for the rewriting of Arab history. Agreed, he wrote, but what method should we choose to accomplish this task? Settling upon the method is prior to addressing the issue of how useful Arab Muslim history can be for the present and future Muslim community.[41] The issue is not just to re-aggregate and reconstruct actual historical events and reclassify them; nor is it to eliminate the narrative traditions characteristic of earlier historians.

ʿImara's chapter, however, raises many more questions than it answers. For example, he asked what had caused Arab Islamic culture to gift its civilization to the world, and what, by contrast, caused it to fall into the rigor mortis of its "dark ages" – a reference to the long centuries of stagnation after the end of the fourteenth century.[42] While he had no ready response, he was sure of one thing: if the Arab Muslims did not abandon their traditional ways of viewing their own historical record, they would compromise any chances for a future of freedom and progress. In fact, they would be unwittingly giving comfort to their enemies, who hoped to maintain the fragmentation of the Muslim Arabs.[43]

What 'Imara was calling for was nothing less than a philosophy of history, which would allow Arab Muslims to view history not as an accumulation of occurrences but as a patterned development of Arab Muslim civilization, a pattern endowed with its own "spirit that is always moving and growing." Note this hypostatization, as though "Arab civilization" is an actor. Viewing history as a patterned tendency would enable Arab Muslims to see the relationships of historical development to social forces, national trends, and big structures.[44] 'Imara did not explain how they were to construct a robust philosophy of history except generally to assert that the gates of ijtihad are open to scholars qualified to exercise it.[45]

'Imara also appealed for recourse to what he variously called the "scientific," "social," "material," "progressive" method. Curiously, he defined this method not according to conceptual categories, its propositions, or its rules for designating evidence. Instead, its central defining feature for him is that research should be aware of economic variables. Beyond this, he proposed that Muslims should use Muslim sources in the rewriting of their history. He then unaccountably proceeded to reject what he had earlier endorsed: the "scientific method" or "materialistic methods," perhaps because of his oversimplified equation of these with Marxism, which he is anxious to reject as a Western "import."[46]

'Imara noted that methods used by earlier Arab Muslim scholars varied, just as do those employed in our time. Today, he wrote, without elaboration, we see Arab historical schools that emphasize a blend of the "non-dialectical, non-social method" with "cognitive and social history."[47] In his view, this represented an evolution away from the idealism in historical thought that had dominated Muslim social theory for a long time. In other words, he held, Muslim writers today were breaking from past patterns by adhering to a new "scientific" paradigm.

'Imara believed that he himself was a proponent of this approach, which, moreover, he felt had been utilized by a few early Muslim chroniclers but had been eclipsed over the centuries by another approach that stressed episodic narrative. 'Imara recalls the Mu'tazili writer Abu Ja'far Muhammad b. 'Abd Allah al-Iskafi (d. 854), who sought to explain the conflict between the fourth caliph, 'Ali, and his adversaries[48] during the first civil war in material/economic terms, rather than relying on the standard idealized explanations rooted in personalities and chronological description. Unfortunately, writes 'Imara, the method used by Iskafi and the few others like him lapsed. His antidote to this idealized historical writing was to resuscitate al-Iskafi's putatively materialist theory while not resorting to Marxist analysis, alien to Islam, in order to affirm the economic roots of conflicts such as that between 'Ali and his rivals.[49] Consequently, contemporary Muslim Arab historians should go directly to indigenous sources to make a materialist argument. This way, they would avoid the trap of importing a method from non-Islamic sources and, 'Imara seems to be suggesting, reach a faulty conclusion. He also demanded the rewriting of the entire record of Arab Muslim history according to the canons of social historiography. In this manner, the older tradition of stressing idiosyncratic factors, such as heroic individuals and their allegedly unique gifts and ideas, would finally be overcome.[50]

Unfortunately, however, 'Imara did not specify in what way a Marxist analysis of this conflict would be faulty; he just implied that it would be unsatisfactory insofar as it was non-Islamic. Neither did he enlighten his reader as to the nature of the "scientific method" that would vindicate al-Iskafi's stress upon economic factors. This failure to articulate the procedure and operation of the "scientific method" is critical. For, in the absence of a more explicit conceptualization of what would be entailed, a scholar would have an equal chance of rediscovering al-Iskafi's "economic materialism" without the benefit of 'Imara's "scientific method" as he would rediscovering him equipped with such a method. Perhaps 'Imara was equating a scientific historical method with one that privileges material causal variables, but saying such variables are important is a far cry from establishing a theoretical conception of historical change.

'Imara evinced little patience for calls by some for the appointment of prestigious boards of historians to rewrite Arab Muslim history. For him, the critical point was that each scholar brings to his or her scholarship certain perspectives and interests that are conditioned by that scholar's social background, experience, and class affiliation. These variations would not be overcome or homogenized, in his opinion, simply by commissioning a larger committee or council of experts to restudy Arab Muslim history. It would be more realistic to acknowledge the authors' own social background characteristics, minimize them as much as possible in the research process, and favor analysis based on social theory.[51]

In his concluding remarks, 'Imara warned that unless the "scientific method" replaced that regnant approach, Arab society would suffer. As he put it:

> The adoption of the scientific, social, material method utilized by al-Iskafi is the primary requisite for transforming our history ... into an effective force that would play its part in the movement of progress, liberation and unity for Arab society and the modern Arab.[52]

About a decade later, 'Imara broached the subject again, though more elliptically. In a work[53] jointly sponsored by al-Azhar's Supreme Council for the Islamic Call and the International Institute for Islamic Thought,[54] he defended recourse to *ijtihad* even in the presence of an explicit canonical text.[55] He then proceeded to lament the displacement of genuine Islamic thought by two rival currents: (1) "Western imported thought";[56] and (2) the "reactionary legacy" that has come down to the Muslims from the era when Islam had fallen into a petrified state. Accordingly, 'Imara believes that Islamic thought was in a state of crisis. But, contrary to Hanafi, who felt that the crisis was due to the domination of a divinely centered *Weltanschauung* in which the individual was marginalized, 'Imara attributed it to the conjuncture of "external pressures"[57] and "shortcomings arising from (our) inability to operationalize the law and the tradition of renewal."[58] It is almost as though 'Imara is ascribing to *tajdid* (renewal) – which, after all, is a mental construct – an independent ability to act. For he does not tell us how to integrate this concept into a theoretical analysis of change.

Later in this work, published in 1991, 'Imara felt it necessary to deny that this failure to implement renewal was due to inadequate conceptualization of causality. That 'Imara on this point was at least implicily arguing against Hanafi seems evident by the former's focus upon al-Ghazali and ibn Rushd. Both of these medieval Muslim thinkers have figured prominently in Hanafi's writings[59] – al-Ghazali, according to him, being responsible for authoritarianism and calcification in Arab Muslim thought because of his attacks on philosophy; and ibn Rushd, among other philosophers, as a hero whose ideas, including the importance of causal explanations, were suppressed at great cost to Arab Muslim civilization.[60]

But 'Imara was having none of this and wished to correct what he believed to be a misperception among some critics (for example, Hasan Hanafi) as to al-Ghazali's and ibn Rushd's notions of causality. 'Imara noted that one can distinguish analytically among three approaches to causality: (1) one that denies it altogether and insists that all occurrences are fortuitous and contingent; (2) one that stresses the causality of natural phenomena and in the world of human beings, whereby God either has no role at all or, as Aristotle had held, intervened initially to set the dynamics of the world going but then entirely extricated Himself from them; (3) one that accepts cause and effect in nature and in the world of human beings but at the same time insists that God plays a central role, both in vesting human beings with the ability to initiate causes to bring about effects and make them responsible for their actions, and in preserving the sovereign power of God to intervene to change the normal course of a cause to bring about an unexpected effect. 'Imara then declared that all Muslims accepted the third approach. In his opinion, the issue regarding al-Ghazali is not whether he had a doctrine of causality (which scholars such as Hanafi, he insists, would deny), but how causality operates.[61]

'Imara then added that ibn Rushd agreed with al-Ghazali that no causes are sufficient in themselves to bring about effects, because such causes are "products of God," whose action is a condition for the operation of these causes."[62] 'Imara is entitled to his opinion, but Hanafi[63] is hardly alone among Arab Muslims in asserting that al-Ghazali abandoned the law of causality in the natural world and the world of human beings. A similar point is made, for example, by the Moroccan philosopher Muhammad 'Abid al-Jabiri. Moreover, ibn Rushd insisted, as we saw earlier, upon separating revelation from the natural and human worlds. Each had its truth(s), and one should not mix the two spheres.

It is true that al-Ghazali's doctrine of causality permits the human being some latitude in acting, but this secondary concept of causality (in which God bestows an act upon a person at the exact moment of the action, and the human being "acquires" this act at that moment) still preserves the gist of the Ash'arite occasionalist ontology and Ash'arism's refusal to grant epistemological autonomy to the human being. Determinism (al-jabr) has loomed large in Arab Muslim thought over the centuries, and al-Ghazali's role in this was central, 'Imara's protests to the contrary notwithstanding. The idea that human beings "acquire" their actions from God, who invests them with the ability to act at that critical juncture, became a way of softening the impacts of pure deterministic thought in the world of human beings. Yet, even here, human action can be no more than contingent upon God's decision to bestow the ability to acquire the impetus for one's acts in society. As for the world of nature, al-Ghazali regarded all phenomena as products of God's direct will and power. God was the motor force of all the particulars and occurrences of the natural world. In this world, a lamp casts light, for example. However, the connection between the lamp and the light that it casts is not a causal but rather purely *ad hoc* one. An individual who sees a lamp producing light would say the lamp is the producer (*al-fa'il*) of the light. But al-Ghazali says this is not necessarily the case, since the "producer" is not a "fabricating producer" (*fa'il sani'*) but rather a "means of action" (*sabab al-fa'il*) actuated by divine will.[64]

Interestingly, 'Imara refrained from probing the distinctions that *do* exist between al-Ghazali and ibn Rushd over how causality operates. 'Imara is correct in noting that all Muslim writers stress God's causal role, but the real question is the nature of that role. Hanafi has a point when he expresses his exasperation that human causality in 'Imara's scheme is *always* contingent. If it is contingent, then this scheme can always trump a perspective that wishes to formulate propositions about social change that allow the initiative to pass to the champions of historical consciousness. According to Ash'arite ontology, the human being's action is circumscribed within the narrowest compass, lamented Hanafi.[65]

Earlier, it was mentioned that 'Imara's solution to the failure of Arab Muslims to implement renewal was use of *ijtihad*. He berated those who insist that *ijtihad* cannot be used in the presence of a canonical text that can be applied to a situation. The problem with such a categorical view, he wrote, was that it failed to distinguish among texts in the first place and furthermore among the subjects and sources of these texts.[66] Those adhering to the slogan "no *ijtihad* if a canonical text exists" believe they are sanctifying these texts, he stated. But, in fact, they are sanctifying "derivative ordinances" whose operative conditions have lapsed.[67] 'Imara's reference here is to the distinction between primary and secondary ordinances of the faith. Primary ordinances, which bear upon matters of worship (the devotional duties, or *'ibadat*), cannot be subject to *ijtihad*, he agreed. But this is not what the opponents of ijtihad are saying. What they want to do is to bar ijtihad in regard to secondary or derivative ordinances, which bear not on matters of worship but on social relations (mu'amalat). The canonical texts that deal with social relations must be subject to ijtihad, 'Imara insists, for these were revealed in the context of the interests (maslaha, pl. masalih) of the Muslims. They pertain to "affairs," to worldly matters. Because worldly matters are subject to change, the interests of the Muslims affected by those matters are also subject to change. Accordingly, ijtihad must be applied to them.[68]

Although 'Imara's point about ijtihad[69] is understood among Muslim modernist writers, it does not address the question of why, if this tool is so readily available, contemporary Arab Muslim thought is considered by so many social theorists to continue in crisis.[70] After all, the tradition in which 'Imara (and Hanafi, too, for that matter) is writing is that of Muhammad 'Abduh and Rashid Rida (d. 1935), which stretches back several generations into the nineteenth century. That tradition has for years now been advocating the resuscitation of ijtihad in Sunni thought. 'Imara's explanation that the writers have been overcome by fear and emotionalism is therefore inadequate. Hanafi would rejoin that a formulaic reply stating that we need to apply ijtihad if we are serious about renewal will not do. What is necessary is not to *reform* our analytical perspectives in this way, as 'Imara seemingly wants to do, but to undertake a major *restructuring* of this thought.[71] Hanafi believes that 'Imara's prescription will simply promote a continuation of the old mindset. "For us," he asserted, "the important thing is not to understand the world as it was in the time of the ancients but rather to transform it, develop it, and control it."[72] For Hanafi, the Achilles heel of the dominant Islamic reform movement, the Salafiya, which 'Imara is advancing as the solution to the Arab Muslims' contemporary problems, is that

> it wanted to transform theory into action without establishing theory. Hence, the reform remained mere preaching and guidance, urging the people to action. But people do not act by preaching.

Rather, they do so by transforming their conceptions of the world, their *Weltanschauung*. Re-establishing knowledge and transforming the unicity of God into a theory is the way to *radical* reform. The transition from reform to revolution is rooted in the consciousness of the masses, furnishing them with a revolutionary conception of the world in advance of the actual revolution.[73]

Even though Hanafi has his own problems in not being able to show how to achieve the goal of revolutionary transformation, he is essentially correct that 'Imara also does not do much in favor of his prescription beyond a rhetorical flourish that one needs to utilize *ijtihad*. An investigation of 'Imara's numerous works reveals that his sympathies do lie with a modernist perspective, featuring an appeal to revive the intellectual perspectives of the Mu'tazila,[74] although Abu Zayd correctly counts him among those who have drifted from modernism to a conservative and even reactionary position in his more recent writings.[75] Recall Hanafi's call for freedom as the path to acquiring a historical consciousness. This, too, has appeal for 'Imara, but he believes such freedom to inhere in Islamic beliefs pure and simple, without the need – as with Hanafi – to reconstruct these beliefs, is the road to this freedom. *Per contra*, 'Imara asserts in a reification: "Islam sees freedom to be the thing that materializes the meaning of life for the human being."[76]

'Imara stresses that it is rule by authoritarian leaders in Islamic history, not Islamic beliefs, that is responsible for oppression over the course of Islamic civilization.[77] But 'Imara seems reluctant to draw the obvious conclusion: if the historical record shows the domination of autocratic rule, despite the fact that freedom is central to Islam's high ideals, how is it that over the long centuries autocracy did in fact prevail? If 'Imara were to say it was due to the lapse of *ijtihad*, the reply must be that if reason is triumphant in Islamic revelation – and 'Imara spends a great deal of energy assuring us that it is[78] – then how could *ijtihad* be permitted to lapse? Or, to put it another way, how could Muslims for so many eras of their history fail to "operationalize the law and tradition of renewal"?[79]

Actually, 'Imara's works are striking for their ahistoricism, despite his obvioius desire to stick to socio-historical context in the development of central ideas such as justice, democracy, and accountability. The following discussion summarizes his thinking about Islam as inherently democratic, even though he does not define democracy or show the evolution of it as an idea and practice across historical time and space.

'Imara wishes to demonstrate that *shura* (consultation) is the foundation of Islam's philosophy and practice of rule. He notes that scant evidence exists in the Islamic heritage about Islamic political institutions in the early period. Was *shura* institutionalized in a recognizeable organizational form? He concedes that direct evidence for this is unavailable. But by digging in the sources, he believes he can infer that it was institutionalized in the form of ten of the Prophet's associates who emigrated with him from Mecca to Medina in 622 AD, with whom the Prophet discussed matters of the moment.[80] 'Imara tells us that the Mosque of Medina became the seat of government in the last ten years of the Prophet's life, and remarks that the doors of the homes of these ten individuals opened out onto the mosque's precincts, that they stood behind the Prophet in prayer and fought in front of him in battle. They were all involved in giving the oath of allegiance to the Rightly Guided Caliphs (ruled collectively 632–661) upon the Prophet's death. He further maintains that the Qur'an's "consultation verses" (42:38 and 3:159) connect the notion of *shura* to *amr* (affair[s]).

'Imara stresses that at the conclave following the Prophet's death the individual who was chosen to be the first caliph, Abu Bakr, declared: "In regard to this matter [*amr* – i.e. the leadership of the Islamic community] there must be someone to undertake it." And 'Umar, who later became the second caliph but who at that meeting supporting Abu Bakr's candidacy, stated: "Consult in this matter." 'Imara then asserts that the word *amr* and its various derived forms, such as *amir* (commander), all related to politics; and that the traditions associated with the Prophet contain a number of sayings showing that the Prophet consulted people, especially in reference to appointing military commanders. Therefore, concludes 'Imara, Islam is characterized by democracy.

Note that 'Imara is exporting his late-twentieth-century understanding of democracy back into the seventh century and finds this democracy full blown in Qur'anic verses and the practice of the Prophet. He does not define democracy; nor does he show the people freely disposing of their will in regard to political matters. There is no analysis of democracy in Islamic history – showing how it arose out of the give and take and contention and cooperation of groups in historical times and places. He does not distinguish between elites making decisions and people actively participating in the determination of decisions. The fact that the Prophet asked for advice prior to appointing military commanders for campaigns by Muslim armies is not evidence for democracy. In fact, 'Imara acknowledges in his book on *Islam and Human Rights* that the historical record has been bereft of democracy in the Islamic world for 1,300 years.[81]

Neither Hasan Hanafi nor Muhammad 'Imara has provided a convincing map of "how to get from here to there," from a crisis in contemporary Sunni thought to the solution to this crisis through radical or reformist paths. In this connection, it is apposite to consider the recommendations of the Moroccan scholar Muhammad 'Abid al-Jabiri. These recommendations are in the form of a methodology of research that entails three steps.

First, one must study the texts that make up the heritage (*turath*) of Islamic thought and refuse to accept the finality of all the commentaries and understandings by others. One must instead take these texts as they are and apply a structural analysis to them. The guiding principle at this stage must be to distill the meaning of the text from the essence of the text itself, utilizing modern semiotic and other methods of structural analysis.

The second step is historical analysis. Here, the contemporary Muslim scholar connects the thought of the writer of a heritage text (for example, al-Ghazali's attack on Islamic philosophy entitled *Tahafut al-Falasifa* – The Incoherence of the Philosophers) to its historical domain and context. This linkage is critical for two reasons: (1) to understand the historicity and genealogy of the ideas that are under study; (2) to understand the sound testing of the structural model associated with the first step above. By sound testing is meant not logical verification but "historical possibility," which allows the contemporary Muslim to know what a text can say, cannot say, and can say but has not explicitly stated.

The third and final step is to reveal the ideological function that the text in which one is interested performs or aspires to perform. This discovery of the ideological content of a heritage text is the only way to return historicity to the text itself and to the overall *turath*.[82]

I believe that Hanafi would welcome this methodology, although it is not clear whether he would be able to utilize it, given the inconsistencies in his thought.[83] By contrast, 'Imara would likely reject it on grounds that it would cause the collapse of the conservative synthesis produced by Muhammad 'Abduh, Rashid Rida and the *salafiya* reform movement associated with them to which 'Imara is so obviously attached. Still, at the rhetorical level, at least, the focus upon historicization of analysis on the part of these two writers – not to mention by secularists – is significant, because it seems the only path by which contemporary Sunni Muslim social thought can come to terms with the concrete issues of society and change.

The contemporary Shi'ite tradition

Thus far, the discussion has centered on contemporary Sunni Muslim political theories with regard to the problem of historicization of social change. In this section, attention will be given to Shi'ite theories, including those identified with Ayatollah Khomeini, the Iranian thinker 'Ali Shari'ati and the contemporary Iranian philosopher 'Abdol Karim Soroush ('Abd al-Karim Surush).

Before turning to their ideas, a word may be in order in regard to two factors that have been much in evidence in recent Shi'ite thinking: (1) *ijtihad* – independent judgment to adduce a legal rule, which is hardly a new principle; (2) *fiqh-i puya*. This expression is not easy to translate into English. *Fiqh* is the venerable word for jurisprudence and is, of course, Arabic in origin. *Puya* is a Persian suffix that, when added to a word, gives that expression a dynamic quality or dimension. Thus, when one speaks of *fiqh-i puya*, one is denoting and connoting a jurisprudence that is sensitive to the element of change. Both of these principles are invoked by Shi'ite thinkers if they are anxious to combine a commitment to two points. On the one hand, they wish to emulate the revered traditions and content of the scriptures in regard to the immutable principles of the faith, often glossed with expressions of monotheism, prophecy (and the finality of Muhammad's prophecy), and the Day of Judgment, plus "the devotional duties." On the other hand, being sensitive to the requirements of the contemporary age, they wish to adapt Islamic principles as may be necessary in order to deal with unexpected contingencies.

I now turn to Ayatollah Khomeini, the single most important figure in the Iranian Revolution of 1978–79. He first emerged on the political scene in 1941 at the time of the exile of Reza Shah, with a book attacking the failure of secular leaders to consult the clergy. Because of the political quietism ordered by the then major religious leader, Ayatollah Burujirdi (d. 1961), Khomeini stayed in the background until the early 1960s, when he emerged as a vehement critic of the policies of Muhammad Reza Pahlavi, especially those pertaining to female suffrage, land reform, eligibility requirements for office-holding, and relations with the United States. The changed historical circumstances in Iran since his initial foray into politics in 1941 eventually led him to argue that Islam and monarchy were incompatible and to demand the clergy take power.

It is my argument that Ayatollah Khomeini, who established a doctrinal principle that the '*ulama*' must rule society and stressed the vindication of this argument through reason, ends up with a theory of social change that makes God, through the vehicle of the Prophet and the Imams, the motor force of such change. For him, the human element in the process of change appears to be epiphenomenal, since humans' activities are regulated by their responses to Prophetic revelation and the course set by the Imams.[84]

On the other hand, Shari'ati appears to make the motor force of social change human beings animated by such principles of the doctrine of the Imamate as *intizar* (anticipation of the return of the Hidden Imam) and *shahadat* (attesting to; and redemptive sacrifice). But he combines with this such secular principles as certain historical laws that work themselves out in dialectical fashion, sometimes involving class conflict. It is not clear how Shari'ati can reconcile as the motor force of historical change such disparate factors as principles associated with the doctrine of the Imamate, on the one hand, and conflicts among contending social classes in society, on the other. It is likely that he either postponed the resolution of the contradictions between these or else never felt that such contradictions were fatal to his philosophy of history.[85]

Soroush's argument for social change stresses the need to separate the *shari'a* from the human interpretation and implementation of its principles, an interpretation and implementation that occur in the context of the social relations and social structures created by human beings. The domain of religion is the domain of God's word; the domain of theory is the domain of the human being. As with Shari'ati, then, Soroush stresses the role of human beings as the generators of change.

Khomeini, historicization, and the motor force of change

In Khomeini's view, that which is real is the hereafter, and all that exists in the terrestrial world is an illusion.[86] Being contingencies, the phenomena of our world are best seen, in his view, as signs of God, who is the only reality.[87] Accordingly, the human being has no independence and, in fact, is appropriately seen as a non-being.[88] Nevertheless, as part of God's design, the human being has the potential to be the "noblest of creatures"; and, though shrouded in veils of darkness, he has been molded in the fairest possible form and is even able to attain absolute perfection – that is, by merging with God.[89] God, as the supreme essence, is the absolute Being, of whom materials and animals are individuations and manifestations. Whatever shape, color and dimension objects and animals assume are accidental contingencies, inasmuch as the only necessary essence is God.

Khomeini's ontology thus stresses that objects and subjects depend upon God's will for their formation, movement, and existence. The basic nature of the universe is the constant creation and re-creation of life through God's will. In his philosophy of history, including the dynamics of historical change, Khomeini appears to argue that the individual is the instrument of God, unless he chooses not to accept the message of the Prophet and the Imams that God makes as a precondition for human salvation. In a word, for Khomeini, all morally upright people are placed by God upon a general path of development toward the discovery of meaning and, ultimately, happiness. Fundamentally, this philosophy of history shares with Sunni Islam the tension that exists between the past and the future. Muslims generally revere their past and hearken to it – especially the period of Muhammad's prophecy – as the golden age of the faith. On the other hand, Islam is an 'optimistic' religion with respect to what lies ahead. The general trend is seen to be linear, upward and forward. Khomeini bifurcates the human being's progress toward pleasing God. On the one hand, the individual "migrates" toward God on his or her own, and the ego is one's worst enemy. It impedes the moral imperative of safeguarding God's rights, in keeping with the Qur'anic injunction "God commands you to return trusts to their owners" (4:58).

However, at another level, the individual placed by God on this path cannot rely upon his or her own resources but must serve as a member of the community of believers. Their guidance is the

Qur'an, the traditions of the Prophet, and the sayings and practices of the Imams, which will "advance man from the defective state in which he finds himself to the higher state that befits him."[90] Thus, in his less mystical and more political writings, Khomeini argues in favor of the establishment of an Islamic state run by the clergy, whose government would implement the laws of God. Were Muslims to fail to achieve this aim, they would be violating their historical mission.[91] Yet, on this level, as well, human beings are but instruments of the divine writ.

Moreover, Khomeini made it clear that the highest jurist acts as the final arbiter of what that writ is. Accordingly, human actions that seek to please God are judged to be worthy or not by this jurist. Additionally, a few months before his death Khomeini issued an authoritative opinion – *fatwa* – that held that whatever the top jurist commanded, including suspending the ordinances of the faith, had to be obeyed by all because he was uniquely situated to declare what Islam is. This position, which his successor has adopted as well, makes it impossible for even enlightened clergymen, much less pious laymen, to confidently utilize *ijtihad* for the purpose of adapting to macro-social change.

Shari'ati, historicization, and the motor force of change

Unlike Khomeini's ontology, which holds that the only reality is God, Shari'ati writes that the basis of reality is the unity of God, nature, and man. This notion of the fusion of God, nature, and man is the key concept in his "integralist world-view" (*jahanbini-yi tawhidi*), and he maintains that the latter permits a good deal of room for the human being as an autonomous individual who bears responsibility for his or her actions. But his ontology may be pursued one step further. The integration of God, man, and nature means the rejection of contradictions, he notes. If the unity of God, man and nature is the foundation of reality, then contradictions are impossible. As he puts it: "the structure of *tawhid* [unicity] cannot accept contradictions or disintegration in the world. Therefore, the world view of *tawhid* does not contain contradiction[s] in man, nature, spirit, body, the world and the hereafter, matter, and meaning."[92]

Despite Shari'ati's apparently emphatic rejection of contradictions, seemingly based on his perceived need to contend against Marxian dialectics, they actually are an important element in his social thought. Here a paradox emerges. On the one hand, Shari'ati applies the logic of dialectics, which rest upon the interaction of mutually contradictory forces, to general historical evolution. On the other hand, he claims that contradictions do not operate in a genuine Shi'i historical community. The strong implication is that God, nature, and the human being are integrated into a unity only for Shi'i Muslims. For non-Shi'a, the doctrine of first principles decidedly features contradictions. But if contradictions are the basis for historical change in non-Shi'i community, the question becomes what constitutes the mechanism of such change in a truly Shi'i community? Shari'ati's writing is highly diffuse on this subject, but one can assume that it consists of a combination of leadership based on justice and the allegiance of the people to the delegated authority, or *wilaya* of the Imams.

Shari'ati's philosophy of history is rich with themes and the interplay of ideas. While eclectic in the borrowing from other traditions, notably Marxism, it contains analysis that is original in the context of existing Shi'i interpretations. According to him, the philosophy of history of Islam is founded upon what he terms "scientific determinism" (*jabr-i 'ilmi*). This signifies that science – especially anthropology, sociology, and political economy – can usefully be applied to gain a true understanding of historical development in Islam.

Influenced by Marx, Shari'ati argues that "history unfolds through dialectical contradictions." History has evolved in the context of a struggle between mutually opposing forces. This struggle, he holds, "began with the first man on earth and has always and everywhere been waged."[93]

Shari'ati's evident teleological perspective and his historicism can be seen in his conviction that history "started from somewhere and of necessity must lead to somewhere; it must have a goal and a direction." He thus seems to be advocating a universal history,[94] within the framework of which the human being can choose, at various stages in his development, to follow the imams, opt for laissez-faire economics, prescribe Marxist solutions, and so forth.

Moreover, Shari'ati maintains that historical change occurs not only through contradictions but through contradictions involving the mode of production. Couching his analysis in terms of the Cain and Abel story, he posits that the brothers in fact provide the archetype of mode-of-production conflict. In the one case, Cain is the agriculturalist; in the other, Abel is the pastoralist. Whereas Cain's social rank and "class" position in society were anchored in his ownership of productive means, those of his brother rested on what he was capable of securing by his hands in hunting, fishing, gleaning. Ultimately, Shari'ati believes that the struggle between Cain and Abel was an "objective" one that sets the stages for all future struggles, themselves each also objective in nature.[95]

In fact, Shari'ati upbraids the clergy for deriving a merely moral lesson from Cain and Abel, namely the admonition "thou shalt not kill." Social science, which garners Shari'ati's enthusiastic regard, shows that this historic dispute between the two brothers was a class conflict. The methodology of the social sciences requires that we establish the causes of certain effects by eliminating constants in comparing two entities, and the only differentiating factor between the two brothers is their social occupation. They had the same parents, grew up in the same environment, had the same influences brought to bear upon their personalities as infants, children, adolescents. Therefore, an ancient legend spawned by the scriptures of the great religions may now be interpreted in a new light, yielding a more powerful explanation through the use of Marxist-influenced sociology.

Shari'ati differentiates between fundamental change and small-scale change. All societies witness the cumulation of many discrete, small changes affecting different facets of life. Hence a social institution such as the family undergoes small-scale change if the basis of authority is broadened from age/wisdom to include virility and valor. But it experiences major change if it moves from the distribution of the estate of the father among survivors to primogeniture. This example is not Shari'ati's, but it is presented here to clarify his meaning.

Shari'ati is convinced that at the level of fundamental change all societies face the problem of the rise and decline of their civilizations. The motor force of historical change being contradiction, is there any escape from decline and disintegration? Historical determinism suggests not, he holds. But continuous revitalization of society is possible, according to him, through the doctrine and practice of permanent revolution. Shari'ati does not mean permanent revolution in Trotsky's sense of periodically intensifying revolutionary ardor and praxis in a society undergoing its travails. Instead, he argues that the three dynamic principles of *ijtihad, al-amr bi al-ma'ruf wa nahy 'an al-munkar* (commanding the good and prohibiting evil – a theme that appears in several verses of the Qur'an), and *muhajirat* (literally, emigration – that is, away from iniquity and toward justice) will protect the Shi'i community from decline.[96]

How can this be so? To begin with, *ijtihad*, correctly applied, renews and rebuilds ideas. The problem in Shi'i society since the disappearance of the twelfth Imam has been that *ijtihad* has been implemented within a narrow compass. Consequently, its scope has been limited to legal specialists deducing derivative ordinances of law, and even then, mainly within the context of hypothetical argumentation. Yet, *ijtihad*'s true meaning is the clarification of one's ideology, Shari'ati remonstrates. And in this sense it becomes "an objective duty (for) every individual to exert himself through *ijtihad* in regard to his own ideology."[97] As for commanding the good and forbidding evil, this is

> the mission and objective duty of all individuals – among the masses, the wretched, the intellectuals, the bazaar merchants – all

are responsible for implementing [it]. This principle will rescue societies from the rise and fall [of their civilizations]. No one can be uncommitted or neutral on this issue.[98]

In regard to emigration, Shari'ati does not go into much detail. He does note, however, that it may refer to an interior journey of the individual or may involve his external relocation. The implication, however, is that emigration prevents routinization and keeps one in touch with newness and thus represents a modality to adapt to change.[99]

Is Shari'ati, then, arguing for free will? Emphatically so. He maintains that the human being is free to choose; the only limiting factors upon his will are the human being's own mortality and the requirements of food, shelter, health, and the biological necessities associated with these. In all other respects, the individual is absolutely free to make his or her own decisions and consequently is fully responsible for the choices he does make.[100]

Shari'ati argues against the materialists, whom he charges with viewing the human being's will as determined and therefore not autonomous. He believes in historical determinism, he tells us, but he prefers the French *determinisme historique* – to him a more flexible concept – to the Persian equivalent, *jabr-i tarikh*. Iranian intellectuals, in his view, have utilized the latter in ways that have led to the caricature of the individual as an automaton. For Shari'ati, by contrast, historical determinism means that history "is a single, ongoing and uninterrupted phenomenon in time that is influenced by specific but not deterministic causes."[101]

Shari'ati then invokes the metaphor of the human being as akin to a fish in a river. The river winds its way through shallows, rapids, narrows, wide gorges, and over waterfalls in a bed shaped by geological formations over time. Yet the fish can go in various directions, even upstream. The individual is influenced by scientific laws of causation; yet he is free to choose his own course, even to the point of taking his own life.[102]

Sometimes, Shariʿati appears to be saying that history (and not the individual) is the motor of change. For example, he declares "History is the fact that changes man from a quasi-savage being into contemporary man. The latter has reached a certain degree of perfection up to the present and will in be, in the distant future, the ideal person, noblest of all creatures in the material world." Yet, at other times, history is a "crucible" in which the human being is transformed.[103] On these occasions, the human being is a social creature in the process of realizing the best that is in him or her: "man is a being in the process of becoming."[104] The goal defines the individual, then, and we have here a teleological conception of the human being, who is on a path toward a certain end.

Ultimately, Shariʿati believed that he had established an interpretation of Islam that differs from both idealism and materialism. Whereas both of those philosophies of life denature the human being (in the case of idealism by making him or her the object of an abstract and disembodied Absolute Idea; in the case of materialism by making him or her derivative of matter), Islam ennobles the individual. He expresses his view in the following passage:

> Islam's doctrine of first principles is based upon belief in the hidden. By "hidden" I mean that unknown reality that exists in the base material, natural phenomena that are accessible to our senses and mental, scientific, and experiential comprehension. This unknown reality is reckoned as a higher grade of truth and the fundamental focus of the totality of movements, laws and manifestations of this world.
> This hidden is, in reality, the absolute spirit and will of existence. Contrary to idealism, which supposes phenomena of the material world to be the product of the Idea; and in contrast to materialism, which imagines ideas to be the emanation of the material world; Islam counts both matter and idea as different appearances (signs) of that "absolute hidden being." Thus, Islam rejects both idealism and materialism simultaneously; Islam recognizes the existence of the world of nature beyond our ideas; and it holds that man, as a being having ideas in the face of material

nature and the material social environment and material production, is autonomous and genuine.[105]

Yet we also have a Shari'ati who, as has been seen, believes in historical determinism. Rejecting happenstance and disjunction in historical development, Shari'ati equates historical determinism with God's will. But that, in turn, is integrated into the principle of *intizar* – anticipation of the return of the Hidden Imam. The exact linkage between causation, God's will, historical determinism, and *intizar* is not clarified by Shari'ati, who simply asserts that ultimately the Shi'i philosophy of history places the human being in the forefront of change.[106]

Unfortunately, Shari'ati's situation was such that he never had the chance to reflect and reconsider ideas that he hurriedly put to paper in what turned out to be a meteoric career as a political activist and orator. Accordingly, his ideas about change are advanced in the context of a historicist and teleological framework, and the linkages between God, human responsibility, historical determinism, the mandate to resort to *ijtihad*, and the like are never really sorted out. Instead, they are presented more in a series of didactic assertions, a mode that cries out for more carefully crafted argumentation.

Soroush and historicization

It was suggested earlier that Soroush contrasts the domain of God's word, whose arena is religion, with the domain of theory, which is the realm of human beings. What kinds of theories? Theories of the universe, anthropological theories, linguistic theories, social theories, the philosophy of science. Because God's word, when it reaches human beings, is construed; it can never thereafter be purely what it was when revealed. Accordingly, the motor force of historical change for Soroush is the human being's utilization of the intellect to grasp science (broadly understood to include the human and social as well as the natural sciences) and metaphysics and to bring the knowledge thus generated to bear on religion. This will permit men and women to make their religion relevant to their current circumstances, rather than relying on received tradition as comprising the totality of religious awareness. Comprehensive knowledge of the sort that Soroush has in mind, once it is applied to the understanding of religion, will alone permit the human being to flourish in the modern and post-modern periods.[107]

As Soroush puts it, in a passage that suggests that human beings make their own history, even if God has hopes for them to fulfill their ultimate ends:

> History does not have an external Other. No external hand can be said to distort and pervert it. War can be imposed on a nation, but no war or dispute can be imposed on history as a whole. This is true even in the divine conception of history, where God's action is realized only through the essence and volition of His creatures, and where the telos of His design and beneficence leads all creatures to their respective ends.[108]

Unlike Khomeini, Soroush rejects the concept of the "Islamization of Knowledge,"[109] maintaining that it is crucial to separate ontological and epistemological principles of science (as that term is broadly understood) from the sacred texts of the religion. And, unlike Shari'ati, Soroush is much more careful and systematic in laying out the principles of his thought. In particular, he is impatient with the tendency of the advocates of Islamization of knowledge to attribute authoritative sanction to sacred texts for the purpose of materializing in those texts anticipations of major contemporary intellectual and political breakthroughs. Among these are scientific breakthroughs achieved in understandings gained from field theories of mathematics, physics, and astronomy; and major social theories, such as those that treat stratification, democratization, and economic markets.

Conclusion

If historical experience is the primary generator of ideas, and if ideas and theories are intended to explain the experiences that are common to a people, then those ideas and theories must be historically grounded. But Middle Eastern political theories by and large do not meet this requirement, the exception being expatriate scholars. Even when scholars call for the historicization of social theory, their own writings do not succeed in achieving this.

Several Sunni Muslim writers who are expatriates living in Europe, such as 'Abd al-Ilah Balqaziz, Burhan Ghalyun, and Mohamed Arkoun, have urged Middle Eastern theorists to move their research in such directions. Although their voices have not made a major difference up to now, the Sunni writers Hasan Hanafi and Muhammad 'Imara, probably under the influence of these expatriates and more specifically the work of the Moroccan scholar 'Abdallah Laroui in the early 1970s, have directed our attention to this issue. But they either could not or would not follow through. In Hanafi's case, he seemingly could not integrate this approach with his own basically ahistorical framework for the renewal of thought. And in 'Imara's case, he seems not to have believed in his own fleeting call to ground analysis in the historical record. And, at any rate, he later drifted increasingly to a perspective supportive of the Islamization of knowledge – which champions the hypostatization of concepts rather than their historical grounding.

In the case of Shi'i writers, Ayatollah Khomeini did not feel it necessary to relate historical change to the adoption of cultural mandates on the part of the clergy, whom he wanted to seize power. His preference was to argue that the application of reason was sufficient not only to show how things came to be the way they are but to demand a change in those conditions by an idealized analysis of the doctrine of the imamate. 'Ali Shari'ati, by contrast, tried to seize the bull by the horns, specifically arguing for the dialectics of historical inquiry. But because of his own commitment to political activism, he never had the opportunity to try to resolve the contradictions in his arguments. In the case of Abdol Karim Soroush, the need for historicization is pushed further along. Because Soroush is far more grounded in the disciplines of philosophical and social theory than Shari'ati, his work probably holds greater promise for historicization. If the younger generation has the opportunity to grasp his explanations and integrate them with some of the more programmatic writings of certain religious leaders, such as Ayatollah Husayn 'Ali Muntaziri, the synthesis could prove to be especially creative.[110]

FOUR

The individual

Among the classic subjects of political theory is the relationship between the interests of the individual and the interests of the community. This relationship does not need ultimately to be conflictual, although many contemporary writers feel it should be posed in these terms.

In her analysis of medieval Islam, Ann Lambton argues that Muslim theorists had not accorded independent attention to the individual. On this argument, whatever may accrue to the individual would do so by virtue of his or her membership in the community. In saying this, Lambton is expressing a consensus view of the literature on this important matter. But when she adds the following thought to this notion, she goes too far: "Islam does not in fact recognize the legal personality of the individual in which his rights are secured to him and vested in him by law."[1]

In fact, the individual in Islamic tradition is entitled to certain rights that *are* secured to and vested in him by the *shari'a*. Among such rights are the right to own property, to inherit it, to bequeath it, to enter into contracts, to present testimony in courts, to represent his or her interests or appoint others to do so in any legal proceeding, to sue for redress of grievances, to pursue gainful employment, to travel, to marry, to divorce, to seek audience with administrators and rulers, to be protected against external enemies by the state, and the like.

The rights enumerated here are similar to rights secured to individuals in Western systems. Indeed, the ability of women to own, inherit, and sell property arose in the West only in recent times, and in this respect Muslims were "ahead" of the West by centuries. This point should be taken into account by certain observers who are overly critical of the status of women in the Middle East and the larger Muslim world. However, it is true that the active promotion of civil and political rights lags, even though entitlement to such rights might be articulated in modern Middle Eastern constitutions and other legal conventions. Lambton no doubt had in mind political and civil rights vested in individuals in certain Western societies. The active promotion of those kinds of rights had their legitimation in such things as Magna Carta (1215), the English Bill of Rights (1689), the American Declaration of Independence (1775), the French Declaration of the Rights of Man and the Citizen (1789), the American Bill of Rights (1791), and the rights inscribed in the British Reform Acts of 1832 (which nevertheless in a retrograde move disenfranchised women, thus sparking in reaction the later suffragette movement that eventually was able to rectify matters) and 1867. These do not have their analogues in the *shari'a*. Such rights as are inscribed in these Western documents appear in nineteenth-century Middle Eastern political theories that were not only themselves influenced by the Western sources but were adopted more or less intact by Middle Eastern administrators and intellectuals who were enamored of the advances in the rights of citizens granted by those sources.

Ultimately, two factors made problematical the evolution of civil and political rights in earlier centuries. The first had to do with the fact that even though in Islamic belief God had given the human being the world in trust, the rights to exploit that world were considered to be Allah's rights and had to be returned to Him, per Qur'an 4:58: "God commands you to return trusts to their owners."

The second factor had to do with the idea that God is sovereign, not the human being. Conservative Muslims interpreted this to mean that the nation and its citizenry, which were products of the American and French revolutions, stood to usurp Allah's entitlements, since they claimed that sovereignty resided in the nation, which could legislate according to the will of the majority.

The fact that conservative Muslims seemed to be saying that only God could legislate does not mean that some Muslims did not believe that their religion allowed broad scope for human beings to take initiatives and to claim sovereign power in the political realm, while conceding God's sovereign power in the purely religious one. However, the conservative viewpoint was the dominant one, and constitutional rights won on behalf of "the sovereign people" were not considered valid by the advocates of that viewpoint. Even when terminology regarding the sovereignty of the nation was inscribed in constitutions in Muslim states, the finality with which such language seemed to be imbued was put in question by references elsewhere to God's sovereignty, or at least to Islam as the state religion, which could be construed to imply that only God was ultimately sovereign. In short, constitutional "victories" on behalf of national sovereignty were always subject to reconsideration as the conservative perspective never faded from the scene and, as we know, reasserted itself in ebb and flow fashion over the decades and generations since the late eighteenth century.

The word in Arabic meaning individual, *fard*, appears in the Qur'an twice (once in the plural, *afrad*), and in both cases the import is one, or by oneself, or alone. Thus, in 6:94, God says: "You have come before Us one by one, as we created you." And in 19:80 we read: "and he will come before Us all alone." This is also how *fard* is used in the Hadith.

Another word denoting individual is *shakhs*. It is this term that resembles the word "individual" in the way that this word is normally understood in the modern context, namely a single person, a neutral attribution without any particularly approbational or pejorative connotation. It is a common expression in Muslim philosophy. Although in Islamic law there is no use of the word *shakhs* or its derivative *shakhsiya* to signify legal personality, Islamic law does have a concept of "the legal capacity of the individual to be a subject of the law." The ability thus bespoken may be that of acquiring rights or that of executing agreements and obligations (and thus fulfilling contracts).[2]

In the Qur'an, one finds oblique references to the individual as the "unit of analysis," as it were. Thus, in sura 10:19, we read the following: "Mankind was but one nation, but differed [later]. Had it not been for a word that went forth before from thy Lord, their differences would have been settled between them." This suggests that in the Muslim tradition, human beings were considered to be similar to each other and lived in one community. But differences developed among them, as God invited them to accept the true religion, in response to which some agreed but others refused. And in 2:213, it is stated: "Mankind was one single nation, and Allah sent Messengers with glad tidings and warnings; and with them He sent the Book in truth, to judge between people in matters wherein they differed." These verses seem to show that the human beings were basically considered to be like creatures. They began to differentiate themselves from one another, however, and one "arena" where these differences began to show was the stage on which they responded to the divine message sent by God's prophets. While some accepted, others rejected, or else they accepted initially but then went astray, necessitating that God send a later prophet in hopes of rectifying their derelictions. God then tried one last time, with the Prophet, Muhammad. Why these differences arose is a matter of considerable reflection on the part of the theologians and jurists of Islam, but the causes that are usually cited are pride, arrogance, greed, opportunism, doubt, and the like.

These generalized references to individuals are hardly enough to permit the development of a theory of individualism in the Islamic tradition. Nor is there a significant body of references in the Sunna (sayings and behavior) of the Prophet to enable one to do this. One should not be surprised at this, given the collectivist ethos inscribed in Muslim society from the outset. However, because of Western political theory's interest in the individual since the seventeenth century, efforts have been made by contemporary writers to come to terms with the concept and praxis of individualism.

In 1965, at the height of the period of Arab nationalism and "Arab socialism," a lecturer in the Law Faculty of Baghdad University, 'Abd al-Karim Zaydan, published a slim volume entitled *The Individual and the State in Islamic Law*.[3] Although the individual is the first word in the title of this book, Zaydan begins with the state. When he gets to the individual, Zaydan declares that his personality in the Islamic state is prominent and is not dissolved by the latter. The individual's personality "arises alongside" the state and works for the latter's maintenance and improvement in the same way that the state works for the maintenance and improvement of the individual's personality. The maintenance and improvement of each is necessary for the maintenance and improvement of the other. "There is no contradiction between the two," and both are subject to "Islam."[4]

> The individual in the Islamic state enjoys all the rights that Islam has established for him... the individual's enjoyment of his rights is considered the greatest guarantee for the Islamic state's remaining strong, sound, and capable of achieving its goals.... The Islamic state has absolutely no right to assail these rights because it was established to enable individuals to live an Islamic life.[5]

Zaydan then provides a discussion of individual rights, which, however, are not analytically examined but rather are asserted in a descriptive narrative form. Most of these rights are those that are to be found in the constitutions of modern states, although some of them are more specific to Islamic tradition, history, and law – as for example the right of consultation, or the community's obligation to implement the ordinances of the *shari'a*, or the role of "the people of loosing and binding" in choosing leaders. At the time the book was published, a number of Arab regimes had adopted some variant of socialism, and this can also be seen in the framework of Zaydan's book, which emphasizes the state's role in providing for the people.

In a similar mode is a book published five years earlier by a prolific Egyptian writer of that era, Mahmud al-Sharqawi, entitled *The Individual and Society in Islam*.[6] In his view, the bases of Islamic society are mental liberation, complete equality among human beings, and "mutual responsibility" – the latter being a term made popular by one of the most prominent Islamist writers, Sayyid Qutb (d. 1966), although it was also a slogan qualified by the leader of the Syrian Muslim Brotherhood, Mustafa al-Siba'i (d. 1964), as "socialist" mutual responsibility, a phrase adopted by the Egyptian regime under Nasser. In his discussion of these concepts, Sharqawi studs his narrative with citations from sacred scriptures. As with Zaydan, the approach is descriptive. The author assembles concepts that are in the contemporary vocabulary of socialist thought – concepts that were central to official state documents issued by such regimes as that of Nasser in Egypt and the Ba'th Party in Syria – and legitimizes them by reference to the Qur'an and the Prophet's traditions.

For example, after establishing the three bases of Islamic society, Sharqawi writes:

> Islam began with the liberation of the human being from the domination of caprices, superstitions, and subjection to that which was neither beneficial nor disadvantageous and of appeals by spurious methods to preserve himself, making some people – rather than God – lords over others.[7]

This passage is footnoted with two attributions, to Qur'an 3:64 and 39:36–38, the import of which is that one should worship the one God and not associate others with Him. With this methodology, it is not possible to develop a theoretical concept of the individual as an active agent. Instead, the individual is seen as an epiphenomenon, a beneficiary of God's munificence and mercy. He does not act on his own but rather is singled out by God for favor, provided he complies with the divine commands.

Nevertheless, in an ad hoc manner, Sharqawi asserts that Islamic values – such as the full equality of believers – motivate the individual to bring about in his actual praxis the upholding, for instance, of the separation of powers, the interpellation and holding to account of the head of state, the decision to run as a candidate for office, the desire to establish a political party, and the like. And he concludes his book with an approving reference to an assessment made in 1932 by a Harvard University professor of philosophy, William Earnest Hocking, that "the path of progress by the Islamic states is not to adopt supposed means that hold that religion has nothing to say about the daily life of the individual or about law or political systems; but rather [to hold that] the human being must find in religion the source of growth and progress."[8]

More than a generation later, in perhaps the most extended treatment of the subject of the individual within an Islamic framework, the Egyptian social psychologist Sayyid 'Abd al-Hamid Mursi published a work under the same title as Sharqawi's book, namely *The Individual and Society in Islam*.[9] Among his works was a book published in 1966 entitled *The Humanism of Arab Socialism*. However, by the time of the 1989 publication, the socialist system of the Nasser period had been significantly undone by his successors, Anwar Sadat (d. 1981) and Hosni Mubarak. At the same time, the rise of radical, violence-prone Islamist groups, and the assertion of influence by non-violent Islamists intent on the application of Islamic law in all areas of life, were in substantial evidence. In the meanwhile, the Soviet reformer Mikhail Gorbachev had commenced an effort, beginning in 1985, to revitalize the Communist system in the USSR – an effort that reverberated in the Soviet-type systems of Eastern Europe. The very year in which Mursi's book was published was the year of the fall of the Berlin Wall and the outbreak of basically peaceful revolutionary movements in those systems. Accordingly, it appeared that the capitalist model, with its stress on the role of the individual, was in the ascendant. It is more than likely that Mursi was influenced by these developments to turn his attention to the role of the individual as viewed within the Islamic tradition.

Mursi tellingly entitles Part I of his book "Toward an Islamic Science of Sociology." In approximately fifty pages, he takes up such topics as the historical development of the concept of human nature, the behavioral sciences, sociology, social and cultural change, social development, the notion of an Islamic sociology, Islam as doctrine and law, the Islamic social system, the goals of an Islamic sociology, the subject and realms of Islamic sociology. In Part II, running for about another fifty pages and entitled "The Masters of Islamic Sociology," Mursi discusses the works of al-Farabi, al-Mas'udi (d. 957), ibn Miskawayh, ibn Sina, ibn al-Haytham (d. 1040), al-Biruni (d. 1048) ibn Hazm (d. 1064), al-Ghazali, ibn Battuta (d. 1368/1377?), and ibn Khaldun.

Mursi defines individualism sociologically. Thus, individualism is expressed by the human being if and when his behavior is not a mere imitation of others and his conduct is not a mere automatic compliance with the exigencies of his social environment. Individualism is shown when the person behaves as an egoistical being, aware of his nature in acting, even while he is simultaneously a member of the group. It is possible for an independent individual with an integrated personality faithfully to express and reflect the characteristics of his country or his time, though he does this not because he is quick to imitate others but because he is sensitive to "the requirements of his era."

Clearly, conflicts will emerge among members of a group who are all strongly individualistic, which will lead them to express themselves in varying ways. But the key is not the degree of deviation in conduct by one individual from that of his colleagues. Rather, it is how the individual behaves in relying upon himself as he establishes relationships with others and how he understands the demands others make of him. If he complies with authority, he does so not because others do but because he sees his compliance to be sound and correct.

Continuing along these lines, Mursi notes that individuality and individualism are not developed in elementary societies as a consequence of the emphasis there upon the collective customs and severe taboos against personally directed conduct, as compared to the situation in complex societies. Although simpler societies lay down sanctions against individualism, complex societies encourage and even require it, a point Mursi believes was made by Durkheim in his classic work *The Division of Labor in Society* (1893). Mursi then approvingly stresses the point that if everybody thought and behaved in the same way, society would not progress but would rather become stagnant and ossified.

Mursi then notes that while an optimum balance must be struck between social and individual interests, this is difficult to achieve. Constant conflicts of interest occur among members of society, and some groups prevail over others. Mussolini and Hitler claimed that their model of totalitarianism was founded upon social integration (*al-takamul al-ijtima'i*); and in the communist systems, similar coercive methods were used to try to achieve this. The effort to create a balance between individualism and collectivism has been going on for centuries, in his opinion. As against overweening authoritarian institutions and values, attempts have been made to empower individuals. On the other hand, efforts to restrain the state and society have often led to willfulness and excessive egotism.

If a person were left to ply his path without any guidance except his own nature, he would move ineluctably toward narcissism. He would want to hold on to whatever he possessed and keep others from having not only what he actually possessed but anything else that they coveted. He would thus be in constant fear that others might be able to take what he has from him or otherwise gain such possessions through their own efforts.[10]

At this point, Mursi wishes to discuss individualism in the context of Islam. Reifying the concept, he says:

> Islam [sic] is not pleased with this individualism and sees it as a deviation, because it does not achieve the happiness of the human being himself or bring about a community consisting of himself and others. For this reason, it [Islam] is wholly intent on centering the human being's existence in belief in God, which would impel him to leave this narrowly circumscribed individualism and therefore this painful psychological constraint. Belief in God is not simply a word spoken by the believer but is a contract and a covenant made by the human being with God. The result of this is that he will live for himself and for others. He has rights but he has duties. He has rights to the extent that he sacrifices freely for the sake of those with whom he associates and interacts... and he has duties to the extent that he considers himself prepared to render them, grasping clearly that his own self is not alone in this life, and that those who share in this life with him have rights before his that require implementation.[11]

This understanding is obviously very different to the original liberal position that considers the human being to be existentially free. Mursi's view is that the rights of others are prior to the rights of the individual. Whether his interpretation of individualism in Islam is the "correct" one, of course, is highly contentious. But his book does stand as an important effort to construe these matters. On its basis, one would have to conclude that the original liberal position would have to be seriously modified to be acceptable. Yet that original position did come to be significantly modified in the Western theory (one should now say Western theories) of liberalism over the course of generations since Locke. Withal, such modifications as have occurred have not led to the result that the rights of others precede one's own rights. In that sense, one is closer to some variant of socialist political theory than to a liberal variant.

Accordingly, are there Islamic "liberals?" Leonard Binder, Professor of Political Science at UCLA and a perceptive observer of Middle Eastern political theories, tends to think so, and he considers Muhammad 'Imara to be one of them.[12] But people such as 'Imara show a deep reluctance to talk about individuals in any formative sense. And certainly, as he sees it, individuals are not sovereign over their persons and property because he believes that only God is sovereign. According to him, the Enlightenment in the West, and its subsequent legacy in the nineteenth and twentieth centuries, taught that the human being's intellect is the source of morality, based on the notion that reason accords with the law of nature. Thus, in a democratic secular system the people are sovereign. In an Islamic system, by contrast, he argues, final sovereignty belongs to God, and God's sovereignty is articulated in the shari'a.[13] Although he insists that Islam is a humanistic religion because God favored the human being and granted him intellect and freedom,[14] he never coherently demonstrates what kind of freedom this is or its locus in the Islamic ontological and epistemological legacies. Nor does he show how the Muslim can convert this putative freedom into individual empowerment to advance his life chances, on the one hand, and protect himself against the state's excesses, on the other. I use the expression "life chances" explicitly as coined by Weber (Lebenschancen) and note that Weber did not reduce this concept to material comforts, amenities, and privileges. For Weber, the expression denotes the individual's opportunity to improve both his ideal (spiritual) and his material well-being.

What 'Imara does say is that in Islamic tradition the human being "has the power to build upon this divine shari'a, set it forth, legally enact its principles, lay out its details. He also has the power to deduce that which the divine law has not sent down, provided that it is subordinated to the framework of that which is divinely permitted and prohibited."[15] It would appear that, from this perspective, the individual's thought and actions are religiously determined, since building upon the shari'a and deducing its unarticulated provisions seem to rule out expressions and emanations of power that touch other spheres not under the purview of Islamic law. He admits that Islam is a "liberal" religion, but he maintains that the meaning and the content of this liberalism cannot be the same as the liberalism of societies such as the United Kingdom, for example. The reason, he states, is that in the case of the Muslims, their liberalism derives from their religion, whereas in the case of non-Muslims it derives from non-religious sources.

The secularist Fu'ad Zakariya, a leading Egyptian critic of the "Islamization of knowledge" trend championed by Islamists, expresses frankly his inability to comprehend the meaning of the terms "divine rule" and "divine sovereignty," both of which are dear to the hearts of the Islamists. Rule (hukm), he maintains, is from beginning to end a human, not a divine, activity. One can invoke texts until the cows come home, but it is clear that humans choose the texts they believe will support their interests. It was only in the age of the prophets that one could speak of divine rule. Thereafter, rule has been human in nature, even though the regulations to which rulers turn might be divine. Expressed dedication to the application of *shari'a* regulations is not in itself a guarantee of better rule than the most despotic systems that the Arabs and Muslims have seen, Zakariya asserts. Instead, the important factor is guarantees to guard against the ruler's perversions. And these guarantees are purely human in origin and nature, evolving over historical time and subject to trial and error, based on bitter experience. Divine rule is a contradiction in terms because it is humans who rule; it is they who implement a divine ordinance in the real world.[16]

If Zakariya says the emphasis on God's sovereignty obscures the reality that it is always human beings who act on what they perceive to be God's commands, Hasan Hanafi wants to know why the human being per se has been absent from the writings of Muslim theologians and jurists who contributed to the heritage of Islam over the centuries. He calls such a state of affairs a "crisis."[17]

The attention paid to the individual in Islam of the pre-modern period is thus a function of God's appointment of the human being as a vicegerent on earth who acts as a custodian of its resources and who is continuously on notice to return that trust at any moment. There is no problematizing of the human being in the sources of the Islamic heritage (the ensemble of holy texts and the writings of the jurists, theologians, historians, philosophers, rhetoricians, philologists, and linguists). This means that no study has been made of the human being as such.[18] When the sources address the human being, it is always in his or her capacity as a believer. For a brief few decades, with the rise to prominence of the Muʻtazila, a movement discussed in an earlier chapter, it seemed possible that explicit treatment might be given to developing a theory of the individual. Their belief in the mastery of reason and free will suggested that the human being was the author of his own actions as well as responsible for them.[19] However, as we have seen, this movement was suppressed beginning in the reign of the caliph Mutawakkil (ruled 847–861), and its influence thus was eclipsed by the early tenth century.

Before proceeding further, however, the following comparative point is worth stressing. Attention to the individual in political theories in Western Europe and North America came only between the seventeenth and nineteenth centuries. The ground for these writings was prepared by Martin Luther (1483–1546) and René Descartes (1596–1650). Luther is important in this regard because of his challenge to the authority of the then universal Catholic Church for its oppressive control over the spiritual realm and the corrupt behavior of its leaders. When others, such as Calvin and the Scottish Presbyters, argued in similar vein, it did not take long for the doctrine to set in that membership in any church was henceforth to be voluntary, and not coerced. Descartes' importance lies in his stand on behalf of reason, which declared that the very definition of the human being was that he was a reasoning creature. This stress on reason as the natural condition of the human being was crucial for the call by the seventeenth-century social-contract theorists Hobbes and Locke, and later by the Swiss thinker Rousseau and the German philosopher Kant in the eighteenth century to develop a theory of the individual in relation to the state.

In short, for many centuries the emphasis upon the entitlements of the group (rather than the individual) was assumed in Western political theory, which had very little to say about the individual.

From the Greeks to Luther, the emphasis was upon the rights of the community. When contemporary observers comment about the lack of attention to the civil and political rights of the individual in the Islamic tradition, the implication seems to be that outside the Muslim world the individual had enjoyed a paramount place for many centuries. Yet this was simply not the case. The individual arises as a theme in Western political theory only around the mid-sixteenth century. The critical explanation for this is that, until the Reformation, spokesmen of the Catholic Church dominated political theory and held that the state was merely a subordinate unit of the religious institution. The human being, as well, was counted merely as a subject of that state and of the Church that dominated it. Obedience to edicts, both religious and political, was what was expected. This did change, of course, but the change was a long time coming. Accordingly, the focus upon the role of the individual as an autonomous actor is only a matter of the last 400 years or so.

We are now in a position to establish the meaning of liberalism, which has perhaps been the regnant political theory in the modern era – if not in the actual operation of the liberal models, then at least in the rhetoric and symbolism and vocabulary of political theorists in this period.[20] Among its key concepts are the following:

- The liberty of the individual: freedom is the individual's natural state.
- Freedom to act as the individual deems appropriate without having to secure the permission of others.
- Faith in the reason of each person.
- Dispersal and diffusion of power.
- Rejection of constraints or limitations on the individual's freedom; if any are imposed, they must be justified.
- Such justifications as may be invoked will in any case be limited.
- Requisite of autonomous and free beings for a just society.
- Entitlement of each person to equal rights with others.

- Necessity of government to protect the liberty of individuals, including challenges to that liberty internally or externally (that is, from foreign attack).
- Private property as an extension of the individual and hence essential to liberty.
- Free market as a mechanism to disperse the state's political power and as a means to extend individual liberty.
- Distinction between negative and positive conceptions of freedom: (i) absence of coercion on the part of others upon myself = negative freedom; (ii) self-direction based on reflection (as opposed to instinctual impulses) = positive freedom.

To these attributes of classic liberalism were added, later on, the basic idea of the state as either a facilitator for or else itself the deliverer of public goods, requiring the taxation of the population according to formulas considered equitable. Among such public goods were education, sanitation, roads, transportation, and the like. By the late nineteenth century, therefore, classic liberalism had changed into a form that permitted a modicum of state-run public operations. Still later, liberalism became increasingly associated with social welfare programs in which the earlier theme of justice for the individual was broadened into the concept of social justice. Here, the Lockean notion that property is the extension of the individual and his or her inalienable right came under challenge. Access to property was considered not to be equal for all, and such differentials in access as were perceived to exist in the "real world" were now the subject of much reformist thinking within liberal theory. Accordingly, in the early decades of the twentieth century in America it was recognized that the state ought to have the authority to assist in the redistribution of wealth through such systems as the progressive income tax. Moreover, the state was recognized to be an important regulator of businesses and the free professions, not by competing with them but by mandating that they conform to certain standards of performance through such mechanisms and licensing.

The evolution of the meaning of liberalism continued after the 1950s with major scholarly works by contractualists and contractarians — terms utilized to refer respectively to those who believed in the principle of "justice as fairness" and those who adhered to utilitarianism. According to the former, the key was to permit inequalities in society only to the extent that allowing them harmed least of all the most disadvantaged members of the society. This position is associated with the writings of John Rawls.[21] A rival interpretation has been argued by David Gauthier[22] which utilizes a game-theoretic model to uphold the nineteenth-century utilitarian model, a model that espouses the greatest good for the greatest number and thereby implies the neglect of the most disadvantaged in society.

Middle Eastern political theories rarely unpack the concept of liberalism the way it has been done here. This makes it relatively easy for the critics of liberalism in the region to generate "straw man" arguments about liberal theory in their effort to uphold Islamist, Marxist, corporatist, or other perspectives. In their treatments, liberalism becomes reified and treated as a monolithic model of politics.

In a typical example, Muhammad 'Imara has this to say about liberty in the Islamic tradition. For Muslims, the credo "there is no God but Allah and Muhammad is His Prophet" establishes the principle of monotheism — *tawhid* — in this faith. From this, he immediately concludes that it is this monotheism that accomplishes the liberation of the human being from enslavement. This is because giving devotion to God alone not only liberates the human being from worshipping idols but represents a profession of faith that makes liberation and freedom one of the linchpins of the Qur'an.[23] This seems tautological. The principle of monotheism is said to have as its goal the liberation of the human being. Why? Because it frees the human being from enslavement. How do we know this? Because Islam makes liberation a major goal. If scripture were sufficient to bring about liberation, would it not be apposite to cite verses from the Old or the New Testaments? After all, in the Old Testament one reads: "The Lord Our God is One" (Deuteronomy 6:4); and in the New Testament, Jesus, speaking of God, says: "And ye shall know the truth, and the truth shall make you free" (John 8:32).

The point is not whether these sacred statements in the Qur'an, the Old Testament and the New Testament are true. The point is that invocations of such sacred texts cannot explain human behavior. One cannot, as 'Imara does, cite Sura 7:157, which talks of the Prophet, sent by God to relieve people of their burdens, and transform this into a theory of liberty – one, not unincidentally, that he maintains preceded "modern" societies' devotion to liberal values by fourteen centuries.[24] 'Imara would do better not to shrug off the fact that the practice of the rulers in the history of the caliphate was to invert (*intakasa*) the ideal model (which he believes included the separation of powers, no less) by asserting that nevertheless "the community and its political thought have redeemed the Islamic model."[25]

It is not that 'Imara is uninterested in change, which he considers a major objective:

> The renewal of the reality of Islamic community by Islam, and the revitalization by Islamic revivification of that which had died in it ... the removal of weaknesses from its present by that which removed its even more severe past weaknesses ... the transformation of its [the community's] contemporary submissiveness into the glory of God and His prophet ... the removal of the Islamic world from the situation of the 'third world' and bringing it into that of the 'first world' into which Islam had placed it centuries ago ... these great objectives are the highest ends of the call to Islam.[26]

'Imara is here calling for "Islamic change." For this to happen, in his view, contemporary Muslims must use the same methods as the early Muslims to bring about the changes they need to make. Positivist ideologies – by which he primarily has in mind liberalism, one supposes – "fall and retreat," while the Islamic religious resurgence "rises." This is the era of the Islamic resurgence, and Muslims must not only benefit from it themselves but ought to offer it to nations whose "positivist outlooks and ideologies" have "collapsed" or are "collapsing" because they lack the power of revitalization.[27]

Why this animus against liberalism by 'Imara, who perhaps in his earlier, post-Marxist phase was someone who had some admiration for liberal views? In my opinion, the reason is that he became caught up in the perspective of the Islamization-of-knowledge movement, to which I have already referred. That movement, though it began in the early 1970s, only came into its own organizationally in the early 1990s. And he felt it necessary to distance himself from positions he had taken by the early 1980s that led Binder, for example, to find liberal tendencies in his thinking.

I do not argue that 'Imara should not change his position in response to changes that occur in the world, the region and within Egyptian society. But it seems to me that he has conflated all the variants of liberal political theory into a single one, perhaps the one identified by C.B. Macpherson as "possessive individualism." This variant, which is essentially a Lockean perspective, would be very difficult for any Muslim thinker to adopt, as it treats the individual

> as essentially the proprietor of his own person or capacities, essentially owing nothing to society for them. The individual was seen neither as a moral whole, nor as part of a larger social whole, but rather as an owner of himself. The relation of ownership, having become for more and more men the critically important relationship determining their actual freedom and actual prospect of realizing their full potentialities, was read back into the nature of the individual. The individual, it was thought, was free inasmuch as he is proprietor of his person and capacities. The human essence is freedom from dependence on the wills of others, and freedom is a function of possession. Society becomes a lot of free equal individuals related to each other as proprietors of their own capacities and of what they have acquired by their exercise. Society consists of relations of exchange between proprietors. Political society becomes a calculated device for the protection of this property and for the maintenance of an orderly relation of exchange.[28]

And yet there is something more basic than the conflating of liberal traditions into a single one such that exploitation is seen to be the inevitable result of the liberal approach. And that is that Muslims believe that when God tells the Prophet to call people to Islam, He is really inviting them to return to their true good natures (fitra). Note the contrast here with the assumption in liberal political theory that the natural condition of the human being is freedom. In Islam, the human being's natural condition is that inherent disposition of goodness to which God assigned each human being upon their birth, a disposition, therefore, that is divinely ordained. The need for a return to this fitra in Muslim belief is based on its perversion as a result of environmental or social circumstances that somehow have diverted the individual away from his or her true nature and led him or her, for example, into excessive pride. Thus, to a Muslim's way of thinking, when Moses and Jesus invited Jews and Christians to accept the message of God, most did not remain consistently faithful but turned away. Islam thus represents an offer by God to people to return to their divinely created good natures.

These considerations have implications for the modern period, as this era is one of highly complex societies. Under these conditions, a return to their natural dispositions may be more difficult, but perhaps not impossible. One problem, however, is the existence of authoritarian states, whose rule is oppressive and exploitative. In the process of trying to return to their "best selves," as it were, Muslims can assist themselves by the establishment of effective civil society organizations that can help to establish and promote their human rights. Such institutions are defined as associations that occupy the space between the family at the most concrete level of social organization and the state at the most abstract. These societies, such as neighborhood associations and religious brotherhoods, represent "niches," as it were, where people occupy social space from which to conduct as autonomously as possible their daily public activities.

In an important effort to clarify the subject of Islam and human rights, including civil society organizations, Mayer[29] has shown that the sacred scriptures of Islam – the Qur'an and the Prophet's Sunna – provide ample support for conceptions of such rights, but failures of omission have occurred in regard to the implementation of scriptural warrants. She concludes that on a broad range of rights issues, interpretations by social conservatives who have historically controlled the levers of power in Islamic societies have prevented meaningful progress in numerous human rights realms. Although Muslims have sought to overcome this regressive control in various ways, including the establishment of effective civil society organizations, progress has been slow.

Western observers often misconstrue this issue. Some attribute the lack of rapid progress in the area of civil society institutions and individual rights to the religion of Islam itself. This is not only absurd but harmful to improving understanding between non-Muslims and Muslims. For example, it is well established in the scholarly literature that Muslim societies have for centuries been characterized not only by the existence of meaningful civil society institutions but also by their dynamic role in representing the interests of their members. These bodies have played a strong role in keeping the state from interfering in the affairs of their members. In short, they have been critical defensive mechanisms to keep overweening states at bay.

In fact, the Lebanese historian Kawtharani maintains that "civil society" is a modern term. A prerequisite for this modern concept is civic politics (*al-siyasa al-madaniya*), and this prerequisite concept harks back to al-Farabi and ibn Khaldun. Ibn Khaldun distinguished *al-siyasa al-madaniya* from politics that were governed by the restraint of the ruler based upon the revealed, canonical law; and also from "rational politics" (*al-siyasa al-'aqliyya*). Kawtharani quotes ibn Khaldun as follows: "what you hear about *al-siyasa al-madaniya* is not of this sort. Among the sages, it means the obligation of every individual in that society in himself, given his nature, to be able to manage directly without leaders."[30]

But in the West the etymology of the first word of the term "civil society" includes the derivatives "city," "civic," "civil," "citizen." By contrast, in Arabic and Middle Eastern languages, such as Persian and Turkish, which often use cognates from Arabic, the words for "city," "civil," and "civic" are *madina* and *madani*, from the root m–d–n, whereas the words for "citizen" (*muwatin*) and "citizenship" (*muwatiniya*) come from a totally different root, w–t–n. *Watan* (fatherland), *muwatin* (citizen), and *muwatiniya* (citizenship) are related to the rise of the Arab territorial state that arose against the backdrop of anti-colonial struggle in the late nineteenth and early twentieth centuries.[31] This means that such concepts did not emerge organically from within the internal political trends of the Arab societies but in response to vocabularies and concepts that were external to them and that arose in Europe.

Given this situation, one may have a clearer understanding of why civil society organizations in the Middle East, despite their lengthy existence and effectiveness in keeping an intrusive state at a distance, were not able to translate this defensive function into the more proactive one of facilitating their members' efforts to make demands upon the state in pursuit of either individual or corporate interests. The argument, in short, is that an indigenous development of the civil society concept would have made it more likely that the actual institutions that arose would be more successful in making demands upon the state. It is in this latter realm that Middle Eastern civil society institutions are typically weak, although this is something that is changing. One area where this weakness can be seen relates to party political activity. In many areas of the world, political parties have emerged as important mobilizing mechanisms, with consequences for recruitment and articulation of programs representing members' views. This sort of development has noticeably lagged in the Middle East region, where political parties continue in the main to follow the lines of patron–client networks in which leaders use party mechanisms for personal purposes.

Since the concept of human rights is really a product of the modern era, an argument that claimed that it was anticipated by "Islam" centuries ago would not be persuasive. This does not mean, as Mayer notes, that a spirit of humanism is absent in this tradition's textual sources. On the contrary, divine mandates to be humane are plentiful in the Islamic revelation. In practice, however, Muslim authorities historically have fallen short of this ideal.

The expression "human being" (*al-insan*), in the general sense of "mankind" (*al-bashar*), appears about seventy times in the Qur'an.[32] Equality is a major theme, the most famous text bearing on this being 49:13: "O people [*nas*], We created you from a male and female, and formed you into nations and tribes so that you may know one another [and not in order that you despise each other]. The most noble among you with God is the most pious." Piety being the mark of distinction among human beings recognized by the Qur'an, the latter are essentially treated in the revelation in terms encouraging mutual recognition of their brotherhood. Moreover, an often-cited Hadith attributed to the Prophet says: "people are as similar to one another as the teeth of a comb."[33] This seems to imply that whatever differences as may arise among them will be less important than the elements that unite them.

Consequences should follow from this position so far as the factor of tolerance is concerned. If people are so similar to one another, presumably there is less need for counseling tolerance, inasmuch as they are likely to agree with each other. By contrast, the value of tolerance is needed when people commit themselves to sharply contrasting views that might otherwise lead to outright conflict. Indeed, the reality in the time of the Prophet was that disagreements arose among his companions and between some of them and him over such things as strategy and tactics in fighting military campaigns, or amnestying prisoners of war. The Qur'an does not convey a consistent message in regard to those who disagree with the believers. In a number of verses, God is prepared to forgive those who repent or who see the error of their ways. But of necessity it is left to interpreters of such verses (for example, 9:5) to determine the commitment to and materialization of such repentance. Such interpretations may not necessarily be benign. In other verses, on the whole, those revealed to the Prophet before his flight to Medina and at a time when he and his supporters were most vulnerable, the message is more forbearing. "You have your religion and I have mine" (109:9). Even after reaching safety in Medina and building the community of believers there, the Prophet received the verse: "there is no compulsion in regard to matters of religion" (2:256). Not surprisingly, certain sayings attributed to the Prophet also convey this notion of living with differences. In one he is stated to have said: "differences among my people are a blessing."[34]

What can one make of these various scriptural statements? That grounds exist for establishing a theory of tolerance in the sacred texts of Islam. But the situation is complicated by an empirical and a theoretical difficulty. On the empirical side, the difficulty is that implementation of the high ideals bespoken in these sacred texts has failed so often in Middle East history since the death of the Prophet. On the theoretical side, the difficulty is that as long as the central concept of punishment for derelictions is that this is one of God's rights, rather than something to be addressed and taken care of by human beings, then it will always be possible for conservatives and cultural relativists to argue that human rights discourse contradicts principles of Islamic law and thus must not be taken seriously.[35]

However, some Muslim theorists have confronted the theoretical difficulty explicitly in an effort to move to a theory of tolerance within an overall Islamic framework. One of the leading efforts in this connection has been provided by the Syrian civil engineer Muhammad Shuhrur. According to Wael Hallaq, Shuhrur is seeking to bring about a paradigm shift ("revolutionary and innovative" are the words he uses) in Islamic jurisprudence with his theory of limits (*nazariyat al-hudud*).[36] Shuhrur, who studied engineering in Moscow and Ireland, has captured the imagination of a significant number of Muslim reformers, beginning with the publication in 1990 of his book *The Book and the Qur'an: A Contemporary Reading*.[37] Since this inaugural publication, he has published several more, including a work on the state and society,[38] one on a reformulation of the foundations of Islamic law,[39] and a proposal for a new Islamic covenant.[40]

Though Shuhrur has things to say about society and state, it is his position on the individual that is of interest here. He believes that plurality is both the natural condition of human beings and also the prerequisite of freedom. Although during the Prophet's lifetime, contending interests were not expressed openly, after his passing from the scene these differences emerged, and became articulated. The entirety of Islamic history since the death of the Prophet, therefore, is a history of contention, as can be seen by the proliferation of sects, schools, and theodicies. These contending interests are not a threat to the integrity of the Islamic system. On the contrary, they are symptoms of its health. The problem, however, arises when people seek to adhere to literal meanings of sacred scriptures, failing to realize that even the most specific (*muhkam*) texts are not to be – nor were they ever intended to be – interpreted literally. According to Shuhrur, the Qur'an has two parts. One deals with prophecy, the other with law and ethics. The message of the Qur'an about prophecy is categorical and does not depend on human knowledge or interpretation. So far as law and ethics go, however, such knowledge and interpretation are very much involved and, among other things, require the ability to distinguish right from wrong.

Shuhrur has been arguing for almost twenty years that, with the exception of that part of the sacred book that bears on prophecy, human beings must bring their interpretive skills to bear upon its contents. In this respect, Shuhrur adopts a position similar to that of the Iranian thinker Abdol Karim Soroush. All interpretations of the Qur'an that are based on exegesis and independent reasoning are by definition human in their motivation, their nature, and their conclusions. Shuhrur is indignant that those in authority in Muslim societies over the centuries – whether rulers and their state bureaucrats or the clergy of Islam – have promoted a sense of fatalism among the people. Such fatalism is not only a recipe for apathy but also a pretext for abandoning responsibility for one's actions (or inactions). As he puts it, the reality is that God may know all the options before me upon which I need to act, but the one who actually chooses among these options is I.

What has happened is that the Qur'an, which, of course, is sacred in that it is God's revelations to human beings, has been sacralized. At first, this seems an absurd statement. But what Shuhrur means is that God intended most of the Qur'an to be open to human reason. He did not intend that those parts should become divine hypostases. The effect of this was to dogmatize passages that had been intended for every generation of human beings to construe as they believed was relevant for their own historical time. The dogmatization of the Qur'an at the hands of authoritarians has produced mimicry and stagnation at best, and oppression at worst. He concludes, as did 'Ali Shari'ati a generation before him, that the clergy of Islam are mainly to blame for this state of affairs. Shari'ati called the Muslim clergy in general "hidebound" (*'ulama'-ye qishri*). Shuhrur couldn't agree more. And both of them believe that most clergymen who have cooperated with rulers have done so for reasons of their own vested interests.

A critique such as Shuhrur's faces the criticism that by training he is not a religious scholar. Accordingly, he is considered insufficiently learned in the sciences of religion to be persuasive. He has, in other words, to undertake an immanent criticism of the condition of Muslim societies historically and today, the state of these societies' intellectual standards, and the role of the professional men of religion in bringing about the circumstances in which these societies have found themselves over the centuries. In order to undertake such a critique, Shuhrur develops what he calls a theory of limits.[41]

The key element in this perspective is that God established limits, not requirements, in regard to behavior in the various realms of human endeavor. These include market transactions, matters of personal status (marriage, divorce, inheritance), torts, felonies, rentals of property, fiduciary issues, and many others. In the area of penal law, the very term for exemplary punishments is *hadd/hudud* – limits. This means that God left it at the discretion of human beings as to what punishment to mete out to a thief. The maximum limit is amputation of a limb, but this need not be the required punishment. Human beings can sentence thieves to periods of incarceration, for example; or even release a thief on grounds of extreme exigency (his family's starvation, for example), leaving the maximum punishment to be imposed only when human beings had established a truly Islamic society, when theft would truly be a wanton act. In Shuhrur's system, *ijtihad* is a critical matter. Because societies change, their requirements change. Independent judgment, grounded in a knowledge of law, is the mechanism that will maintain the dynamism required to adapt to changing circumstances.

Shuhrur's project resonates with the ideas of Muhammad 'Abduh and his followers that the only way to get away from stultifying imitation of past practices is to revive the doctrine of *ijtihad*. Shuhrur is a Sunni Muslim who wants to valorize the use of independent judgment as the essential vehicle for reforming Muslim society. 'Abduh and his followers were Sunnis as well, and they tried to draw upon the *ijtihad* tradition of Mu'tazilism – the rationalist school discussed earlier in this book. Because of the marginalization of the Mu'tazilites, Sunni jurists in the modern period have always been ambivalent about the utilization of *ijtihad*. Indeed, it is the Shi'i jurists or intellectuals (such as 'Ali Shari'ati) who are identified most closely with this principle. Thus, Shuhrur faces the same kind of opposition encountered by 'Abduh a century ago, even though major thinkers of the Mu'tazili school, such as al-Jahiz (d. 868/69) – who insisted that every Muslim must resort to *ijtihad* – continue for contemporary Sunni '*ulama*' to be influential in non-legal realms of Sunni thought, such as prose and rhetoric.

Shuhrur's theory of limits and his insistence on the individual's right to engage in independent judgment is not unlike the concept among Iranian pietists of the last two generations termed *fiqh-i puya* (dynamic jurisprudence). The idea behind this is that traditional jurisprudence (fiqh-i sunnati) is time-bound and not adaptable to the requirements of the modern era.

While Shuhrur wants to utilize ijtihad as a way of liberating the individual from repressive interpretations of religion, Sourush wants to separate religion from the search for democracy. Dynamic jurisprudence can, in his view, lead to such separation and emancipation because it advocates the application of ijtihad even on primary principles of the faith.[42] Soroush insists that religion must remain in its own sphere, which is an orientation to otherworldly salvation. He writes: "I am of the view that religion is, basically and fundamentally, for ameliorating our hereafter."[43]

This is not to suggest that Soroush is an advocate of secular liberalism. In fact, he blames the latter for producing an individual who is "very close to a morally deterring egoism." Asked whether rights-based (liberalism) and duty-based (communitarianism) views can be reconciled, he concludes that both have shortcomings and suggests a third paradigm, virtue, which can bridge the differences between them but shed their negative qualities.[44]

Conclusion

Middle Eastern political theories accord more attention to the rights of society than they do to the rights of the individual. This is the case whether one is discussing the early period of the consolidation of the schools of law, or, later on, the medieval, early modern or modern periods. Although British and French imperialism in the Middle East in the nineteenth and twentieth centuries, through the cultural diffusion of certain Western political ideas about constitutionalism and democracy, did attract the interest of some Middle Eastern theorists in individualism, this was not sufficient to displace the primacy of place accorded to collectivist theories. In the post-independence period, most state narratives adopted some variant of socialism, which again placed the emphasis upon communal rights and interests.

Nonetheless, contemporary Middle Eastern political theorists feel that they must address the question of individual rights, given their understanding that political liberalism has played a leading role in certain circles in the West. The tendency of the writing on individual rights is somewhat apologetic, the effort being to show that Middle Eastern cultural traditions also vindicate such rights. However, these writers do not demonstrate this by argumentation so much as they assert it on the basis of scriptural references that they believe promote and protect individual interests. The presentation tends to be narrative and descriptive. Even the more sophisticated theorists, such as the Egyptian social psychologist 'Abd al-Hamid Mursi, who acknowledges that complex societies require a more salient role for individualism and individual interests, maintains that Islamic culture mandates the supervention of others' rights and interests over one's own. Indeed, he holds that "Islam" (sic) is "displeased with individualism" and imposes upon the human being belief in God; once this is achieved, that person must, by the nature of things, give primacy to the rights of the community.

Perhaps the prolific writer Muhammad 'Imara is one of the best-known among Islamist intellectuals for his writings on Islamic topics. Though some regard him as an Islamic liberal, this appellation begs the question. At any rate, he seems to believe that recognition of the rights of the individual inevitably defies God's sovereignty. Such defiance, he sarcastically implies, may be suitable in Western civilization, because in the latter it is the intellect that is placed on the altar of obedience. But Muslim societies are God-centered and hence constrain individualism within a narrow compass. It is true that he has called Islam a "liberal" religion, but he states bluntly that what this means is very different from its meaning in the United Kingdom, for instance. Liberalism deriving from religion, he asserts, is different from liberalism that derives from non-religious sources. But, rather than settling matters, such an assertion merely raises many questions about why that is the case. If he responds that it is because liberalism derived from religion necessitates that the individual accord sovereignty to God, we are left in a vicious circle inasmuch as we are free to act because God gives us the right to be free, but our freedom is based on according primacy not to our self-determination but to that of God.

Although the meaning of liberalism has evolved across geographical space and over historical time in the West, Middle Eastern political theorists – especially apologists for Islamic political theories – tend to treat the concept in highly simplistic ways, essentially equating it with greediness, selfishness, egotism, and enmity towards the rights of others. The reality, however, is that many variants of liberalism, and hence different interpretations of the rights and the role of individuals, may be found. Today, some of the most interesting debates in the field of liberalism are taking place between the advocates of Rawls's theory of "justice as fairness" and those espousing Gauthier's utilitarian ideas of "the greatest good for the greatest number." Middle Eastern political theorists, in the urge to support communitarian values, seem oblivious to these debates.

Yet we do need to bear in mind two factors: (1) colonialism often trumpeted the advantages of liberalism but perversely denied colonized Middle Easterners the opportunity to apply it; (2) it cannot be denied that one interpretation of liberalism, which Macpherson has called "the political theory of possessive individualism," is particularly contrary to the collectivist ethos that has dominated Middle Eastern political theories over the centuries. This variant makes the individual over into a proprietor of his own self, an atomized unit living in near blithe disregard of the surrounding society. It is virtually impossible for Middle Eastern political theorists to credit such an interpretation of liberalism with any validity for the people living in that part of the world – even if we can admit that Macpherson's model is highly skewed and exaggerated.

Ultimately, the acceptability of the rights of the individual as against society's rights (which are deemed actually to be the rights of God) has to be seen in the light of how liberalism and how Islam interpret human nature. God's call to human beings to accept

Islam is tantamount to calling them to return to their original true good natures. But this is a divinely ordained condition. Liberalism, by contrast, maintains that the natural condition of the human being is freedom. It therefore seems that we are up against a basic contradiction. However, the Syrian thinker Muhammad Shuhrur, in a novel interpretation of the scripture as establishing "limits" and not "requirements," reasons that God does not require obedience to supposed strictures but counsels human beings to make choices. Even if those choices are not fully open-ended (since God does, after all, expect obedience in regard to certain basic points, such as monotheism), human discretion is the key to dealing with changing historical circumstances.

Whether Shuhrur's theory of limits, and similar notions on the part of Abdol Karim Soroush, can reconcile Middle Eastern political theories with liberal individualism is the question. The really interesting point is that Shuhrur emphasizes the importance of historical circumstances in changing the way we theorize about politics. Once again, therefore, the theme emerges that reality shapes our thinking, and we need to ground our ideas in the historical record if we want to talk convincingly about solutions to major problems of the modern world.

FIVE

Society

In the period known as the "age of ignorance" (*jahiliya*), prior to the rise of Islam, the clan, consisting of several families, constituted the basic unit of society. According to the ethos of pre-Islamic tribal society, membership in the collectivity was imperative, since, without it, the human being could not exist, much less prosper. With the onset of Islam, the preceding period in retrospect came to be seen as one of contention, rancor, hostility, and instability. These traits were then contrasted to those that were believed to qualify the new society, which, although still tribal in its organization, was now understood to be animated by an ethos of reciprocity and mutuality, underpinned by a moral and spiritual cultural unity.

Contemporary anthropologists, sociologists or political scientists would not characterize the tribal order prior to the rise of Islam as "a state of nature" – the phrase used by Western social contract theorists to depict human existence prior to individuals joining together in communal life. That is because pre-Islamic Arabian tribal life was indeed societally based and possessed a recognizable structure and processes. But Muslim writers, with their jaundiced view of life prior to Islam, would have used the "state of nature" characterization had it been available to them. The reason is that they believed (and continue to do so) that the *jahiliya* era was chaotic and lacked continuity, regularity, calculability, order.

Society, as an analytical construct, involves "the guiding notion ... that collective life made up a whole, a totality, perhaps even a system."[1] Eric Wolf, the author of these words, however, warns us not to think compartmentally about society. His point is that no society is hermetically sealed off from other societies. For example, he notes that social science scholars known as "diffusionists" have emphasized the tendency of cultural and even structural traits to "travel" from one social setting to another. Because of this, it begs the question to suggest, for example, that French society is "French," or Russian society is "Russian," because they are unique terrains. However, this caveat should not cause us to jettison the concept of society, so long as we are aware that any particular one is subject to significant influences from the outside.

Tracing the evolution of the term "society" in Western thinking, Wolf notes that the concept of the state or the political community was not separated from that of (civil) society until well into the seventeenth century. However, by the time of Locke (1632–1704) the concept of society had come to mean "the arena of interplay of private rights against the state."[2]

Meanwhile, in the Muslim world, this Lockean perspective did not come to obtain because the existence of private rights, much less their being wielded against the state, would have been highly anomalous. The terms Muslims utilized to bespeak collectivities were *umma* and *jama'a* (the generic word for an aggregation of people, a group). This does not mean that Lockean notions of society did not enter into both the vocabulary and the practice of Muslims, but that would come subsequent to the colonial encounter of the West and the Middle East.

Until then, the classic theory of society among Muslims stressed God's role in calling people to join together under the aegis of the divine commands. These commands constituted a legal system that God, in His wisdom, bestowed as a device to regulate social relations among human beings. It was up to them to accept or not to accept the jural conditions laid down by the Almighty, but His role in any case was to articulate the requirements in a language of promises of reward and threats of punishment. If people chose to obey these rules, the Muslim theory of society holds, then they were thereby entering into society; if they chose to disobey them, they were *ipso facto* opting to remain in a state of unrelieved ignorance – that is, to remain in the state of nature.

Classical Muslim theories of social contract

Is there a Muslim theory of why human beings join together and leave the state of nature and enter society? The answer to this question is yes, such a theory (or theories) does/do exist, although it/they came not at the origins of the Islamic community but rather in the modern period. This is true for both Sunnism and Shi'ism. The following discussion takes up the discourse of social contract theorizing in Sunnism. Afterward Shi'i theories of social contract will also be examined.

Social-contract theorists in the West differ on a number of points. They do, however, concur that human beings choose to form associations to promote their interests. An important corollary is that tension exists between the individual's inherent independence and freedom, on the one hand, and the authority to which he must submit to achieve compliance with the goals of the contract, on the other. Occasionally, a theorist discusses God in the overall scheme of things. But the conception is deistic, so that the God who created the world, as Aristotle held, does not intervene in its operation. Contractualist theories privilege natural law and natural rights, according to which the individual is treated as a social being who is fully rational, free, and independent. Fundamentally, three steps are taken in the process of making the social contract: (1) creating society; (2) creating the sovereign state; (3) discharging obligations and enjoying benefits.

Because mainstream Ash'ari Sunni Islam views God as continuously intervening in the operation of the universe and insists on the human being's "acquisition" of his or her actions from God, it did not generate a theory of social contract.[3] The theory was introduced as a convention to the Muslim world in the nineteenth century, when reformers such as the Egyptian Azharite scholar Rifa'a Rafi' al-Tahtawi (d. 1873) and the Young Ottoman writer Namik Kemal (d. 1888) became interested in Western contractualist writings.[4] This is not to say that Muslim traditions lack ideas and concepts that are important to the elaboration of a theory of social contract, such as justice, obligation, mutuality, and interests.[5] But before the nineteenth century, jurists would not have referred to individual Muslims ceding their discrete interests to the community as a whole and converting them into a collective interest for which that community would be the trustee.

Contemporary Sunni writers are raising critical issues about political community. Their writing variously deals with such concepts as representation, interest, organization, obligation, authority, justice, sovereignty, and leadership. Despite the seriousness of their motivations and commitments, their theoretical arguments are characterized by the ad hoc manner by which they incorporate the propositions that bear on the above concepts in their efforts to construct a theory of social contract. They are forced into this by an assumption that, in Islam, natural law is to be equated with divine law, but then ignore the implications of this for autonomous social action by individual Muslims in constructing and consolidating political community.

Before discussing some of these contemporary theorists, it is fitting to examine earlier writing relevant to the concept of contract. In the Qur'an a number of words appear that have the connotation of contract. These include *'ahd*,[6] *'aqd*,[7] *bay'*,[8] *mawthiq*,[9] and *mithaq*.[10] Although it is impossible to be certain as to what constituted the contemporary understandings of these terms, it is unikely that they were understood as betokening social contract.

According to Ash'ari non-modernist Sunnism, God had sent prophets to various peoples and made covenants with them, which they have broken for various reasons. Pained, God made a final effort with those who agreed to submit, choosing Muhammad as His Prophet. The Muslims who agreed did so because they believed that they would benefit from God's revelational knowledge as well as from His offer of the earth's resources to them in their capacity as his vicegerents. Note that they are not the architects of this covenant, although they are its beneficiaries. Their role is passive, even though in accepting what is offered they have gained so much.

The Prophet's part in this "single contract" was to articulate the message and persuade people to accept it. Muslims differ as to whether the Prophet's role went beyond proselytizing to include political leadership. Or, rather, they agree that he also was a political leader, but they disagree as to the grounds by which he achieved that station. Some believe it was *ex officio* from the fact that he was the Prophet. Others maintain that it was due to the people's perception that he was best qualified to lead based on his endowment of leadership skills but that this had nothing to do with his Prophecy. Over the centuries, non-modernist Sunni mainstream interpretations support the first scenario, whereas many modernists support the second.

As a merchant, the Prophet knew the importance of contracts. As an arbiter of disputes and initiator of tribal alliances, he gained important legal and political experience. But these compacts were not social contracts, which are formed when "each man, by right of nature, that is, by right of his human character ... possessed the quality of freedom."[11] This sort of individualism was precluded by tribal society's collectivist ethos prior to the rise of Islam and by Ash'arism's belief that God ordained the Prophet's office, which was to induce the people to obey God's commands and, thereby, to obtain the blessings of salvation and fulfillment. This differs from individuals freely disposing of their wills in response to the dictates of reason for the defense of their interests by entering into a civil union. Ash'arism denied that human beings voluntarily entrust some of their rights and interests to society and its state, which would be merely custodians of these and must return them on demand. By contrast, God's role is as initiator of all contracts with the believers, as already seen by the reference in Qur'an 4:58: "God commands you to return trusts to their owners." God is the trustor in this tradition, not individuals, who in fact are his trustees. If they fail to return them to God, He may take them back, as stated in 3:26: "You give whom it pleases You the kingdom, and You take away the power from whomsoever You will." Ultimately, then, Muslims may accept or reject the revelation, but they may not negotiate or renegotiate the covenant.

With the Prophet's death, a "double contract" came into force in the Ash'ari view.[12] In addition to the original contract between God and the believers came a second contract in which the leaders of the community identified one of themselves to administer the law. This caliph could not promulgate new law, but he retained the Prophet's function of implementing existing law. Over the centuries, most Muslim writers have characterized the second contract as being founded on popular choice, basing their arguments on works by medieval constitutionalist theorists such as al-Mawardi, whose works we reviewed earlier. This claim of "popular election" became particularly prominent in the writings of Muslims in the nineteenth century and thereafter, as European theories of social contract began to be known. However, the early caliphs were chosen not by the people but by the close companions of the Prophet. Moreover, with Umayyad dynastic rule, whatever "popular" element putatively had existed in the first twenty-nine years of Islam vanished. Meanwhile, although the constitutional scholars implied or stated the right to replace an unjust caliph, their greater concern was over the possible chaos that disobedience to a ruler might unleash, making it impossible to fulfill the devotional obligations. Hence their writings had a strongly apologetic cast, and this overrode their weakly stated arguments that sinning rulers need not be obeyed. At any rate, they established neither a threshold of oppression nor a procedure to oust a derelict leader. Additionally, these theorists discussed relations between the caliphs and Muslims in the context of fulfilling religious, not worldly, obligations and rights. It would therefore be greatly stretching matters to consider the caliphs of Islam as representing the people's trust and obligated to returning those trusts to them were they to feel that these caliphs were unjust or oppressive.

Western theories of social contract

Conditions seemed more favorable to social contract thought in the post-Reformation West. It is true that Christ's statement, "Render unto Caesar that which is Caesar's and unto God that which is God's," and St Paul's injunction, "Let every soul be subject to the highest powers," which equated obedience to magistrates with obedience to God (Romans 13:1–7), were hardly conducive to contactarian ideas.

But matters were to change. St Thomas Aquinas (d. 1274) asserted the people's right to determine the form of government, to authorize individual rulers, and to revoke the rule – although he entered the reservation that the harm they caused in doing so must be less than the oppression of the tyrant they sought to remove. In addition, the system of feudalism itself was based on notions of contractually based mutual obligations and rights among lords, vassals and villeins. Finally, considerations of natural law were important for the emergence of Western social contract theory. The theory arose on the belief, as Cicero had stated it, that "there is in fact a true law, namely right reason, which is in accordance with nature, applies to all men and is unchangeable and eternal." If there is such a natural law, then there must be natural rights associated with such a law. As Barker put it, "if there were any limitations imposed on natural rights, those limitations must be due to a voluntary contract made by the possessors of such rights."[13]

The conception of natural law here is that the operation of the universe exists independently of the will of God. Even if, as with Aquinas, the creation is due to God's will, it is maintained that God nevertheless thereupon refrained from interfering in its dynamics.

This is quite different from Ash'arite perspectives, which stress God's immanence in nature, whereby all development results from His recurring intervention to bring about each individual action.

Under the influence of European encounters with the Muslim world after the French Revolution, Muslim interest in contracts took a somewhat different turn. Now, it was deemed important somehow to integrate the traditional view on contracts as (a) covenants offered by God to a people passively accepting it, supplemented by (b) the secondary contract made by the leaders of the community among themselves to choose a supreme leader, with (c) contracts as social conventions stressing the free will of people to manage their own affairs. The European influence in this area was captured by themes in the writings of Hobbes, Locke, Rousseau, and Kant. Hobbes based his interpretation of why humans enter society from a state of nature on their fear of death in the latter and their rational calculation of the benefits accruing to them in the former. To that end, they entrusted their lives and property to an omnipotent Legislator (Leviathan). Locke held that people were the properties of God and had the duty to protect their own property lest harm befall God's interests. Human beings find it increasingly difficult to implement in a state of nature those duties with which God has charged them because of the absence of a final authority there. People have an entitlement to their lives and property (considered an extension of that life); and every one is naturally free, equal, and independent. Human insecurity in the state of nature was due to the inability to enforce these entitlements. Hence, people entering into society drew up a contract with the legislature to enforce their entitlements. The legislature was vested with a "fiduciary power to act for certain ends."[14] If the legislature failed in its fiduciary power for whatever reason, the people had the right to change it.

Rousseau's interpretation was that people entered into society because in the state of nature, even though free they were dominated by their animal natures and low levels of rational and moral development, whereas it behoved them to refine these. According to him, to rescue oneself from doltish lethargy, each individual made a reciprocal commitment with the sovereign (not with other individuals) to overcome this dilemma, an act that vested him with moral integrity. Thus, for Rousseau, the social contract was a means for converting the human being from a dullard to the creature he was destined to be. He admitted that in doing so the individual "loses ... his *natural* liberty and his unqualified right to lay hands on all that tempts him, provided only that he can compass its possession. [However,] what he gains is *civil* liberty."[15] As for Kant, he sought to answer the question that bothered Rousseau: how to reconcile natural rights and natural freedom with submission to authority. Kant was clear in his own mind about the moral obligation of human beings to enter into community. His solution to the problem was to suggest that autonomy and authority were not mutually exclusive, and he maintained that only in a community was justice possible. In the state of nature, the freedom that people possessed was lawless and could be actualized – in the form of legislation advancing the interests of the self – only in civil society.[16]

Sunni theories of social contract

Acting as a bridge from the late nineteenth to the mid-twentieth century were members of a group of reformers from Muhammad 'Abduh to Khalid Muhammad Khalid (prior to his 1980 recantation). Their objectives were to reconcile reason and revelation, and in this manner to revivify the faith. Attacking the blind imitation of earlier jurists and theologians, they upheld the cause of *ijtihad* as the only way to keep the element of dynamism at the forefront of efforts to resolve the problems of contemporary society. 'Abduh and his followers also rescued the general good and public interest (*maslaha mursala*), a forgotten juristic principle, and made it central to their reform efforts. On this view, if the ultimate value for the community of believers is their good and welfare, then strictures that on the face of it may be interpreted as impeding the attainment of that good and welfare are to be superseded by more liberal interpretations.

The problem in all of this is whether Muslims, who, upon accepting the message of Islam and thus entering into the umma, are seen to be freely disposing of their will to do so and freely choosing a leader or leaders who would be the trustee of their rights. It was Rashid Rida – Muhammad 'Abduh's illustrious student – more than the master himself, who paid some attention to matters relevant to social contract. Rida argued that the Islamic community's sovereignty is manifested in the elite, which the sources had termed "the people of loosing and binding" (ahd al-hall wa al-'aqd).

Although he fails to specify in any detail who these people are, Rida identified them generally as the community's leaders and those of prominent rank whom the believers trust. In his opinion, the Muslims, having accepted God's covenant, thereupon endowed the people of loosing and binding with the authority to nominate the head of that community, provided the believers are consulted and allowed to ratify the elite's choice. Note that Rida has recourse here to modern notions of representative rule that had long been current in the non-Muslim world. Rida thus bestows the community's delegated sovereignty upon a poorly identified elite, a step that Kerr rightly maintains is unacceptable for two reasons.

First, Rida seems to be saying tautologically that authority devolves upon those who have it or are able to exercise it, since the Constitutionalist theorists – such as al-Mawardi (d. 1058) – who wrote on this group never specified in what manner the Muslims appointed its members to be their trustees. Accordingly, that theory ends (with ibn Jama'a, for instance) by justifying the rule of he who seizes it, "which is another way of saying that might makes right."[17] Second, the people of loosing and binding would appear to be a semi-closed elite to whom the Muslims as a whole must submit: they are not delegates of the Muslims but a group whose members "seemingly enjoy their status by virtue of what is assumed to be an undeniable and absolute capacity.... Their authority then appears to be in the nature of an oligarchy rather than a kind of publicly exercised sovereignty."[18]

Accordingly, Rida cannot be considered an advocate of Muslim popular delegation of authority based on free will and choice and exercising social contractualist rights. It is 'Ali 'Abd al-Raziq (d. 1966) who came closer to contractualist thought. In his view, God offered His covenant to the believers, and they joined His community to implement their religious obligations. But 'Abd al-Raziq then maintained that the Prophet's successors established the caliphate not as a result of doctrinal necessity or divine ordainment but in response to historically contingent factors. Muslims, as with any human beings, possess natural rights and reason, which permit them to act in accordance with their own calculus of what is best for themselves. This being so, Muslims do not have to model their government on the historical caliphate but may establish any form of government they wish. The Prophet himself was solely a religious leader who left it up to each new generation of Muslims to decide this matter.[19]

Since 'Abd al-Raziq wrote these views in 1925, we may ask if more recent writings relevant to social contract theory by Sunni Muslims go beyond his contributions. In a way, the answer to this question is both yes and no. Yes, in the sense that the more recent scholars are more self-conscious about the contradictions between divine law and natural law; but no, in the sense that their attempts to resolve these contradictions have not significantly advanced the argument beyond 'Abd al-Raziq's efforts. I would like to examine the writings of three Egyptian Muslim modernists in this area. Modernists in this context are those who believe in the importance of *ijtihad* and *maslaha* and simultaneously are historically minded. But before I address their positions, it is well to review the social, economic, and political trends in Egypt since the June War of 1967, following which secular thought, which had enjoyed the patronage of the Egyptian government, gradually became eclipsed and is currently decidedly on the defensive in the face of theories rooted in one way or another in Islamic orientations toward politics.[20] Although most such orientations have stressed peaceful transition to the era of the "Islamic state," some have professed and engaged in violent behavior to bring about this state of affairs.

Since 1967, intellectuals have been writing against the backdrop of internal, regional, and international developments that have been highly unsettling. In the approximately forty years since the June War of 1967 and the death of President Nasser in 1970, his two successors have moved away from his secular socialist policies, including pan-Arabism abroad. Such a transition has involved privatization and structural readjustment in the economy, although the entire edifice of state capitalism built in the 1957–70 era has even now not been completely dismantled. Still, with President Sadat's policies favoring foreign investment and private property, and generally more liberal trade policies, Egypt has experienced dramatic shifts in class structure, land-tenure relations, the role of labor, and the efficacy of state health and welfare programs.

Continuing high rates of population growth have contributed to the widening of the rich–poor gap. Meanwhile, deterioration of the country's infrastructure, increasingly burdensome bureaucratization of politics, mounting corruption within the state administration and economic sectors, and failure to establish government accountability and transparency have all plagued the social order in Egypt. In foreign policy, the major change has been the orientation to the United States, the (cold) peace with Israel, and rivalry with Saudi Arabia and Iraq for leadership in regional affairs. Meanwhile, Egypt's economy has been increasingly integrated into the global capitalist economy, and the trends of globalization have been negative for most of the country's population. A consumer culture has been generated, according to which rapid gratification of desires is the watchword. Private businessmen have been far more active in the realms of land and financial speculation, resort construction, and housing projects than in the traditional areas of interest to the members of the middle class, such as investment in industry, manufacturing, and the technology sector. In the meanwhile, the earlier programs that erected a social safety net for the mass of the population have been dismantled. Although state subsidies have not been eliminated, they have been greatly reduced.

This is a formidable catalog of negatives, although it is fitting also to note some positive aspects. The media enjoy significant autonomy, professional and voluntary associations have proliferated, and certain judicial bodies (such as the Constitutional Court) have stood up to the authoritarian policies of the regime by invalidating election results or efforts to change the electoral law in the direction of narrowing the franchise. Yet, if civil society has grown, its associations and groups have not really been able to transform their historical successes in keeping the state at arm's length into the ability to make demands upon that state to promote their interests.

Meanwhile, violence has flared at various points since the mid-1970s, as opposition forces have formed and engaged in confrontations with the security forces. Although the high-water mark of such incidents, especially those that pitted groups animated by a radical interpretation of Islam against the state, was reached by the mid-1990s and appears to have subsided to significantly lower levels, alienation of the society from the state had reached unprecedented levels by the turn of the twentieth to the twenty-first century. Muslim modernists have become increasingly alarmed at the appropriation of religious discourse by the violence-prone or rhetorically militant Islamist groups. The dilemma that they have faced is that the state has cynically tried to co-opt them in its struggle against the radical Islamists, whereas they do not wish to appear as complicit in state repression. On the other hand, they believe that violence-prone Islamist groups should not be allowed to appropriate and monopolize religious discourse, since in their view the behavior and thought of these Islamists does not represent the "true" Islam. The secularist intellectuals, meanwhile, are highly critical of state corruption and repression.

With the preceding in mind, I will examine the writing of two modernist writers who have tried to construe what ought to be the appropriate understanding by Muslims of themes at the heart of social contract theory. One is Muhammad Ahmad Khalaf Allah (d. 1983), a Nasserist who sought to integrate Islamic principles with a leftist understanding of politics. The other is Tariq al-Bishri, a leftist structuralist historian and lawyer who has abandoned his earlier views in favor of a conservative modernist position.

Muhammad Ahmad Khalaf Allah

Khalaf Allah represents the Nasserist legacy. His theoretical position can be said to reflect the most liberal modernist Muslim perspective. That is, he supports the principle of *ijtihad* in its most unencumbered form because of the importance of dealing with changed historical circumstances. Hence, he stands as a counter to Bishri (who, however, in his earlier work, positioned himself in that same perspective). At the same time, Khalaf Allah's "Islamic credentials" are hard for his rivals to refute because his work is replete with analyses of Qur'anic verse, which in turn are anchored in the interpretations of Muhammad 'Abduh and his school. Even though the logic of his arguments is to separate religion and politics in the tradition of 'Abd al-Raziq, he does not advocate this explicitly.

As a student, Khalaf Allah specialized in the literature of the Qur'an. He graduated from the Dar al-'Ulum, a Western-style academy that was the forerunner of Cairo University. He was a student of the famous Shaykh Amin al-Khuli (d. 1967), "who developed a theory of the literary exegesis of the Qur'an ... [that] promoted the use of all accessible scientific methods, irrespective of religious considerations, the view being that the Qur'an's message could only be understood after its historical literal meaning for the first addressees ... had been identified."[21] Khalaf Allah also earned bachelor's and master's degrees in philosophy from the University of London. From 1965 to 1983, he served as director of the Institute for Arabic Research and Studies in Cairo. After Nasser's death, he affiliated with the leftist political party the Unitary National Progressive Bloc and became the secretary of its political affairs committee.

Khalaf Allah accepted the traditional contractualist premiss that God summoned the people to accept His message, granting them in return use of the earth's resources to enable them to prosper. God's initiative in creating the community is seen in Qur'an 8:62–63: "It is He Who has strengthened you [Muhammad] with His help and with believers whose hearts he cemented with love."[22] Divine love, then, becomes God's motive that leads the people to enter into a contract with Him and ccreate a new society. However, Khalaf Allah mainly focuses on what occurs once the new society is established. He is particularly interested in the idea of the state, including the motive behind its establishment.

At one point, Khalaf Allah asserts that God ordains this state, citing Qur'an 2:247 ("God gives authority to whomsoever He wills") and 3:26 ("You give whom it pleases You the Kingdom and take away the power from whomsoever You will").[23] Elsewhere, though, he holds that Muslims established the institution of rule as a matter of reason.[24] On this view, rule was required not by the holy law but by the fact that it is rational for human beings to submit to a leader who prevents abuses and arbitrates their disputes. I take this to be his general position, as can be seen in the following passage: "the development of human thought guided human reason to the theory of natural rights emanating from human nature and social life, to the effect that the people are the source of all authority."[25] Note the attribution to natural rights, which presupposes natural law. He holds that the people are the authors of their own progress,[26] and each member of the community takes full responsibility for his or her actions, based on reason.[27]

Khalaf Allah says that each of the first four caliphs was chosen in a different manner, which shows that the form of government in Muslim societies is subject to debate and historical contingencies. No invariant blueprint exists for an Islamic state and government. The only givens are devotional matters ('*ibadat*) pertaining to the absolute unity of God, the finality of Muhammad's prophecy, the Day of Judgment, and communal expression of belief in these principles, including the statement of the credo, prayer, alms-giving, Ramadan fasting, and pilgrimage to Mecca. The daily affairs of the people are considered social relations (mu'amalat), and these are arranged according to the constraints of circumstances. Muslims no longer choose a caliph by the decision of one, three, or five people but elect a government by means of an articulated public opinion and a national electorate.[28]

In Khalaf Allah's opinion, the Qur'an mandated accountable government in the consultation verses, which, in his opinion, are actually warrants for heeding public opinion. He believes that they require that "opinion in public matters be collective, not individual."[29] The Prophet's role was to assist in the articulation of public opinion: "It was necessary for the Prophet ... to clarify to the people the practical meaning of this verse, 3:159 – "so consult them in affairs" – and advise them on how to form public opinion and to take decisions bearing on public matters."[30]

In Khalaf Allah's opinion, the dynamic influencing the state and its government is "the public interest and the public good" (maslaha 'amma and khayr 'amm),[31] concepts that he does not define but unhesitatingly applies anachronistically to the early Islamic period. In the modern era, he argues, the separation of powers is the chief means of securing the public interest and public good. No Qur'anic basis for this is necessary because, as he has already noted, the Prophet left social matters to the devising of each Muslim generation. Thus, the basis of contemporary political systems is "human interests and the public good."[32] Because he has already referred to the human being's "natural rights emanating from human nature," a fair reading of his view of the state is that it is the property of freely disposing individuals. In this regard, he radically interprets Qur'an 3:159 as God commanding the Prophet to acknowledge that the people create their own history.[33]

The government that the people establish is to be accountable to them. Although in early Islam those to be consulted were the

Prophet's companions, termed in the Qur'an "those in authority among you" (4:59), and by the early commentators as "the people of loosing and binding," in the modern period they include economic, political, and social elites who act as delegated representatives. He approvingly cites 'Abduh on this point. Both government and the people can freely borrow non-Islamic laws if they do not contravene the core beliefs. After all, early jurists adopted aspects of Greek, Roman, Persian, Assyrian, and Babylonian law in regard to administration, finance, and the dispensation of justice. Moreover, the early jurists clearly never intended that their opinions on such secular matters be final. Hence, contemporary Islamist calls for re-establishing the *shari'a*'s sway can only mean a demand to observe the devotional duties. Because those areas of the *shari'a* that refer to social relations are constantly changing, later generations can use their own discretion in arranging them.[34]

In doing so, they are led by their representatives. These people, whom we have already seen, are referenced as "those in authority among you," are the subject of two Qur'anic verses. In the first, 4:59, God commands believers to obey Him, His Prophet, and "those in authority among you." In the second, 4:83, God laments the fact that people waste their time in idle speculation when receiving news about war or peace affecting the community. He admonishes them to take such news to "those in authority among them," who will be able to check and scrutinize the news and authenticate or reject its veracity and interpret its significance for the community.[35] But Khalaf Allah states that such persons in authority are mere mortals and cannot make *ex cathedra* statements of final import about critical matters affecting the people's secular affairs.

He finds the strongest scriptural warrant for the establishment of non-religious authority among the believers in 3:104: "So let there be among you [believers] a body [*umma*] that may call to the good, enjoying what is beneficial and forbid what is evil." He acknowledges 'Abduh's commentary on this verse that establishing such a body is a categorical imperative (*fard 'ayn*) incumbent on every believer. He also raises the issue of accountability of this body to the general population that, in his opinion, elects it. The people as voters exercise oversight and dominion over this body, in his view. In the event that it falls short in meeting its obligations, the believers will replace it.[36] Withal, one must note that Khalaf Allah's idea that Qur'an 3:104 supports the concept of an accountable elected legislature that calls for good and prohibits evil is a radical modernist interpretation that was not anticipated by earlier commentators. After all, the verse was revealed in reference to a merciful God stepping in to separate warring combatants and seeking to elicit their conversion into a whole community of believers.

Khalaf Allah notes that nothing in the Prophet's Sunna details the nature of the state. There are, however, traditions attributed to him that indicate that he wanted to leave these specifics to later Muslims. This is also in keeping with God's intent in the Qur'an, which avoids details of this sort, he maintains.[37] What the Qur'an does specify is the end or the purpose of the state that the Muslims establish, and that is the public good, which Khalaf Allah equates with the distribution of wealth.[38]

As for whether the human being is fully autonomous in participating in these processes, Khalaf Allah declares:

> There is no doubt that God has guided us to the most preferable and complete foundations and principles upon which we are to build our government and establish our state. He entrusted to us this establishment by giving us in this regard full freedom and complete independence in our daily affairs and social interests.[39]

In other words, for Khalaf Allah, God is the creator of the cosmos but leaves the operation of His creation to humans.

Oddly, in view of his comments about the full autonomy of the believers to organize their politics as they see fit, Khalaf Allah claims that God chose Muhammad to be both the Prophet of the believers and the head of the first Islamic state.[40] He did not need to take this position. He could have argued, instead, that the people chose the

Prophet for this secular office because of their conviction that he was the best person for the job, not because he needed to be the ruler *ex officio* as a result of his role as religious messenger.

Noting that Qur'an 4:58 specifies that "God commands you to return trusts to their owners," Khalaf Allah thence proceeds to inquire into the nature of such trusts, identifying them as security, tranquility of the soul, and absence of fear. A trust is given over to a trustee who deposits it for safekeeping and, in doing so, creates a bond with the trustor. There are three kinds of trust: that which the human being has with God, that with another human being, and that with himself. The government receives the trust of the people, and its officials discharge their duties in fulfillment of this trust.[41] Unfortunately, Khalaf Allah does not dwell on this topic, averting thereby any discussion of the contradiction between free disposition by the people of decisions by the people and God's entitlement to all trusts. He seems to believe that a state and its government belong in practice to the believers, who make it available to officials, and it is the officials' task to implement policies based on the interests of the community. He declares that "rule" (*al-hukm*) in Islam belongs to the nation (*li al-umma*).[42]

In other words, Khalaf Allah adopts the robust position that the administration of the affairs of Muslim society after the Prophet was based on the authority of Muslim society itself, and not of God. The authority of the caliph derived from the people. Therefore he rejects the claim that Islam is both religion and politics. This is a view of contract that differs markedly from that adopted by Islamist groups, which assert that the rule belongs only to God.[43]

As with most Muslim modernists, Khalaf Allah berates those who interpret various verses of the Qur'an, collectively termed the *hakimiyya* or sovereignty verses, to mean that God is a continuous permanent sovereign intervener in the secular affairs of the believers. He carefully provides a contextual analysis of these five verses, which we have already considered earlier, to conclude that it is the people themselves (*al-nas, al-sha'b*) who dispose of their daily affairs.[44] They do so initially as members of the Islamic community (*umma islamiyya*), but in the modern period they constitute a body politic, forming a national community (*umma qawmiyya*), united by where they live, their language, their "common interests," and their common history. Crucially, regardless of the historical era, he is absolutely clear that the individual members of these collectivities are freely disposing of their affairs as human beings and not automatically responding to direct or indirect divine commands.[45] In fact, in one place he seems to suggest that the revelation itself was a response to the need of the Arabs to make progress. The content of the message of the Qur'an, on this view, was a demand for Arab society to create radical changes in the Arabs' views, beliefs, traditions, customs, moral values, and standard of behavior.[46]

Tariq al-Bishri

Tariq al-Bishri is considered by Egyptians to be one of Egypt's most important contemporary intellectuals. His work, as Leonard Binder notes, is "widely respected" and "has attracted a good deal of political interest, including that of the Egyptian government."[47] He is sufficiently distinguished that when the Islamist journal *al-Manar al-Jadid* commenced publication in 1998 he was invited to contribute an article to its initial issue. Bishri is a conservative modernist advocate of national unity, Islamic authenticity, Egyptian independence and cultural autonomy. His ideas enjoy credibility – although more liberal Muslim thinkers of course do not agree with all that he says. A Marxist-influenced nationalist in the Nasser years, Bishri has filled top positions in Egypt's legal system. In 1998, he was appointed to and briefly held the post of first deputy chair of the Council of State (Majlis al-Dawla), an organ modeled after the French Conseil d'État, which represents the country's highest jurisdiction in matters of public administration. His grandfather served as Shaykh al-Azhar, so he has strong connections to the country's official religious institution. He believes that one must treat Islam as a historical phenomenon, examining it in terms not of ideal types but of institutions and processes shaped by the actual conditions of Muslims in any given historical era.

Today, Bishri is one of the leading interpreters of conservative modernism. Although Bishri upholds independent judgment as critical for adapting to changing circumstances, and has long been associated with the cause of the independence of the judiciary from the government, Meijer is essentially correct in saying that virtually every institution or social force that Bishri regards as authentic is "hierarchical."[48] Since the 1973 October War involving Egypt, Syria and Israel, Bishri's focus has moved from secular historical analysis and become increasingly abstract. His message is a call for Egyptian unity but retains a diffuse commitment to institutional pluralism in which elites listen and the masses take action.

Bishri has consistently had an almost romantic faith in the perspicacity of the masses, an instinctive trust in their "healthy instincts."[49] While providing a lengthy narrative, he assumes rather than demonstrates that British imperialism and elite corruption generated a high level of political consciousness in the Egyptian masses, inferring this consciousness from mass participation in events. As for elites, he criticizes leaders of all political persuasions – capitalist, corporatist, Nasserist, and Islamist – for having failed to deliver a truly independent society whose foundations are cultural authenticity and social pluralism.

Unlike Khalaf Allah, Bishri does not systematically comb through the scriptural texts to find explanations for the ideas and behavior of the masses. Instead, he emphasizes that social circumstances constrain human behavior, and he tends to valorize that behavior as the key to knowledge about the world. In a word, his is an epistemology of praxis. Bishri often refers to "reality" (*al-waqi'*), and, although he does not problematize it, he maintains that individuals are social actors who must understand this reality before they can act to promote their welfare. The general implication seems to be that the masses are the prime actors.

The following reconstructs the general outlines of Bishri's position. First, he seemingly accepts the mainstream Sunni contractualist view that God in His mercy offered His covenant to those who would believe, and they accepted in order to "walk pleasingly" in His sight and also to better themselves and prosper. Second, after Muhammad's death, the doctrine of the double contract inhered. Third, over historical time the institutional structures of the Islamic community became ossified. Fourth, the eighteenth- and nineteenth-century revivalist movements that spread across the Islamic world were salutary efforts to restore a healthy balance between knowledge and action, because the Muslims then understood their real conditions, brought their ideas to bear on their actual realities, and developed their ideas in directions permitted by those realities. Fifth, Western imperialism and the opportunism of regional elites aborted these movements, which were replaced by state-led reform in the nineteenth and twentieth centuries that created a dualism in society, the hallmark of which was the simultaneous existence of Islamic and Western institutions and processes. This was a recipe for inertia at best, and failures in distributive justice at worst. And sixth, the only way to resolve society's many problems is through unity, tolerance of diversity and cultural authenticity.

How did people originally contract to form a human society from a state of nature? Bishri does not seem to speculate. Before Islam, Arabian society was tribally based. How it became so is of little interest to Bishri. In what way the new Muslim society evolved once it was formed is also not very clear from his essays. He does maintain generally in a reification that Islam put an end to tribal *'asabiyya* (which translates roughly as social solidarity, with overtones of clannish zealotry) and replaced it with a bond of religious affiliation. How did this happen? he asks. He does not give a direct response but notes contentiously that the process ended inter-tribal enmity. The new community retained tribalism's ethos of collectivism and its lineage relationships, while smashing its familistic particularism. In his typically abstract language, Bishri adds:

In this way, factors of collectivism followed that were mutually compatible and nourishing. There was thus established among these factors mutual connections and gradual advance from the particular to the general, until matters reached the stage of the great Islamic society ... Fustat in Egypt ... arose as a layout of land for troops from every tribe, living as neighbors alongside one another, rather than dispersed against one another, being united by a single effort to spread the call of monotheism.[50]

This propitious evolution did not last, according to Bishri. Centuries of stagnation followed until the eighteenth- and nineteenth-century revivalist movements. Wahhabis in Arabia, Dihlawis in India, Sanusis in North Africa, and Mahdists in Sudan rose up to end centuries of torpor, characterized by blind imitation of eighth- and ninth-century jurists. In doing so, they created a new reality, and it is this new reality that is the arena for social contract.[51]

It was these revivalist movements, and not the official reform efforts of the Ottoman and Egyptian states in the nineteenth century, that had the best chance of constituting a new social contract for the Muslims of the Middle East. Western-sponsored reform efforts could not work because, while they may have been appropriate for the European societies that gave rise to them, they could not flourish in the soil of the Middle East. Unfortunately, the official state reform efforts were imposed from above, in rank imitation of the West, and in the process the traditional associational groups of Muslim society, which were not only viable but integral to the concept of representation of interests of the people as a whole, were destroyed. The results can be seen today, when Muslim leaders seem infatuated with the concept, if not the reality, of party pluralism as the best guarantee for assuring genuine elections. But, in fact, the associational groups that have in the meanwhile been destroyed, such as Sufi brotherhoods and the extended family, would be much more effective in ensuring this.[52]

When writing of imitation of the West, Bishri has in mind not only the modernization policies associated with the Industrial

Revolution but also the emphasis that Western thinkers have long placed upon the individual. Whereas governments of Egypt in the nineteenth and twentieth centuries pursued arbitrary and authoritarian policies, the Western model they wished to imitate privileged the interests of the individual, and not the community. This may be seen in the various constitutions of Egypt during the era of British rule. The motivation for privileging the individual in the West was to emancipate him or her from the oppression of the state, and this permitted the individual then to join associations of various kinds, as de Tocqueville witnessed when he went to the United States in the early decades of the nineteenth century.

In a country such as Egypt, Bishri holds, this has led to conceiving society through the interests of the individual, separated from the national community because his or her ties to vital intermediate associations such as guilds, brotherhoods and the extended family have been sundered. When the people become reduced to individuals who are then tied from above to the state or the mass party, the ruler becomes an individual who extinguishes "pressure groups" (takwinat daghita) that otherwise could successfully represent their interests before state or ruling party bodies.[53]

Having made these points, Bishri proceeds to uphold the Qur'anic injunction to believers to "command the good and forbid evil." The trouble is, he notes, that this stricture has long been abandoned. A disease is therefore harming the community, and this requires remedial intervention. Again reifying Islam, he alleges that it considers the community to be a single body, and this body's various parts must preserve themselves. Commanding the good and forbidding wrongdoing is one of the most urgent canonical duties, because sustaining the community is the fundamental task of the Muslim. And the right of the community is God's right. Commanding the good and forbidding evil is a duty that depends upon the people observing the religious obligations (al-fara'id). This is what the public interest is.[54] One needs to emphasize here Bishri's implication that God's rights and His law are tantamount to natural rights and natural law, from which is generated the concept of the public interest in the first place.

Does Bishri, then, problematize natural law and natural rights? The picture is not clear. In his 1972 book on the Egyptian nationalist movement, he rebuts religious critics of Egypt's legal system for subordinating religious to positive law. Positive law is not the problem, he wrote, and indeed it can be a tool to eliminate the skewed concentration of wealth.[55] But the connection positive law has with natural law is disregarded. Later, in his book on the Copts,[56] Bishri makes the national – not the religious – community the exemplar of human life. The ties that bind are territorial and rooted in Egyptian nationality, a large tent under which Muslims and Copts are brought together. Left to themselves, the Egyptian people would make this national community cohere, using the vehicle of political parties and groups to institutionalize their presumably contractual agreements. But unfortunately, he holds, the leaders of these parties and groups have been the problem. And here Bishri spreads the blame around equally. However, more recently Bishri has chosen to blame the Copts for the growing sense of alienation that this community has experienced in the wake of incidents such as the "Constantine Affair" – which has to do with the putative conversion of a Christian woman to Islam and her statement that this was never the case.[57]

Thus, where do we stand in regard to natural law and rights? The role of a continually intervening God seems to be eclipsed in favor of people acting in history. But are they autonomous actors because of their rationality? Compared with Khalaf Allah, Bishri deals much less with reason. This is not to say he disregards it. On the contrary, he holds that the only way that Muslims can avoid regressing is to keep open the gates of *ijtihad* and reason.[58] But whether and how believers use reason to derive their own identity and their interests remains unexplored. Seemingly, identity and entitlements based on it emerge in some elemental way in direct response to notions of who people think they are; these notions are in turn shaped by their reality. For example, he writes that Islam was from the very start a doctrine or belief (*'aqida*), an association (*ribat*), a comprehensive culture embracing modes of expression, intellectual activity, organizations, and individual and social conduct. This beginning, he feels, "is sound from the point of view of historical reality."[59] But did autonomous, free and rational individuals intentionally bring about this state of affairs? If so, how?

In a discussion of pluralism in Islam, he writes that Muslims joined groups and bodies (*tawa'if wa hay'at*). The community's traditional social structure featured various similar, cohesive institutions that were founded on concepts and laws that connected prevailing ideas, structures, systems of mutual rights, and duties and norms of conduct. These social units, such as the extended family, the tribe, the village, the ward, trade syndicates, professional societies, lodges, schools, and mosques formed a stable equilibrium, each unit providing a check on the others.[60] Meanwhile, he maintains that the interests of the community and the spread of justice guide the believers to establish conditions in society that are appropriate for the principles of Islam.[61] In short, it is their religious beliefs that in the broadest manner drive their conduct.

Yet, how those interests are specifically formed in the first place is not clear, except for general references to adverse social circumstances and the determination not to give in to Western imperialism. Ironically, though Bishri is a historian and repeatedly calls for a method of analysis that links thought to actual historical circumstances, he does not show how these thoughts emerge and shape the actions of the people, nor how those actions in turn affect further development of those thoughts. He seems to believe that it is enough to recapitulate historical events and assume that these events shape consciousness in certain ways at critical historical junctures.

Bishri has, however, appealed for what one might regard as a basis for a new social contract for Egypt, which he glosses under the rubric of a new "national project." Egyptians need to create a new, dynamic social equilibrium in society. It would reflect the proper arrangement of power between the state and social forces and among those social forces themselves. This new equilibrium would end the zero-sum mentality that characterizes Egyptian politics today, he contends. It would retain the concentration of power in the community (as against its state and government?) so that it can achieve its goals.[62]

This so-called national project will be characterized by "the prevailing political trend." This seems suggestive of Rousseau's concept of the General Will. Bishri calls such a trend "the general framework for the [social] forces of the community," a framework that embraces these forces yet preserves their plurality and variety. The prevailing political trend expresses the unity of the community in terms of its overall cultural make-up without sacrificing the pluralism bespoken by its separate units. It is a distillation of "isolated details" (mufradat) of presumably modern Egyptian social, political and cultural movements. Inevitably, these "details" initially are not well integrated with one another, and contradictions may appear among them. But a wide-scale debate will ultimately harmonize these details, although Bishri is basically silent about how this might transpire.[63] He warns that this prevailing trend cannot be "created" out of whole cloth. It can only be "extracted" from the movement of history and society. It is reality here that is master, he asserts.[64]

I have stated that Bishri is basically silent on how the national debate will harmonize the various conflicting preferences and trends. However, at one juncture he does refer to the need to restore what he believes was the integration of religious and secular sciences in Islam until secularist thought allegedly triumphed in Egypt beginning in the 1920s. This would allow Egyptians to view existential reality with an Islamic outlook that would link up with rationalism and its method of viewing the actual world as it is. To succeed, Egyptians would have to resort to scientific methods of inquiry, deduction, empirical inquiry, inferring meanings, and discovering the laws of social change. The process will not be easy and will take at least a generation of educating youth in these methods "from an Islamic point of view."[65] The dynamic by which this linking up of "the" Islamic outlook with rationalism will occur is not explored. An Islamist such as Sayyid Qutb (d. 1966) would say that the linkage between Islam and right reason, which is the major ingredient of natural law, is intrinsic. "The claim that *Shari'a* is in harmony with natural law is verified with the assertion that natural law follows *Shari'a*." But this is a tautology.[66]

Bishri admits that this is all very abstract but excuses the abstraction on grounds that he wanted the discussion to be general and comprehensive.[67] Ultimately, he seems to hold that the national project, animated by the prevailing political trend, must be the product of a learning process in which people come to understand their religious and social interests at the same time. In this learning process, Egyptians will not have to choose between Arabism and Islam. These are predetermined givens for them. Their active choice centers instead on how to integrate them effectively. "In this way, we can operate our will," he asserts, taking into account the prevailing reality.[68]

Shi'ite perspectives on social contract

Although Shi'ites agree with Sunnis on three primary principles of the faith, God's unicity, the final prophecy of Muhammad, and the Day of Judgment, they go beyond Sunnis in acknowledging a fourth: the doctrine of the Imamate. Since this doctrine has been reviewed earlier, it is not necessary to reprise it here. The doctrine is unabashedly elitist when compared to Sunnism, since it foregrounds the role of the Imams, whose very existence is considered a prerequisite to the certainty of God's existence and who exclusively are entitled to rule. Although the commandment to follow the Imams was suspended at the time of Imam Ja'far al-Sadiq (d. 765) on grounds of prudence in view of the persecution of the Shi'a, it was never eliminated in theory. Meanwhile, over time, the Shi'i clergy claimed that they had become the general agents of the Imams. They took these developments even further at the end of the eighteenth century, when they vindicated their right to exercise independent judgment, which however was denied to others in the community. As a consequence, the clergy's self-confidence grew immeasurably.

Although it was to be another century before the clergy would demand formal rights to represent the Iranian people, they secured full consultation of the rulers with them in the 1800s. Eventually, largely because of the monarchs' growing tendency to grant economic concessions and commercial privileges to foreigners and cede territories to them, many clergymen joined the Constitutional Revolution of 1905–09 to restrict royal autocracy. The theoretical tools that they used for this purpose included the Qur'anic tenet (in 3:104, 3:110, 3:114, 7:157, and 9:71) of commanding the good and forbidding evil as a device to combat the ruler's *zulm* (oppression of the Imams' justice). They also utilized the legal stipulation of accountability in conduct (*hisba*). However, their discourse was not couched in terms of natural rights or natural law but rather oriented to the impiety of the ruler. Such impiety was seen to be a violation of Allah's rights and the rights of the Prophet and Imams.

The clergy remained content with their status as the general agents of the Imams and were clearly sensitive to the accusation that they were trying to replace Islamic law with Western constitutionalism. Hence, their discourse was one of *mashrutah-yi mashru'ah* – literally, making (rule) contingent on the requirements of *shari'a*. At the time there was no Shi'ite equivalent of 'Ali 'Abd al-Raziq who might announce that it was up to every generation of Shi'ites to establish their own model of state and government and to declare that in Islam religion and poitics were separable. So concerned were the "constitutionalist" *'ulama'* about the charge that they were stalking horses for outright republicanism that they eventually abandoned the Constitutionalist cause by 1909.

Indeed, the clergy supported Reza Khan's claims to be the new Shah of Iran in the mid-1920s. The fact that he later turned upon them in pursuing Westernizing reforms does not alter this fact.

In fact, upon the Shah's forced abdication by the wartime allies, Ayatollah Khomeini published a book, *Revealing the Secrets*, in which he condemned secular rulers for failing to consult the clergy, but he explicitly disclaimed the notion that he was attacking the monarchical system itself. During the oil crisis of the late 1940s and early 1950s, most of the clergy supported the pro-British monarch in his conflict with the nationalist prime minister Muhammad Musaddiq. Even in 1963, when Khomeini condemned the policies of Muhammad Reza Pahlavi, he did not articulate a position founded on contractualist principles. At most, he upbraided the government for its failure to consult with the clergy on such issues as eligibility requirements to hold office, female enfranchisement, and land redistribution.

But in 1970, Khomeini changed his position and argued in favor of clerical rule and the overthrow of the monarchy. After he seized power during the Iranian Revolution of 1978–79, matters took a new turn. He and his associates became the effective rulers of Iran. And shortly before his death, he ruled that whatever the top jurist – *faqih* – said was Islam was Islam. In fact, he went beyond this and maintained that the *faqih* could suspend the pillars of the faith if he thought that by doing so it would help "Islam" survive in the context of plots by its enemies to undo it. Because the state was "Islamic," whatever decisions it made were *ipso facto* in defense of Islam.

Although certain Shi'i theorists today, especially those close to the ruling establishment in the Islamic Republic of Iran, maintain that Shi'ism is rooted in contractualist notions, its elitist character in both theory and practice undermines this claim. I shall focus on three individuals whom I believe have contributed to the discussion that is relevant for social contract: Ayatollah Ruhollah Khomeini, Ayatollah Ni'matallah Salihi Najafabadi, and Ayatollah Dr Mahdi Ha'iri (d. 1999). The rationale for including Khomeini is that his book *Islamic Government* (Hukumat-i Islami) of 1971 bears centrally, though negatively, on social contract ideas. Najafabadi is Khomeini's faithful disciple and a firm advocate of his elitist doctrine of the "guardianship of the jurist" (*wilayat al-faqih*).

Najafabadi's book *Guardianship of the Jurist: Government by the Righteous* (*Wilayat al-Faqih: Hukhumat-i Salihan*) was published in 1984. He goes well beyond Khomeini's position, converting it into a model of rule based on popular sovereignty, presumably because he felt the need to "update" or modernize Khomeini's argument. This breathtaking conversion of an elitist doctrine into a principle of popular democracy ends by reversing the words of the famous adage *vox populi vox dei* – the voice of the people is the voice of God – to read instead "the voice of God is the voice of the people."

Mahdi Ha'iri, by contrast, rejects the doctrine of the guardianship of the jurist by maintaining that government is totally outside the purview of religion. Here, indeed, is the Shi'ite version of 'Ali 'Abd al-Raziq, and it is revealing that Ha'iri's emergence within the public discourse on the clergy and politics was heralded by a book he had to publish in the West. Ha'iri is a son of the founder of the modern seminary at Qom, Shaykh 'Abd al-Karim Ha'iri Yazdi (d. 1937). A graduate of the Qom seminary with the degree of *ijtihad*, he received his Ph.D. in philosophy from the University of Toronto. Like Khomeini, he was a student of the eminent Husayn Burujirdi (d. 1961).

As noted, Khomeini did not initially oppose secular rule and explicitly said so in a work published in 1943.[69] At that time, he complained that the secular rulers had failed to consult the clergy and called upon them to do so. But in 1970 he dramatically altered his position and thereafter held that the clergy alone must rule.[70] Now, he was maintaining that the Imams had vested their substantive authority in the jurists (*wilayat al-faqih*), pending the return of the Hidden Imam. In this scenario of rule the ordinary believer, whether as an individual or collectively, has no role to play, since the course of events is divinely driven. Khomeini's approach, first, is to show logically that Islam, since it mandates a community of believers, necessitates a state and government. He appeals to the authority of Mulla Ahmad Naraqi (d. 1829), who established nineteen arguments to confirm the validity of the concept of the guardianship of the jurist. In Naraqi's view, according to Khomeini, this guardianship was substantive in nature and not residual. In short, it amounted to authority to be an executive ruler and could not be restricted to narrow, technical matters, such as the legal authority to represent the interests of minors or widows or to arbitrate legal disputes involving legacies or debts. Because Naraqi had not allowed such broad powers, Khomeini needed to furnish proof of his argument, which he believed he had found in Qur'an 4:58–59 and in a Hadith (oral tradition) called *maqbula 'Umar ibn Hanzala* – "the accepted [tradition] of 'Umar ibn Hanzala. This tradition involves a set of questions and replies posed by this 'Umar and answered by the sixth Imam of Twelver Shi'ism, Ja'far al-Sadiq.[21]

The verses of Qur'an 4:58–59 are as follows: "God commands you to return trusts to their owners, and when you judge among the people to do so equitably. Noble are the counsels of God, and God hears all and sees everything. O ye who believe, obey God, obey the Prophet, and those in authority among you." The tradition of 'Umar ibn Hanzala has 'Umar asking about a situation in which two Shi'ites dispute a matter of debt or inheritance. May they have recourse to the courts of the Sunni caliphate for a ruling? Imam Ja'far al-Sadiq forbids this recourse, and when asked for instructions as to what they should do replies that they must identify a Shi'ite believer whom they believe is especially well versed in imamite law and abide by his ruling, "for I appointed him a judge over you" (*la qad ja'altuhu 'alaykum hakiman*).

Khomeini maintains that the traditional rendering of the verb in the clause "when you judge among the people" (4:58) is mistaken and should be understood to mean "rule." Furthermore, he translates the noun in the quoted passage of the tradition of 'Umar ibn Hanzala as "ruler" rather than "judge." Just to make sure that his reader knows what he means, he inserts the pre-Islamic Persian word *farmanrava* (sovereign ruler) in parentheses after the Arabic word in the accusative case, *hakiman*.[71] He justifies this innovative rendering of these words in the following way. First, the Qur'anic verses and the Hadith must be read in tandem. The verb in verse

4:58 "modifies secular princes."[72] These princes are being put on notice that they must return trusts loaned to them by God back to Him and must rule justly. In the Hadith the Imam is being asked whether the disputants could seek judgment from the Sunni authorities and replies that he who does so is in effect asking illegitimate governmental authorities. Khomeini then says that it is clear that there are legitimate and illegitimate government authorities and their judges to whom one might possibly have recourse for a decision. The Imam tells 'Umar that the disputants must find a knowledgeable and fair-minded person and that that individual is not just a judge but represents legitimate governmental authorities and their judges. Khomeini holds that the Imam says:

> I appointed a person who has these qualifications to be a ruler (*farmanrava*) over you, and he who has such qualifications has been appointed by me for the governmental and judicial affairs of the Muslims; and the Muslims do not have the right to refer to anyone else.[73]

Elsewhere, Khomeini had held that the caliphs in the period of the sixth Imam had carefully avoided interfering in the jurisdiction of judges, and judges took the same care not to intrude into the bailiwicks of the caliphs. From this, he concludes that the sixth Imam was clearly making a distinction between the jurisdictions of rulers and those of judges, and in the operative phrase of his reply to 'Umar ibn Hanzalah – *laqad ja'altuhu 'alaykum hakiman* – he is referring to a person whom he has appointed to be both ruler (*wali*) and judge (*qadi*). The Imam refers to such a person as *hakim*. This word can mean both ruler and judge. If, Khomeini adds, the Imam wanted to restrict his appointment merely to judges rather than rulers and judges, he would have used the phrase *laqad ja'altuhu 'alaykum qadiyan*. The word *qadi*, here in the accusative case, cannot mean ruler and can only mean judge. But this is not what the Imam said.[74]

As for verse 4:59, Khomeini innovatively asserts that "those in authority among you" are the clergy. This represents a sharp departure from the traditional interpretation among Shi'ite commentators on the Qur'an that the phrase referred to the Imams. For example, the author of the most authoritative twentieth-century Shi'ite Qur'anic commentary, Muhammad Husayn Taba'taba'i (d. 1981), explicitly rejected the contention that the referent was the clergy.[75]

At any rate, no warrant exists for interpreting this argument for the entitlement of the clergy to be rulers in the absence of the Hidden Imam as grounds to endorse social contract notions, but this is what the cleric Ni'matullah Salihi Najafabadi maintains. Borrowing terminology from rhetoric, he holds that the doctrine of *wilayat al-faqih* may be considered from two perspectives: its "originative" meaning (*mafum insha'i*) and its "notificatory" meaning (*mafum khabari*). He claims that the doctrine was classically understood only in its restrictive sense, as something indicative and notificatory. He then seeks to "restore" the originative and creative meaning, which renders the doctrine into "one of the firmest and clearest rational, social, and political principles, and one in which the voice of the people is the key defining element."[76] In his opinion, the jurist, in whom the authority of the Imam is vested, has no independent authority to rule over the people. Rather, the relationship is reversed. In his construction, it is the *vox populi* that is the driving force for the operationalization of the doctrine. On what basis does he maintain this? Reason tells us that popular sovereignty is the linchpin of *wilayat al-faqih*.

In Najafabadi's analysis, he who has *wilaya* may possess it as a result of one of three modalities: (1) God grants it; (2) it is legitimately acquired by the use of power — all clergymen have *wilaya* in this sense, but in order to prevent chaos only one of them is the final authority in its implementation; (3) it is rule "in fact," as occurs when others persuade an individual to assume and exercise it, which happened with Imam 'Ali in 656. This vesting of the *wilaya* according to the third modality occurs in an allegedly free environment, with the majority of the people taking the oath of allegiance (*bay'a*) to the designee.[77] This passage is remarkable for more than one reason.

First, Khomeini would adamantly maintain that the jurists have the Imam's authority as a consequence of the first modality, pure and simple. Second, Najafabadi appears to be eroding the forcefulness of the concept by suggesting that Imam 'Ali, no less, possessed the *wilaya* of God and the Prophet because ordinary human beings gave it to him. On this argument, the designation of Imam 'Ali resulted from a mass election in the modern sense of the term, and the Prophet's investiture of him fades into the background. Najafabadi applies the same pattern to Khomeini's status – a mass election through majority vote.

Najafabadi appears to be arguing in the direction of social contract notions. The jurist thus "elected" is endowed with exemplary knowledge, justice, political consciousness, administrative skills, planning abilities, farsightedness, courage, and decisiveness. Once he is chosen, all must support his rule as an incumbent duty akin to the obligation to implement the secondary principles of the faith: prayer, almsgiving, fasting during Ramadan, and making the pilgrimage. Whatever happened to the classical formulation that *wilaya* was bestowed from above? Najafabadi maintains that to hold this "limiting" view of the process would be a "contravention of divine law, the interest of society, and the glory, nobility, and freedom of the people."[78]

How can Najafabadi uphold this view? His reply is: through the principle of reason. Since government is a "social necessity," it would be wrong to dispense with it.[79] The way to establish a government is not by imposing a system on the people, because this violates the principle of reason. It is innate reason that is the dynamic force in all discussions of *wilayat al-faqih*. The people, animated by rational understandings of their interests, play the key role in the devolution of authority to the *faqih*,[80] and Najafabadi anchors his interpretation upon majority rule.[81] If he is correct about the role of reason, then what is the point of adhering to the doctrine of the Imamate, since according to that doctrine it is not reason that provides the dynamic of social life, but rather the imperative of divine grace?

Undeterred by such an objection, Najafabadi seeks to clinch his argument by alleging that the *wilaya* of the jurist is based upon the foundations of a contract between the people and the *faqih*. He uses the expressions '*aqd va qarardad-i ijtima'i* (social contract) and *mithaq-i ijtima'i* (social compact) and offers "Islamic" grounds to support this view. Thus, he cites Qur'an 5:1: "O ye who believe, fulfill your contracts." In this, he blithely ignores the fact that this verse is devoid of the connotation of members of a community making a contract with a leader and voluntarily ceding their rights to that individual, who then becomes the trustee of such interests in the classic seventeenth- and eighteenth-century theories of social contract. He owns that the *faqih* can be dismissed by the Council of Experts, a body inaugurated by the Constitution of the Islamic Republic of Iran he notes. But he fails to add that the Council of Experts is an elite body whose members are themselves vetted for candidacy to that body by the *faqih* and his appointees, not by the masses.

Ayatollah Mahdi Ha'iri rejects these ideas out of hand. He totally opposes Khomeini's doctrine of the jurist's mandate by specifically denying that Islam has anything to do with politics. Politics are a human contrivance and convention in his view. In the first part of his book *Philosophical Wisdom and Government*, Ha'iri sets forth a dense discussion of being and existence that leads to a later discussion of government and politics.[82]

Hukuma (government) and *hukm* (rule) come from the Arabic verb *hakama* and connote judging, arbitrating. They indicate stability, firmness, certitude, and decisiveness. In contemporary politics and political science, the Arabic word *hukuma* means statecraft, administration, and managing a country's affairs. In logic *hukm* and *hukuma* mean submission to arbitration based on sure and certifiable knowledge, and *hikma* (wisdom) comes from *hukm*, signifying not command but judgment. In other words, *hukm* and *hukuma* mean decisive knowledge and, by extension, awareness of reality.[83]

Accordingly, says Ha'iri, government and statecraft refer to wisdom and not command, power, dominion, *wilaya* (authority), or *qaymuma* (mandate, guardianship).[84] He invokes Aristotle to show that statesmanship is the highest virtue because it centers on the interests of society as a whole. Therefore, it has nothing to do with ordering and commanding a people.[85]

Ha'iri writes that societies before the modern era were either dictatorships with some role for religious groups or simple tribal systems. In neither did the people have the chance to express themselves to their rulers, and the individual counted for little. Modern democracy, however, is founded on individual rights and freedoms. These qualities emanate from the rights and privileges that individuals have to their own property.[86]

As Ha'iri sees it, in the modern period thinkers have maintained that for a society to establish government a social contract must exist, and the citizens and individuals, no matter how unaware, enter such a contract, transferring to an individual or a body the right to defend some of their own rights.[87] He is unconvinced and posits that government and politics are not complex phenomena that must be conveyed through the rational processors of the theoretical mind. On the contrary, as concepts they are the product of the most basic and elemental needs of the natural life of the people. Government is not a metaphysical matter in the manner of Plato's theory of forms, nor a superior, rational manifestation for which theoretical reason is a guide by means of axioms and rational proofs. Instead, it is the result of the humdrum experience of people who face daily, transient, and contingent needs in living as neighbors. It is simply an artifact and cannot come under the rubric of the immutable divine laws.[88] From ancient times, in fact, government and administration have been dealt with as derivations of practical reason. Accordingly, there can be no doubt that the administration of towns is completely outside the orbit of the universal divine laws.[89]

The upshot is that government (Ha'iri means the state) is not in any way a mental construct that, as Hegel saw it, represents the Spirit of History. Nor is it, as Rousseau maintained, a mere possibility (*padida-yi i'tibari*) that results from a transactional contract between citizens and rulers. Neither is it a logical necessity that, in Kant's view, embraces analytical judgments. Instead, it is a natural necessity and is always epiphenomenal.

Ha'iri's perspective therefore rejects the idea that government is rooted in the foundations and universals of rational or non-rational religious thought. Philosophy and jurisprudence are theories in the abstract, whereas politics is in the realm of the immediate. If, somehow, philosophers or jurists take political office, the exigencies of *practical* reason will mandate their dismissal, because they would be totally unqualified to rule. The holding of political office by philosophers or jurists would in itself constitute an injustice and provoke disorder and corruption in society. These dangers would be magnified should religious leaders take charge of government because of the passions religious motivations stir. Making religious credentials a prerequisite for office-holding is a logical error because religious deference and leadership are not grounds for qualifying one to be a political leader. The logical place for the religious leader is the realm of *theoretical* reason and not that of the personal affairs of the citizens and the governments of countries.

Ha'iri then invokes scripture to argue that practical reason is not the realm of the religious leader, the jurist, or the philosopher. He claims that the Qur'an vests politics completely in the hands of the people, citing Qur'an 42:38, a verse we have encountered in another context. This text states: "Their [the people's] affairs are a matter of counsel." He interprets this verse categorically by maintaining that the people themselves determine their affairs without any recourse to revelation.[90]

Thus, for Ha'iri, the human being is a rational creature for whom "a natural-rational" existence is secured through the workings of practical reason on the empirical environmental conditions surrounding him, and decidedly not by any higher order of thinking. To Ha'iri, Rousseau mistakenly believes that humans enter into society through a deliberate, discursive process of reflection in which they solve the basic problem of surrendering their independence to the public person (legislator) while retaining their individual freedom as private persons. In denying this, Ha'iri attributes their coming together to the obvious and unmediated requirements of security for their lives and their livelihoods. As he puts it,

> The counsels and guidance of practical reason concerning the need for an arrangement and management of the affairs of the country are so obvious and necessary that they are decisively accepted by every person without the slightest awareness or rational comprehension, without the slightest need for being educated about any factors outside themselves.[91]

This is the essence of Ha'iri's argument: every person is an individual who crystallizes in himself or herself all the traits of the universal type called the human being and is naturally independent and free of reliance upon others. Hence, he must be endowed with all the rights that have been supposed and confirmed (by philosophers?) for the individual, among which is freedom to decide matters for himself or herself. Accordingly, he has no need for society and social contract in the use of these natural rights. The reason for this is that these rights stem from the nature and essence of his being human, irrespective of time and/or place. It is impossible to violate this principle of his existence. Since this freedom is a natural rather than a positive or contractual right, the latter inheres for him for all time and anywhere. If an individual gets together with other individuals, they form an aggregate. But if he decides to leave this aggregate, he takes all his natural rights along.

The problem with Rousseau, according to Ha'iri, is that he cannot resolve the contradiction that arises when he says that people voluntarily cede their independence to the legislator, but in doing so they are as free as before because everyone has an interest in cooperating and hence willingly does so. There is nothing free about that choice, according to Ha'iri. As he puts it, "No human being ... can really change his true person into an unreal or public personality ... and deprive himself of an independent and free existence."[92]

He then investigates another model, proposed by the Dutch legist Hugo Grotius (d. 1645), which is based on servitude to the state. Grotius holds that people contractually agree to their submission and servitude to a masterful state, a process akin to a mercantile exchange between seller and buyer. Rousseau rejects the analogy by noting that the transaction is coerced because often the masterful state turns out to be despotic and corrupt. But Ha'iri believes that Rousseau's rebuttal itself is faulty because whether the state does behave corruptly or despotically does not vitiate the idea that a bargain is struck in the first place between insecure sellers and self-assured buyer. It merely shows that the terms of the contract have been violated. "Do not forget," says Ha'iri, "that violations occur also in normal contracts between sellers and buyers."[93]

Instead, the criticism of Grotius must be both empirical and theoretical. Empirically, no government historically has "owned" its people. If a herder buys a cow from another, he owns that cow as his property. But the relationship between government and citizens is one of guardianship, not ownership. It is true that some governments have behaved tyrannically, as though they regarded themselves as slave masters, but that does not validate the argument that Grotius is making that the people in actual societies have voluntarily enslaved themselves in some contractual way.

The theoretical rebuttal to Grotius's doctrine of state servitude goes as follows. In the Islamic law of contract the buyer and seller must always be identified in advance, whether one is speaking of material goods, marriages, or leases. Failing this, the contract cannot be considered valid. In a contract of personal servitude, which is the standard of Grotius's doctrine, one of the parties is indigent and offers himself as a slave, while the other is the masterful state as purchaser of the slave. Once they have been identified as the parties, the process of the transactions can begin and be concluded. Note that before they have been identified, the concluding or non-concluding of the transaction is inconceivable. Yet Grotius, without acknowledging this logical impossibility, presents his doctrine simply on the basis of a verbal analogy (*tashabuh-i lafzi*). Grotius and, indeed, social contract theorists more generally ignore the fact that before the contract all citizens are equal in their privileges and rights.[94] Accordingly, no individual can alienate his inherent equality in rights and privileges to another, even if he wills to do so.

If both Rousseau and Grotius are wrong, then what is the correct interpretation? Ha'iri declares that it is a law of nature that human beings require a location on which to live, from which derives a second law that holds that anyone who has acquired territory that has not been otherwise claimed may rightly possess it. In the beginning the human being individualistically chooses his plot, which is for him alone and for his family. But in a later, second stage, he acquires ownership of adjacent land, over which others, however, also exercise some ownership rights. In both stages the human being is making the choice of where to live on the basis of existential exigency, and so property ownership in both stages has been achieved as a matter of natural necessity. The difference is that in the first stage the property is a "private natural possession" (*ta'alluq va malikiyyat-i khususi va tabi'i*), whereas in the second stage it becomes diffused and conflated with the properties of others. In the first stage the requirement was for monopolization of the location by the individual, whereas in the second stage the erstwhile private ownership (*malikiyat-i khususi*) is transformed into private joint ownership (*malikiyyat-i khusui-yi musha'*). The property continues to remain private in the second stage but no longer monopolistically or exclusively so in the hands of a lone individual.

Under both individual and joint ownership the principle of private possession is retained in the sense that every person independently possesses these two kinds of locales – places that have been allocated to him to live on by his nature. The lone individual has moved from the small location in the first stage to the larger space in the second stage because of the natural requirements of finding food and making a living. He has thus responded to purely physiological needs. And there is nothing in all this that has anything to do with legislation, a collective will, or even the will and rational understanding of the human mind that concludes it is beneficial to enter into a social contract. In both stages the location where he lives is the human being's as a result of natural right and cannot in the first instance be legally established for nor alienated from him by some external power. Positive, legal, and nominal ownership are established only later and would not be possible without the prior establishment of natural ownership.[95]

Ha'iri believes that in the second stage society has not yet appeared because there is no need for it, given that each individual's right of exclusive private and joint private ownership accrues to him from his natural need for subsistence. Joint private ownership does not equal collective ownership in the modern sense. In this pre-society phase ownership of the larger space is individual for every human being – which means that he has the unfettered right of access to that space, just as his neighbors do. He has no need to cooperate with others. When they do encounter one another, it is a product of their natural interaction, not of a contract between them. Moreover, just as he can bequeath his smaller space to his heirs, he can pass on the large space to those heirs.[96]

But this situation cannot last because, as each individual uses his practical reason to improve his life chances, eventually this brings him into contact with arrant outsiders, who could make competing claims on his larger living space. At this point, the individuals who are neighbors, still guided by their practical reason, deputize some person or some entity, compensate that person or entity, and task him or it with the mandate of ensuring the good life and peaceful coexistence for them all in the face of outside pretensions to their living spaces. In case of disagreement among the individuals as to the identity of the deputy, the opinion of the majority is followed. Ha'iri insists that they are still acting as equal individuals endowed with equal natural inherent rights. He cites the Hadith "the people are masters of their wealth" (*al-nas musallatun 'ala amwalihim*) to maintain his identification of this process as a natural one that has nothing to do with the workings of an Islamic society and its law of contracts.[97]

The contract that is effected between the individuals and the deputy is purely private in nature, not social, collective, or public. This deputy is totally dependent upon the individuals. He or it is not a deputy for a collective unit. There is no public legal body in which, as Rousseau would have it, each citizen would have membership, bound in a net of unity, and in which the citizens have lost their identity and independence. Consequently, this model of private joint property with its deputy is in the sense of all the individual citizens, not in the sense of a collective entity. The expression that Ha'iri uses for this model is the deputyship of private joint property (*vikalat-i malikiyyat-i shakhsi-yi musha'*).[98]

In sum, Ha'iri establishes an independent domain for natural law and, in the process, suggests that politics and government have nothing to do with Islam. If the argument about natural law necessarily establishes the irrelevance of revelation for forming a government, can there be a concept of social contract in a Muslim society? Ha'iri seems to be saying that an Islamic society is Islamic by dint of the private beliefs of its members in respect to the primary and secondary principles of pietistic faith (God's unicity, Muhammad's prophecy, the Day of Judgment, prayer, *zakat*, Ramadan fasting, and pilgrimage). Everything else is in the realm of secular affairs and is totally independent of religion. He may be right, but if so he seems to be implying that there cannot be an Islamic theory of social contract. Is this necessarily so? Might not reconciliation between Ash'arism and Mu'tazilism keep this issue open?

Second, Ha'iri has embraced the concept of natural law as separate from revealed law. Hobbes, Locke, and other social contract theorists also held this view, but they then went on to anchor natural law's independence to a concept of social contract. Ha'iri, by contrast, implies that the separation of divine and natural law guarantees that social contract doctrines cannot be maintained. Ha'iri's arguments about joint private property are not convincing because he maintains that people are acting out of their intrinsic and inherent individual rights to live and to own. Even when they appoint someone or some body to arbitrate their disputes and protect them from the claims of outsiders, Ha'iri has to assume that they are still acting as individual, atomized units and are not fusing into a large collectivity. This begs the question. It would appear that at that stage they have, indeed, constituted themselves as a public, legal, corporate personality.

Conclusion

Middle Eastern political theories across different historical periods since the rise of Islam have accorded greater importance to society than to the individual. As seen in the previous chapter, the notion of private civil and political rights attached to the individual (a post-Reformation development in the West) did not exist in the Middle East until the writings of the nineteenth-century reformists.

Social contract theories by Western writers were premissed on the concept that autonomous human beings deliberately chose to leave the state of nature by entering into society on grounds of security, morality, or other values that did not require religious prescriptions. In the writings of Middle Eastern political theorists prior to the nineteenth century, the contract was one between God and the human being, and the contract was one not devised by the latter but rather offered by the former. The individual could choose to reject the offer, of course, but in doing so he would have forfeited the opportunity to construct a life of fulfillment and prosperity.

If they chose to accept the contract, they would not retain control over any rights that they surrendered, because the owner of those rights was considered to be God. Ultimately, the different views of contract between Middle Eastern political theories and Western theories has to do with the difference between revealed or divine law, on the one hand, and natural law, on the other. Natural law holds that human beings are autonomous, endowed with reason and entitlements to promote their own welfare. Divine law, no matter how liberally interpreted, stops short of this and rather conditions such well-being upon obedience to God's commands.

The Sunni modernist theories of social contract examined in this chapter variously assess the opportunities for the human being and for the social groups in which they are members to advance their life chances. Khalaf Allah's interpretation insists that God willingly vests the individual with maximum autonomy and enlightenment in an arrangement that does not threaten the revelation in any way. Bishri's interpretation, by contrast, is much more cautious and in any case circumscribes the individual's role by deploying not the latter but rather the social group as his unit of analysis.

Shi'i theories, by their very nature, have greater difficulty in according autonomy to the individual, since the doctrine of the Imamate basically disempowers them and vests initiative in the hands of the Imams, or, in the Khomeini version, the clergy in their capacity as the deputies of the Imams. Finally, Ha'iri's understanding is that politics is always a matter that exists in a sphere separate from religion. He denies the validity of social contract thinking because he believes that human beings enter into communities on the basis of their practical needs, and not some putative calculation of optimizing their interests. Withal, Ha'iri leaves the door open for the individual as the effective agent of political thought and practice precisely because of his insistence that revealed law has nothing to do with politics.

The contemporary theories examined in this chapter in their various ways were very significantly influenced by historical changes affecting the societies in which their authors lived. Khalaf Allah, Bishri, and Huwaydi were all products of the Nasserist system, one that in terms of commitment went far down the road of applying the principles of collectivism and egalitarianism. Khomeini's understanding of the doctrine of the Imamate and the authority of the Imams was, in its turn, dramatically changed by the social history of Iran in the years following World War II. Admittedly, the situation is less clear in the case of Ha'iri, whose speculations and theorizing appear somewhat more independently of actual historical developments occurring on the ground. But even he was moved to reject the connection between religion and politics because of Khomeini's historical effort to consolidate that connection and, eventually, to construct an absolutist model of hierocratic rule.

SIX

The state

The state in Middle Eastern political theory lends itself well to a sociology-of-knowledge perspective. Conceptualizations of the state in these theories in the contemporary era clearly were and have been influenced by the actual historical experiences of the people in the region. This is true whether we speak of Islamist perspectives, moderate *din wa dawla* arguments, or liberal, Marxist, or corporatist theories that have diffused into the region largely from the outside. Even theories of the state that appear to have the strongest continuity with the past traditions and ideas of the people of the region (and so might be expected to owe their existence to some essentialized model of the state that has been basically handed down without any empirical referents because of that model's scriptural legitimacy) cannot escape the impact of concrete historical developments on the rise of conceptual systems.

In this connection, the crucial historical event for the region of the Middle East is the encounter with the West. While this encounter did have some positive aspects, including the spread of ideas about constitutionalism, the overall effect was more negative than positive. Wars, annexations of territory, encouraging nationalities to secede from Muslim rule, economic domination and exploitation, and cultural imperialism were some of the major motifs of this encounter. In reaction to these destructive trends, Muslim intellectuals in particular sought to conceptualize politics, the state, and its relations with society in terms that made sense, given the historical development of the region over the centuries.

But how does one conceptualize the state? Is Weber's definition general enough to fit any social and historical context? Perhaps so. Or, expressed differently, it would be hard to find an example of a state that did not approximate to his conception, even if it contains ambiguities that need to be recognized. To Weber, then, the state is "a human community that (successfully) claims the *monopoly of the legitimate use of physical force* within a given territory."[1] In her book *God's Rule: Government and Islam*, Patricia Crone has examined the concept and reality of the state in Islamic history. Adhering to the Weberian model, she holds that the concept of the state as it has developed in the West has come to mean (1) territorially based sovereign governmental institutions; (2) a politically organized society – a polity – in which such institutions may be found. In her view, medieval Muslims (or those in the classical period, for that matter) lacked a word for the state in either of these two senses. Unfortunately, she does not clearly distinguish between state and government, but her meaning is nevertheless clear. Her point, which has been made by many contemporary Middle Eastern theorists themselves,[2] is that state and government were grasped by reference to personalities. Even when it was a matter of the abstract conception of supreme political authority, Muslims understood matters through the lens of personalization. If Muslims wanted to refer to the society ruled by such a leader, whether a caliph, a king, a sultan, or an emir, they would use the religious terms *umma* or *milla*. And if they wanted to refer to the caliphate (*khilafa*), their attribution was to the office of that incumbent, rather than to the polity of which he was the leader.[3]

The word for state in the languages of the contemporary Middle East is *dawla* (Arabic), *dawlat* (Persian), *devlet* (Turkish). Sometimes, especially in Persian and Turkish, the word can also mean government, while in Arabic this concept is glossed by another term, hukuma. Derivatives of the last are also in use in modern Persian (hukumat) and modern Turkish (hukumet), though, as mentioned, writers in these two languages may substitute dawlat or devlet for hukumat or hukumet. Lewis[4] and others have studied the evolution of the term dawla from its origins in referring to the turning or rotation of bodies (such as planets) to the later metaphor of a ruler's "turn in office." It took centuries before the word came to refer to sovereign territorial state, even though by as early as the eighth century it was used to refer to the panoply of institutions that rudimentary states such as the caliphate possess – such as the bayt al-mal (treasury), juyush al-amsar (garrison troops), or diwan/dawawin al-mazalim (judicial bodies charged with investigating administrative derelictions).

Although dawla is the widely accepted term for sovereign territorial state, this acceptance has not solved the abiding problem in Middle Eastern political theory of how to devolve authority and rule from the person of the leader to abstract institutions and constitutional mandates that require accountability and transparency. It may be said that very few groups in Middle Eastern societies are comfortable with the current situation involving the state.

Sunni Islamist perspectives on the state

Sunni Islamists – those seeking the immediate application of the shari'a in all areas of life – are unhappy with the contemporary conception and praxis of Middle Eastern states because they believe such states have appropriated ("eaten") Allah's rights. The Pakistani thinker Abu al-A'la Mawdudi (d. 1979) and the Egyptian theorist Sayyid Qutb (d. 1966) both maintained that Muslim states are apostate, as it were, because they have arrogated to secular authority the sovereignty of God. In their view, the only legitimate rule is the rule of God. To justify this conception, they refer to a series of verses in the Qur'an that have come to be known as the hakimiya or sovereignty verses. These include three verses in Sura 5 and two in Sura 12.

Much controversy exists over the meanings of these verses. It is safe to say that Mawdudi's and Qutb's interpretations are novel in the context of the centuries-old process of Qur'anic commentary (tafsir). In Qur'an 5:44, 45, and 47, and in Qur'an 12:40 and 67, verses appear that condemn those who do not obey God. The verses are as follows:

> Those who do not judge according to God's revelations are unbelievers [fa man lam yahkum bi ma anzala Allah, fa ha'ula'i hum al-kafirun]. (Qur'an 5:44)

> Those who do not judge according to God's revelations are oppressors [fa man lam yahkum bi ma anzala Allah, fa ha'ula'i hum al-zalimun]. (Qur'an 5:45)

> Those who do not judge according to God's revelations are evil doers [fa man lam yahkum bi ma anzala Allah, fa ha'ula'i hum al-fasiqun]. (Qur'an 5:47)

> Judgment belongs to God, alone [inna al-hukm illa li Allah]. (Qur'an 12:40)

> Judgment belongs to God, alone [inna al-hukm illa li Allah]. (Qur'an 12:67)

Both writers substituted for the verb "to judge" and the noun, "judgment" the verb "to rule" and the noun "rule" for the Arabic expressions yahkum and hukm. The secondary meanings of the verbal and noun forms of the root h–k–m do signify to rule and rule. But the primary meaning relates to judging and arbitrating between contending viewpoints or interests. Mawdudi and Qutb were keen to show that existing states in Pakistan and Egypt, respectively, had failed to obey the commands of God in their public policies and therefore considered them as irredeemably hostile to Islam. Their followers have used such arguments to attempt the forcible destruction of these states and their governments, in hopes of replacing them with ones that would be true to the original intentions and requirements of God.[5]

Shi'i Islamist views of the state

In the previous chapter, the dominant Shi'ite Islamist perspective held by Ayatollah Khomeini was detailed. Hence it is not necessary to recapitulate it here. Recall that he, too, changed the meaning of these terms in exactly the way Mawdudi and Qutb had done, although it is not certain whether he had read or heard about their works.[6]

Accordingly, existing Middle Eastern states, so far as the Islamist tendency is concerned, are "apostate" because they have failed to obey God and to apply Islamic law in all areas of life. The Sunni Islamists appear to feel that the resurrection of the Islamic caliphate is the answer to the contemporary Middle Eastern state that they characterize as apostate on grounds – contested vigorously by their opponents – that such a state would be one in which God is sovereign and God rules. The Shi'ite Islamists, by contrast, do not accept the restoration of the caliphate, because it was an institution established by the Sunnis and would presumably continue to be controlled by them today as well. For them, therefore, the solution is to emulate the Islamic Republic of Iran, or at least to take guidance from its leaders as to the nature of the state that they wish to establish. For example, Hizbullah in Lebanon today is a Shi'ite movement. Controversy exists over whether they wish to apply Khomeini's (absolute) mandate of the jurist to the Lebanese state. Many believe they do not want to do this, but even if they do not, seeking advice from the *faqih* in the Islamic Republic of Iran is important to the Lebanese Hizbullah leadership.

We have so far been discussing Sunni and Shi'ite Islamist theories of the state in the contemporary Middle East. It must be acknowledged that even within the Sunni Islamist and Shi'ite Islamist perspectives, differences exist, and no monolithic model has emerged. When we come to non-Islamist contemporary theorists of the state, we must make the same point. Indeed, the differences among them may be more numerous than the differences among the Islamists.

'Ali 'Abd al-Raziq's Sunni reformist theory of the state

Among contemporary Sunni non-Islamist theories, perhaps the earliest is that of 'Ali 'Abd al-Raziq (d. 1966), a scholar at al-Azhar at the time that he wrote his influential book *Islam and the Foundations of Rule* (1925).[7] The book was published about a year after the abolition of the caliphate by the Turkish government, which was the successor government of the defunct Ottoman Empire. It created controversy almost at once, and its author was barred from his teaching post at al-Azhar, the book was banned, and 'Abd al-Raziq himself, although not his ideas, became marginalized. In this work, 'Abd al-Raziq denies that there is such a thing as Islamic government by showing that the Qur'an and the Sunna of the Prophet were silent in regard to this issue, apart from vague references to authority needing to be obeyed.

He agreed that the Muslim community needed a government and state, because without them communal worship and community welfare would be virtually impossible to achieve, but he denied that they had to be of a specific kind. In that sense, Islam, to him, is decidedly not *din wa dawla* (religion and state/politics). Because the political system of the Muslims could change from generation to generation, one must avoid this shibboleth, because it suggests that the same political system should inhere over historical periods. One of the worst results of such a perspective is the actual caliphate that history has documented. Indeed the actual caliphate that arose was not a blessing for the Muslims, in 'Abd al-Raziq's view, but a disaster, in view of its despotism, corruption, reliance upon coercion, and intolerance of opinions that pointed out its injustices. Its disappearance after the Mongol sack of Baghdad in 1258 made no difference to the ability of Muslims to conduct their worship or pursue their welfare.

'Abd al-Raziq declares that God never intended that the model of rule by the Prophet during the years he was in Medina (622–630/32) should be the blueprint for government and state for Muslims thereafter. He added that the political model chosen by the Prophet was that of a limited form of monarchy, based on how the tribes of Arabia governed themselves prior to the onset of the Prophecy of Muhammad. (On this point, a number of scholars, who otherwise agree with the gist of 'Abd al-Raziq's argument, part ways with him, incidentally.) Even if there are references in the sayings of the Prophet to the imam (a term that was more current at the time than caliph, which came to be used after the demise of the Prophet), he stated, that did not mean that there must always be an imam.

To those who maintained that the caliph and the caliphate were divinely ordained and thus mandated because there was no opposition to the founding of the institution and its incumbent, he replied that the lack of opposition is not evidence of their necessity or legitimacy. Such lack of opposition, after all, could be explained by the people's fear of incurring the wrath and retribution of the caliph and his caliphate. Because freedom of expression did not exist at that time, there was nothing to stop elites from establishing the form of government – the caliphate – that they actually did establish. Moreover, it was precisely this lack of freedom of expression that explains why no systematic analysis of politics had ever been undertaken by the jurists and clergy in Islamic history.

'Abd al-Raziq wrote that either the Prophet saw his mission to be limited to Prophecy, or he believed that this mission also included political activities (which in his view would have been incompatible with his mission as Prophet), or he had in mind the creation of a simple form of state and government (which seems inapplicable because there was no budget, no administrative structure, no recognizable feature of even the most rudimentary forms of state and government). Thus, his mission was limited to Prophecy, and he left it up to each future generation to devise the form of government it believed best suited the Muslims of that era.

Looking at the historical record, 'Abd al-Raziq notes that all agree that the Prophet died without having made provision for the leadership of the umma. To him, therefore, this is proof that God had never meant to concern Himself with matters of government or state. For if he had, then the fact that the Prophet died without resolution of this issue would have meant that his mission remained incomplete at the time of his death. Yet Muslims believe that Muhammad's prophecy was the final and complete one. Consequently, this must mean that founding a state or government that would be applicable for all time was never part of his mission.

Finally, speaking of the contemporary era, 'Abd al-Raziq maintained that Muslims have reached such a stage that it is impossible to unite them all politically. Rather than this being a drawback, this state of affairs actually conforms to God's design. For it has always been His intention to have variations and differences among people. As evidence, he cites Qur'an 49:13: "We have made you into nations and tribes so that you may come to know each other."

As noted earlier, 'Abd al-Raziq's theses about the state and government sent shock waves throughout the Islamic world. Many wrote responses, and in the subcontinent of India the "Khilafat Movement" suggested that a large body of the Islamic community worldwide was keen to re-establish the caliphate. In the Arab world, one of the major efforts to save the institution, albeit in a reformed guise, was made in Syria by Shaykh Rashid Rida (d. 1935). On the other hand, some Muslims intellectuals, such as the Egyptian writer and man of letters Taha Husayn, applauded 'Abd al-Raziq's efforts, seeing in them the necessary beginning for releasing the creativity of the Muslim mind, as it were, and using that creativity to address and solve many of the pressing economic, political, and social problems facing Muslims in the twentieth century.

Two conservative Sunni rejoinders to 'Abd al-Raziq's thesis

The ubiquitous Muhammad 'Imara edited 'Abd al-Raziq's book in the mid-1970s and included an introduction mainly devoted to criticizing the author. According to 'Imara, 'Abd al-Raziq's motivation for writing his book was to ensure that King Fu'ad of Egypt, who saw himself as the logical choice to be the new caliph of the Muslim world in a restored caliphate, not succeed to this post. 'Imara was somewhat sympathetic to 'Abd al-Raziq in that the latter was a disciple of Muhammad 'Abduh and of the *salafiya* movement associated with that thinker. This was a tradition that 'Imara has sought to uphold, considering it "the mid-most path" – that is, a kind of "golden mean" between extreme interpretations of Islam that are either too conservative or too liberal.

Nevertheless, 'Imara attacked 'Abd al-Raziq's argument for being overly simplistic and rife with internal inconsistencies. For example, 'Abd al-Raziq's major thesis is that the Prophet did not try to establish a state but was a purely religious leader; yet, in some passages he seems to contradict this, as when he writes: "it [the Prophet's authority] included the spiritual aspects of the life of the human being – which is a characteristic of prophecy – and also included the sensory aspects [*jawanib hayat al-insan al-hissiya*] – which is a characteristic of governments."[8] 'Imara concludes from this that 'Abd al-Raziq seems to be suggesting in this passage that politics, government, and state in their civil meaning did figure significantly after all in the system that the Prophet established.

Yet, 'Imara seems to be distorting 'Abd al-Raziq's argument on this point. 'Abd al-Raziq is seemingly here maintaining that the stature of the Prophet was far greater than that of kings, rulers, and other secular leaders. He admits that the nature of the Prophet's authority was such that it could have subsumed politics under it. As 'Abd al-Raziq puts it, in fact, the Prophet

> has the politics of the world and of the hereafter. Therefore, the Prophet's authority was a general authority, by virtue of his mission. His command among the Muslims was a matter of obedience; his rule was total. There was nothing to which the hand of rule extended but that the authority of the Prophet incorporated it; nor was any kind of leadership or authority conceivable but that it was subsumed under the authority of the Prophet over the believers.[9]

Clearly, 'Abd al-Raziq is describing in metaphorical language the Prophet's stature in this passage. He does not mean to say the Prophet actually was interested in ruling in a political sense. He is trying to show that the Prophet's stature is exceptional and so could, if he chose to make it so, be utilized for the purposes of kingly rule. Thus, what 'Abd al-Raziq argues is that the Prophet did not have the intention of political rule, even if his authority was broad enough to include political leadership, because he saw his role in timeless terms. He did not envision his role in the form of the tenure of kings and magistrates but in the form of warner, missionizer, propagator of the divine message. What he seems to be suggesting is that the Prophet did after all perform a political role. But that role was secondary, and – upon his departure – he expected others to lead the Muslims according to whatever pattern they believed suited them. On this argument, the Prophet's reputation was so legendary that people forget that he did not lead the community of Medina *ex officio* – that is, by virtue of the fact that he was the religious leader. He played a political role insofar as the Muslims of the time considered him to have the best skills for that role. So he played it reluctantly. The religious mission was what motivated him. If people considered him the best candidate to lead politically, so be it. But he was hardly interested in such leadership, lest it undermine his role as Islam's Prophet. This meant that after him, the Muslims could choose someone with qualities better suited for that era, rather than someone who came closest to reflecting the Prophet's own attributes. This was all the more the case in that the Prophet's attributes were inimitable.

In other respects, too, 'Imara's criticism of 'Abd al-Raziq is not persuasive and begs the question of whether that criticism is sound. He attacks 'Abd al-Raziq for confusing the noble ideals of the caliphate with the reality of the historical record of the caliphate. In short, 'Imara wants 'Abd al-Raziq to drop the analysis of the caliphate as an actually operating institution and somehow equate an idealized theory of the caliphate provided by the rule of the first four "Rightly Guided" caliphs with "true Islam."[10]

At the end of the day, 'Imara is saying, Islam is very much in fact *din wa dawla*. He seems to be scandalized by the denial of this.[11] To 'Imara Islam must have a state in order to prosper and develop. The state must be Islamic. He consequently defends the *din wa dawla* thesis. In doing so, he seems to set up a straw man argument by maintaining that the opponents of the *din wa dawla* thesis believe that the Prophet did not establish a state.

But further reflection would show 'Imara that very few (if any) opponents of the *din wa dawla* argument deny that the early Muslims had a state and a government. The question is, what is to be the nature and the role of those institutions? 'Imara seems to want to have it both ways: the state's nature and role are to be left to future generations; but those generations have to be constrained by the caliphate, which alone is legitimate rule and is, in fact, divinely mandated. He somehow expects that this idealized caliphate can be in some manner materialized and by that very fact will perform surpassingly well. He does not see any structural deficiencies in the institution of the caliphate *per se*. Nor does he believe, for example, that the institution of *shura* needs to be problematized, anatomized, and analyzed to make sure that it empowers the people. He is perfectly content to say, well there are two Qur'anic verses regarding *shura* (42:38 and 3:159) and on their foundations the Islamic state realizes its democracy. To resolve the problems of the contemporary Muslim state, all that is really needed is for incumbent leaders to be moral.

Among those problems, as he sees it, is secularization, which he considers a threat to the Islamic order that he wishes to defend. Most thoughtful religious-minded opponents of *din wa dawla* hold that a secular state is acceptable, so long as it permits the people to discharge their devotional obligations. The obverse of this is that they fear *din wa dawla* as a formula for coerced belief, no matter how often its advocates cite scriptural verses that project a liberal attitude upon the resulting political system, such as Qur'an 2:256: "There is no coercion in matters of religion" or Qur'an 109:6: "To you your religion and to me mine." 'Imara, for his part, seems to believe that the mere invoking of these sacred texts is sufficient to calm the fears that haunt *din wa dawla* opponents.

We can juxtapose to 'Imara's conception of the state that which has been developed by Muhammad Salim al 'Awwa, an Egyptian, a member of the Muslim Brotherhood, with several years of residence in Saudi Arabia and currently secretary-general of the International Union for Muslim Scholars, with its headquarters in Dublin and a branch in Cairo. Recall that the 'Imara, who in his earlier years was influenced by leftist thought, had evolved in his thinking to the point of advocating the "Islamization of Knowledge."[12] This is certainly a stance dear to al-'Awwa's heart, as he is an active participant in that movement. Although al-'Awwa is not as prolific a writer as 'Imara, his work is among the more substantive efforts to conceptualize the state. We have already discussed his ideas to some extent earlier in this volume. We return to his thought here with specific reference to how he conceptualizes the state.

'Awwa reads back into Islamic history the Jeffersonian idea that "this is a government of laws, not of men," when he says the Islamic community at the time of the Prophet followed *shari'a* principles and that the *shari'a* mandated the accountability of individuals and government institutions to the law. Indeed, he says hyperbolically that Islam was the first system to establish this mandate.[13] But this begs the question of whether indeed it was. It assumes the *shari'a* was the basis of government and state and citizenship. In fact, one could argue that the accountability the *shari'a* mandated related to the believer's faith in God, and not to civil institutions such as government, state, and so on. This is exactly the point made by Fauzi Najjar, whose book was published two years after 'Awwa's and likely was a rejoinder to it on the same basis as 'Ali 'Abd al-Raziq's work fifty years earlier.[14] The jurists, who wrote on the Imamate, did not elaborate a concept of citizenship or a political theory. This took time – the philosophers, who came later, took up some of these issues, and, in doing so were influenced by Plato and Aristotle. The jurists wrote about certain functions of the Imam, such as jihad, commanding the good and forbidding evil, and so on. But there were no works that problematized the state. It would not have occurred to them to do so, since the system was a religious one.[15] Moreover, he seems to ignore the precedent of the Athenian *polis*, which was founded on the *nomos* (traditions of law), and the representation of interests in the Assembly. And was not the state in the era of the Roman Republic founded on the law?

In short, 'Awwa, instead of deductively and empirically showing how the first Muslim community established a state founded on law, merely assumes it. He says the source of the law was divine revelation, but he does not show how such divine revelation problematized the state, government and politics. Nor should one be surprised at this, since the revelation was a message of ethical principles and religious salvation. To be sure, the ethical and religious message of Islam might contain certain "entry points" to an eventually broad conceptualization of state and politics that was grounded in theory and the empirical record. But this is very different from saying that the Qur'an and the Prophet's Sunna materialized Jeffersonian democracy.[16]

'Awwa finds in sayings of the early caliphs additional evidence for contemporary democratic values. For example, the first caliph, Abu Bakr, is reputed to have stated: "Obey me if I obey God, but if I disobey Him, disobey me." Presumably, one of the commands that Abu Bakr needed to follow was the often cited verse (2:256) that there is no compulsion in matters of religion. But if that were so, then why did Abu Bakr spend the bulk of his short tenure as caliph fighting what came to be known as the wars of apostasy? The point is not that Abu Bakr may have been inconsistent in saying do not obey me if I disobey Allah but leading the effort in the wars of apostasy despite Qur'an 2:256. The point is that in such statements one cannot find a theory of democracy.[17]

The argument of 'Awwa as it unfolds becomes the more dubious as he seeks to develop a theory of the state. For example, he cites a seemingly sound Hadith (its chain of transmission back to the Prophet is unbroken in the sense that those who conveyed it over time were all considered to be trustworthy and hence not in the business of fabricating) from al-Suyuti (d. 1505) that urges: "Do not obey a creature against his Creator." This means that if a ruler conducts himself or herself in violation of God's ordinances, do not obey him. This Hadith, he insists, provides the basis for a theory of revolution. He maintains that the jurists elaborated on this doctrine of obeying the caliph only if he applies the *shari'a*, but having the right to overthrow him if he follows his own inclination, acts arbitrarily, or becomes despotic. He cites al-Mawardi and ibn Hazm on this.[18] But, in fact, as we saw earlier in this volume, the jurists ended up by legitimating the rule of caliphs even if the actual power and authority lay in the hands of the secular rulers, such as the Saljuq sultans. Indeed, by al-Ghazali, and certainly by ibn Jama'a, the theory basically amounted to support for the principle of "might makes right" because it legitimated the rule of the actual secular ruler, whoever he was and however he acceded to his position. In other words, the constitutional theory chose to look the other way in the face of the grossest violations of *shari'a* principles. Moreover, one would expect that if the jurists were serious about this, and the people were aware of their rights in this regard, they would create a mechanism that would empower the courts to hear complaints against derelict rulers and (1) establish the criteria on the basis of which to say whether or not a caliph were sinning; (2) devise a mechanism to punish such derelict rulers. But this was never done.

In the effort to promote the caliphate, 'Awwa next makes the following observations, which cannot pass unchallenged. He asserts that ever since the Turks abolished the caliphate in 1924, the masses of Muslims have supported its restoration as the single most important call that they have made. No evidence for this is given except a bald assertion that "the Islamic movements that have, in their programs, connected religion and life or the system of rule and the call to Islam have been the most successful movements."[19] Even if this is true (and there is no evidence that it is), it does not mean the people demand the restoration of the caliphate. It could mean that they want some other system – for example, a civil government that respects the faith but does not seek to impose a model of politics on them.

In fairness to him, 'Awwa does call for sensitivity to the requirements of historical change and the needs of the times in the effort to recapture the congruence he believes existed between the political system and Islamic principles during the era of the Rightly Guided Caliphs.[20] But as we have already seen, he later on in the book criticizes those who assess the performance of the caliphate by reference to the actual historical record, preferring that assessment be based only on the ideals of its principles plus the praxis of the first four caliphs. Therefore, if we take him at his word, then his expressed desire to factor into the analysis actual historical developments appears misplaced. Moreover, his preferred sources appear to be secondary literature, including the writings of his professors, such as Muhammad Taha Badawi and Muhammad Mustafa Shalabi. The problem is that the early sources, such as al-Tabari (d. 923) or al-Mas'udi or ibn Kathir (d. 1373), would not provide the evidence he is looking for to show the Islamic state of that era as founded on democratic principles, whereas the later secondary literature, which would be apologetic on this point, could be counted upon to do exactly that.

For example, 'Awwa asserts that the basis of the state created by the Prophet upon his emigration to Medina in 622 had already been laid by the second oath at 'Aqaba, a ravine outside the city, just before he entered it in response to an invitation by certain people there for him to come and assist them resolve some disputes they were having among themselves. This oath, taken by seventy-four persons (including two women), committed these people to go to war and to defend the Prophet. This oath of allegiance (bay'a) is stressed by 'Awwa and like-minded writers to support the argument that the system that was established at that time was democratic. But Hourani is probably closer to understanding the significance of such oaths of allegiance when he says that

> after the first age [i.e., after the end of the Rightly Guided Caliphate] this [the bay'a] was no more than a formality, and even in theory it was not, in the full sense, a process of election. It was rather a recognition than a choice: in the view of most thinkers, in the bay'a the community acquiesced in authority, it did not confer it.[21]

The next step in the building of this state, according to 'Awwa, was the drafting of a document later called the "Constitution of Medina." As 'Awwa sees it, if the second oath at 'Aqaba set the stage for creating the state, the Constitution of Medina was the basis for the Prophet's assumption of his political leadership role. In his opinion the document delimited the foundations of "citizenship" in the new state.[22] Note his anachronistic reference to citizenship, a concept that was unknown at that time. But for 'Awwa, it is important to establish that this state was the first truly democratic state, resting on the foundation of citizen rights and obligations. Perhaps not realizing the import of what he is about to say, 'Awwa next asserts that the Constitution of Medina replaced tribal linkages with religious ties.[23] In fact, this is the argument made by 'Ali 'Abd al-Raziq, who had insisted that the Islamic community established by the Prophet was a religious, not a political, community. If religious ties prevail, one wonders about the putative citizenship of the members of this community.

'Awwa writes only three pages on the new Islamic state's implementation of its tasks, by comparison to the description of its goals, such as the defense of the interests of the Muslims, the advancement of social justice, the provision of equality and its "citizens," the spread of education, the organization of finances, and the conduct of international relations. Perhaps the reason for such brief allusions is that the evidence did not exist to support his claim of a functioning state as this is commonly understood today. Recall that his effort is to read back into the era of the Prophet concepts and practices associated with the functioning of the modern state, with its system of separation of powers into judicial, legislative, and executive branches.[24] He admits that political theory did not exist at the time of the Prophet, but he asserts that "it reached its final form ... in the books of the jurists and theologians."[25] Yet, as we have already seen, the works of the jurists considered only a few topics of concern to political theory – such as *jihad* – and developed no general theories of such familiar concerns of political theory as the state, civil society, or the individual. Where he might have found evidence for such issues, in the writers of the Muslim philosophers, he failed to look.

Finally, 'Awwa's "theory" of the state leaves out the empirical record for almost the entire period of Islamic history. Acknowledging that some have argued the need to assess the degree to which the idealized Islamic state lived up to its principles in actual practice, he finesses the issue by saying that one cannot evaluate a divinely ordained system by reference to human actions, especially as those actions contained so many derelictions and instances of malfeasance.[26] But, of course, the reply to such a dismissal of the empirical record must be that if all the corruptions, distortions, oppressions of the state from the end of the era of the Rightly Guided Caliphs until the modern period were due to the systematic violations by leaders ruling in the name of Islam, then might it not be possible that the system devised in theory was itself defective because it contained no institutionalized means to prevent those violations? As Muhammad Sa'id al-'Ashmawi, a critic of Islamism, puts it: "How can it be that the [structural] foundations and antecedents of the caliphate were not responsible for [the corruptions that] ensued?"[27]

'Awwa, 'Imara, and others who share their views are asking us to accept that personally idiosyncratic behavior by virtually all the caliphs was responsible, and that the answer must lie elsewhere. The system itself was at fault, and the reason for that in turn was that

Islam indeed was a religious call, and not a political order. If it had been a political order, and if it was characterized by all the political virtues adumbrated by 'Awwa and others — such as consultation, social justice, and meaningful representation of interests — then the Muslims would have established the institutions and processes to ensure the implementation of those values. No such thing happened, however, and thus, when rulers ruled "politically," no mechanisms existed to restrain them effectively.

Muhammad Shuhrur's reformist theory of limits and the Arab Islamic state

We have already encountered the "theory of limits" (*nazariyyat al-hudud*) of Muhammad Shuhrur in a previous chapter on the individual in contemporary Middle Eastern political theories. His model of the state is eclectic, combining elements of the thought of ibn Rushd, Rousseau, Hegel, and Marx.

Shuhrur calls the state the peak institution in society, a distinctly Hegelian notion; but then defers also to Marx:

> Through [its] institutions, the state is a mechanism for the expression of a reality in which a people live.... The state is considered the peak of the prevailing epistemological, moral, social and political consciousness in a society. Thus, it is the superstructure resting upon a base and represents prevailing social and economic relations and levels of knowledge. If these relationships are backward, the state is backward; if they are advanced, then so is the state.[28]

Shuhrur employs the Marxist categories of base and superstructure as descriptive categories rather than analytical constructs. Hence, we are not sure how theoretically useful they are. He asserts that if the "influence" of the base is stronger than that of the superstructure, the state will be more democratic; if it is weaker, then it will be less democratic. He follows Marx in considering the state part of the superstructure. But he has earlier stated that it is the peak institution in society, a clear contradiction of Marx.[29]

THE STATE 213

In Shuhrur's opinion, the state embraces the relationships that exist between an individual in himself and the collective whole. When we speak of people, we are really speaking of the dialectical connection between the one, the individual, and the whole, the collective.[30] Shuhrur does not, however, spell out how the state comprehends the individual's relations with the collective group or community. It seems he has an organic conception of the state that, as indicated earlier, implicitly rests upon a corporatist model. That model stresses the state as the orchestrator of the interests of all classes, groups, and individuals in society. In classic corporatism, it does this because it is the benevolent guardian and is rationally capable of advocating on behalf of all the actors in society. This conception differs from the liberal model of the state, which in its classical version acts minimally to prevent competition in economic and political markets from becoming lethal but otherwise does not intervene. It also differs from the Marxist model, which holds that the state is "the executive committee of the ruling class" and hence cannot act as the neutral arbiter characterized in the liberal conception, or as the supervening power that coordinates the representation of interests held by social groups. It further differs from the state in the original Muslim conception as the facilitator of obedience to God's commands by the members of the community as a whole (as opposed to any specific individual one of them).

In Shuhrur's conception, all economic, social and political relationships are latent (ready to be actualized?) in the general level of knowledge and moral values of those living in the community, both as its members as a whole but also as discrete individuals. Although he does not utilize the concept of sovereignty, it seems that he believes that the state is the sovereign instrument that stands ready to give expression to such knowledge and values, although vehicles at lesser grades of abstraction (such as the family, lineage group, clan, etc.) also do this.[31]

People's values can also be seen at the economic level. Here, Shuhrur again invokes Marxist language, specifically the mode and forces of production. Two possibilities exist: a production model and a "profiteering" (ri'i) model. In the former, wealth accumulates as a consequence of productive labor and scientific administration and the adequate distribution of the forces of production among the economic sectors – presumably he means agriculture, industry, manufactures, services. The state's role is to regulate and maintain a balance in such distribution and among the sectors, but he also adds a further state function: contributing to the credentialization of human beings – that is, making them qualified to perform certain tasks. In the profiteering model, however, the state takes resources from the people and spends these on itself, primarily to preserve itself against the people. Such a state can only be established if the mode of production is "backward." Its wealth is not productive but rather venal in nature.[32]

Finally, people's values may also be seen at the level of epistemological awareness. This level is reflected in the other two levels. One who knows nothing will not ask for, nor will he do, anything. It is this level that explains the scientific advancement or lagging behind of a society. If the epistemological level is advanced, so is the society.

To Shuhrur, the civilized state rests on "wise revelation," with its twin aspects of prophecy (nubuwa) and message (risala). The prophecy aspect contains clarifications (bayyinat) that must be laid out in order to authenticate the laws that are passed. The message part contains commands and proscriptions. These carry no clarifications as they are God's commands, and God does not explain His imperatives. These must be obeyed on the basis of promises of good things to come if they are heeded and of threats of dire consequences if they are not. The structure of the Arab Islamic state should rest upon clarifications that must be furnished before proposing any legislation. Such clarifications are material and scientific in nature. God's limits are the only things that can constrain such a state. These limits represent in fact a range of possibilities, so that the state "turns or curves" within the limits established by God. How it does so depends upon "the prevailing epistemological level" – which seems to mean the stock of knowledge available in the society in question – and the prevailing conditions. However, the highly abstract level of this discussion makes it difficult to understand the bearing of these concepts on the actual operation of the state under concrete historical circumstances.

At any rate, the problem as Shuhrur sees it is that Arab Islamic societies are still dominated by families and clans and are of the profiteering type (in contrast to societies where productivity prevails). When this is the case, it always drives the epistemological level backwards and suppresses it. The state, in short, either ignores or eviscerates the activities of scientific research institutes that could otherwise provide it with rationalizations for good and effective policies. This backwardness is accompanied by moral backwardness, because social relations in society and in the state become an expression of those connections that suppress moral values on behalf of the existing relations of power that are based on narrow self-interest, opportunism, and the like.[33]

All states have institutions that clarify, on the one hand, and those that are jural, on the other hand. Shuhrur stresses that the purpose of the legislative, executive, and judicial branches is to serve these two types of institution. In an apparent *non sequitur*, he then maintains that many more prophets have existed historically than messengers (bearing in mind again that prophets are sent with clarifications, and messengers are sent to provide laws). God used prophets to teach people about things that were hidden from their knowledge. Muhammad, who was both a Prophet and a Messenger, was the last of God's apostles, and consequently the people were left to their own devices following his death. From that time until today, our knowledge of the universe has reached unprecedented levels.

Shuhrur next argues that God legislated by way of his messengers in ways suitable for the development of societies at the time the particular messenger was sent. People in ancient times did not understand the dichotomies of good and evil, light and darkness, fertility and sterility. They thus attributed these things to deities endowed with awesome power. They came to be associated with rule on earth, and from this situation arose the concept of despotic, monarchical rule. The ruler's power on earth was coordinate with the deity's rule from on high.[34]

Rule thus became divinely ordained, even among tribal systems, where the leader and the shaman (religious official) became "epistemological authorities." Even today, we find systems in which we see the "philosophy of God–the universe–the human being," another of Shuhrur's unexplained expressions. In the Arab world, this philosophy is Islamic, which, if it is truly followed, would provide different results from what we see in reality, since that reality consists of deviations from the true, pristine model.[35]

In Shuhrur's opinion, every state without exception has been founded on a religious basis. Additionally, the spread of states by religion has given indispensable concepts to humankind, including legitimation, moral law, reliance on customs as a basis for the state's structure, and the liberty of the human being. Both of these assertions are contentious, as some states (for instance, the USSR) were not founded on a religious basis, and it is far from clear how the religious impetus for the creation of certain states provided the concept of liberty of the human being, for example.

Withal, the "clarificatory" and jural institutions that are latent in all state structures are the fundamental motive forces of the desired Arab Islamic state. That state's structure amounts to the revelation that was revealed to the Prophet, Muhammad. Besides clarification and law, a third element, which Shuhrur calls "particularization," is also part of the state structure. This term refers to the classification and expounding of the rules and laws that are generated by the process of *ijtihad*, or independent judgment, to find a legal ruling to cover a set of circumstances. Particularization thus refers to the process of determining the law, including the state constitution, by a properly established body, such as the supreme court of the land. A state that spends more than half of its budget on education and scientific research (to which he gives the label *bayyinat* – or clarifications) is closer to the Islamic ideal, because "Islam" holds that the advancement of knowledge is important for human progress. In light of innovations in knowledge, such a state enacts new laws suitable for the level of civilization it has attained.[36]

Without the dialectical relationship between clarifications and legislation, no state can arise and endure. Lacking it, the state remains a mere superstructure for the base of society, which is extremely backward. It is human beings who animate this relationship, of course, and Shuhrur adds that these human beings have a dialectic of their own, central to which is freedom to choose options without compulsion. This freedom consists in the liberty to believe, which is a gift from God, and the liberty to express one's opinions. The concept of consultation known as *shura* is a means of implementing these freedoms by a group of people who are at an epistemological and moral level that is in keeping with the social and economic structure of society. Today, Shuhrur notes, freedom of opinion and following the will of the majority is called democracy, although the early concept of *shura* is certainly one of its requisites.[37]

The Prophet undertook consultation within the structure of the state that existed in his time. His pattern of consultation[38] did not restrict that structure to one particular form. The "wise revelation" mentioned "those in authority" (4:59), without saying who they were, how they are chosen, what their qualifications are, and the like. Rather, that body of ideas was mainly concerned with determining the moral basis of society.[39] The contemporary Islamic concept of *shura* is democracy, according to Shuhrur. It signifies expressing one's views based on information that has come to hand and upon the basis of which the human being forms opinions. Shura cannot be legislated by statute but rather "enters into the structure of the constitutional state ... because freedom and democracy ... are a scientific mode [*namat 'ilmi*] of human life."[40]

Shuhrur next examines the constitution of the state, since that is the framework that expresses the state's structure. State structures evolve slowly, and constitutions are amended accordingly, only at occasional intervals. The crisis of the "Arab political mind" (sic) lies in its failure to attach any importance to the constitution. The Arab political mind feels no constraints about the ruler continuing in power with lifetime tenure; nor is it conscious of the latter's near absolute power, nor the means by which he achieved it. Rather, it concerns itself less with important issues of daily life, such as red traffic-light violations or unfair customs duties. Why is this? Shuhrur's reply is that it is because the law organizes the people's daily lives in the same manner as Islamic jurisprudence (fiqh) did in early Islamic history. Judges acted in settling disputes and ordering relations among individuals in those days, and this is how the law is administered by rulers today. Among the Arabs, the "Islamic legal mind" is not concerned with deficiencies, just implementation. But the "constitutional mind" ought to be (and is) concerned with deficiencies, and seeks to remedy them.

Since the first caliph after the end of the Rightly Guided Caliphate (632–661) seized power and made rule inheritable, the role of the Muslims themselves became marginalized. This situation continues to prevail in our own time. Constitutions of contemporary Arab states, which are supposed to organize their structures, are free from any previous (constraining?) historical structures, because these structures were never deemed obligatory. Such is the practice, although in theory – in Shuhrur's opinion, at any rate – "Islam" is supposed to deal with every structure according to its historicity. Why should this be so? His reply is that it is due to the central place of "the law of development" in Islamic belief.[41] Exactly what this law of development constitutes, or how it demonstrates that "Islam" treats structures in terms of their historicity, is not examined, however. This is a real shame, since historicization is, as I have maintained, a *sine qua non* for Middle Eastern political theories. Shuhrur has brought us right to the edge of a crucial issue but has demurred on its elaboration.

Shuhrur's analysis of the state then moves in the direction of the role of political parties. Again, the inquiry is elliptical and begs certain questions. He notes that when *shura*, which he equates with democracy, "entered the fundamental structure of Islamic belief" and when it was implemented, the ideal form for it was party pluralism. He does not seem to believe it necessary to demonstrate that *shura* did become central to belief and practice, nor show precisely why party pluralism was its ideal manifestation, much less its practice. Notwithstanding this lacuna, he presses on with a definition of party pluralism as the expression of opinion and the right to differ in an organized, scientific, methodical manner. Surprisingly, he claims that party pluralism is characteristic of Islam (no doubt, he means that it *should be* one of the fundamentals). "Islam" has a right and a left, and the right and the left in Islam have wings. What is rightist today could be leftist tomorrow. He then reverts to the "wise revelation" and lists the following points:

- God accepted opposition and deferred His anger against its possible excesses to Judgment Day. If God was willing to accept opposition, why should we not do so?
- The human being's expression of freedom began as opposition to God. If all had obeyed God's commands, we would never have known that the human being is free and not an automaton.
- If majority opinion errs, this is no reason to abandon the principle.[42]

In Shuhrur's opinion, the political party expresses the collective consciousness of a group. It has an action program that seeks to move the state and society forward. It is animated by popular opinion, he feels (though many would say that it takes its cues not from popular opinion but rather from the ideology of its members, especially its elites). In earlier times, differences were settled by force, and the people had no say. Today, the people not only have a say, but they "rule."[43]

Party pluralism is a sort of master key for Shuhrur. But, he asks, how can an Islamic party be established alongside non-Islamic ones? And how can the exclusionary poll tax (*jizya*) of earlier periods continue to be imposed on Jews, Christians, and other "people of the book" (ahl al-kitab) in an age of party pluralism? If all opinions are important, then what might "Islam's" view be on the opinions of "the other"?[44]

At this point, Shuhrur engages in Qur'anic exegesis to demonstrate that God laid the ground for political pluralism. In this effort, he believes he can logically show that apparently categorical divine commands to distrust non-believers referred only to specific contexts; and that in general God's instructions were that human beings must accept diversity. He reminds us that the scripture contains unambiguous (muhkam) as well as ambiguous (mashbuh) verses as to their meaning. Sura 9 contains verses that are all unambiguous. Among them is 29, which states: "Fight those people of the book who do not believe in God and the Last Day, who do not prohibit what God and His Apostle have forbidden, nor accept divine law, until all of them pay jizya in submission." But in Qur'an 60:8–9, we read:

> God does not forbid you from being kind and acting justly towards those who did not fight over faith with you, and who have not expelled you from your homes. God indeed loves those who are just. He only forbids you from making friends with those who fought over faith with you and banished you from your homes and aided in your exile. Whoever makes friends with them is a transgressor.

These two verses from different suras regulate the Arab and Islamic political mind in particular in regard to the principle of force and that mind's position on "the other" – the non-Muslim. We need to determine whether it is established categorically for all times and places, or limited to the period of the mission of the Prophet.[45]

Continuing, Shuhrur notes that Sura 9 was revealed in Medina, after the Prophet emigrated there in 622. Medina was the site for the establishment of the Islamic community and its embryonic political system. It was characterized by politics and wars. Such matters are the topic of these two suras. Sura 60 contains the declaration about those who fight the believers and those who do not, without considering if they belong to the people of the book or not. God has left the door of justice and piety open until the Day of Judgment. He has not determined the conditions of the piety or justice that need to be fulfilled. But He did define the justifications and conditions of fighting that must be acknowledged and carried out. In Sura 9 God has determined the conditions for implementing 60:9 ("He only forbids you from befriending those who fought over faith with you and banished you from your homes and aided in your exile. Whoever befriends them is a transgressor"). Consequently, we see that the language of Sura 9:29 is not unambiguous after all but is rather governed by 60:9. So, how can we collect the *jizya* from those who are a minority and who do not fight us, and who have not expelled us from our homes? Where is the piety and justice in that?[46]

This is a vivid example of his theory of limits at work. Shuhrur, who began by admitting that Sura 9 contains unambiguous verses, ends up restricting the application of one of these, number 29, by bringing in two verses, 60:8–9, that have the effect not of abrogating 9:29 but qualifying it to the point of allowing Muslims to drop the poll tax on at least some of the people of the book.[47]

From all of the foregoing, Shuhrur concludes that the constitution of any Arab Islamic state must contain the following: a guarantee of freedom to form political parties, without the need for approval by any authority; a guarantee of freedom of expression in meetings and peaceful demonstrations, in associations, and in the media; irrelevance of the devotional duties (such as prayer, alms-giving, Ramadan fasting, and the pilgrimage to Mecca) for the programs of the political parties, since they are unrelated to economics, politics, or social issues; state guarantee of the people's undertaking their devotional duties (for example, during a period of religiously mandated fasting, work hours must be shortened); equality among individuals without regard to their nationality; the right of minority nationalities to develop their cultures in total freedom; civilian supremacy over the military.[48]

Shuhrur next asks what appears to be an unusual question. Is the Islamic state a secular state? He concludes that in fact it is (or at least that it should be). A secular state is one whose legitimacy rests not upon priests or professional men of religion but rather on the people (al-nas). Since Islam knows no priesthood, and the 'ulama' are not a priesthood, the important role played by the latter as among the "people of loosing and binding" (ahl al-hall wa al-'aqd) should be seen for what it is: as the representatives of the people. In a modern setting, the people of loosing and binding are elected deputies of the people in parliament. The secular state is one where opinions are expressed freely, and such freedom of opinion is protected.[49]

Surprisingly, though, after trying to show that the Arab Islamic state is secular, Shuhrur avers that as a religion Islam cannot be separated from the state. The reason is that Islam contains the components of truth, legislation, morality, and aesthetics. Moreover, it contains the dialectic of straightness (istiqama) and curvature (hanifiyya).[50] The Islamicity of the state is verified by the fact that its laws do not go beyond God's limits; and by its adoption of truth and inquiry for its structure, through science and reason; and by its reliance upon directives and tutelage in its educational methodology.

As for the devotional duties, they are pursued by individuals seeking piety. They are unrelated to the state and lack the aspect of curvature, being anchored in place. It is the aspect of curvature that relates to the possibilities of development or regress, whereas the aspect of straightness is not open to change in either of these directions because God's commands regarding these devotional duties are straightforward and brook no questioning if one accepts Islam. Since the state is constantly subject to development (or regress, one presumes), it is natural that it be separated from the devotional duties. The Prophet himself made that separation. Consequently, we see that the Islamic state is a purely secular one. Islam encompasses the dialectic of straightness and curvature. This provides room for party pluralism and freedom of expression. Islam contains leftist and rightist positions in solving the same problem. The only thing that is needed is to provide the clarifications and the agreement of the majority of the people, not that of the 'ulama' qua religious stratum. In that capacity, they have no connection to the agreement of the majority, and they have no right to give legitimacy to the state or to its laws.[51]

What, then, about the Islamic Arab state? In theory, at any rate, Islam is simultaneously a liberal and a conservative religion. Its liberalism appears in its acceptance of the different customs, traditions, and habits of all the peoples on earth, as long as they do not transcend God's limits. It also believes that freedom and nobility are God's gifts to the people, both male and female, equally. It does not prevent their integration in public. But it prevents their isolation in a confined space with those who are marriageable. Islamic personal status law (pertaining to marriage, divorce, inheritance, and the like) is humane and civil, within the limits established by God. Those limits are set on the basis of the degree of historical development of the society, the proffer of clarifications, and agreement to accept the majority's will. Relative justice is believed to be achievable historically via legislative enactments. In such a state, women's and men's dress follows social customs within the limits established by God. Some states are more patriarchal and hence are bound by maximum limits, whereas others are committed to less patriarchal rules and hence do not follow maximum limits.[52]

In practice, however, the situation is different. Authoritarianism has been the great problem of Arab Islamic societies since the rule of the Rightly Guided Caliphs. A supreme effort is required to extricate such societies from the "crisis of democracy," an effort that must begin within the "Arab political mind" before it can be addressed in institutions. Authoritarianism has become entrenched as a philosophy. Islamic jurisprudence and Sufism have acted as handmaidens to facilitate this tendency, giving it legitimacy. The watchword of this authoritarianism has been the phrase "obey those in authority," no matter how they achieved it. Fatalism on the part of the Muslim masses is the other side of this coin, as they have come to view their lives as fated and prescribed.[53] In making this point, Shuhrur iterates a recurring theme in the writing of reformist-minded Middle Eastern political theorists: the law is supposed to be the repository of right conduct, and the jurists the guardians of that law. However, instead of articulating it in a manner most conducive to constructive outcomes and well-being for Muslims, these jurists have interpreted the law in such a way that populations have become disenfranchised and wholly dependent upon others to make decisions affecting their most important interests. Sufism, too, with its tendency to stress inner contemplation, has the same effect of eliminating initiative and fostering attitudes of indifference on the part of the masses.

However, Shuhrur does not offer much guidance on the way out of this dilemma, beyond the Hegelian notion, one supposes, that thought must change prior to action. How the rise in belief in democracy is to happen is left somewhat mysterious. To be fair to him, though, he does add that democracy is worth struggling and dying for, because it is the "scientific civilized mode" for human existence.[54]

One knows when one has attained democracy when the following requisites have been fulfilled. The constitution, which aggregates the principles that drive the operation of the state, is applicable for all individuals in the society, irrespective of their nationality or belief. The laws that order the daily operations of the state institutions and the people derive their authority from that constitution. Both the constitution and the laws may be changed, but only through due process. Meanwhile, they may not be contravened. The moral system defining the values and standards of the society is understood holistically and not considered divisible — there is no such thing as a big truth and a small truth, a major lie and a minor lie. But moral infractions may only be punished if a tort or a crime is committed. One may not sanction a person for thinking ill of another. Finally, customs — which are aggregates of local traditions — must be allowed to differ from one region of the state territory to the next. They may change, and while moral systems may also be transformed, this will always be slower than changes in customs. It is correct to talk of Arab customs, but there is no such thing as Arab morality, since morality itself is universal.[55] Although he does not elaborate on this point, Shuhrur here is taking a position against moral relativism. This has implications for the debate on human rights, among other things, and whether the leaders of a society may excuse themselves from compliance with rights schemes that contain provisions from which they believe their societies may be exempted.[56]

Towards the end of his analysis, Shuhrur provides a coda to the themes he has highlighted in his compositional essay on the state. He seeks to move the discussion on the state from dead center, where he believes it has remained for many centuries because of the tendency of those who have bothered to comment on the subject in the first place to talk at a highly abstract, idealized level. Hence, he declares that the Arab Islamic state must "believe" that this universe in which we live is material, real, based on contradiction and the merging of opposites. It must believe in change and the development of things and of societies. It must believe that contradictions internal to society necessarily lead to changes in forms, relations, and structures, both of society and of the state. Thus, the Arab Islamic state is evolving, and the motor force of such development is the clear material evidence furnished by objective knowledge and reason. This dynamic will not cease until the Day of Judgment, when a new world without contradictions comes into existence. The human being is a factor in this process and can intervene to shape the development that is going on. But he cannot eliminate it.[57]

The reader cannot have failed to notice the Hegelian and Marxist influences in Shuhrur's thinking as reflected in these passages. Change occurs dialectically; contradictions are the motor force of development. Shuhrur seems to be saying, with Marx, that the individual "is no abstract being, squatting outside the world" and indeed can "make his own history, but not out of whole cloth."[58] But he does not integrate these concepts theoretically into his analysis. Rather, they appear as denotative remarks that, he believes, help his argument along. He never strays far from the Islamic context, however. For example, he notes that scientific research, making knowledge relevant to life, and moving the wheel of progress forward are all functions of the state in the Islamic *Weltanschauung*, since "the doctrine of divine unicity is latent" in such functions. In other words, he believes that God wants states to be configured so as to provide the science and technology needed for the well-being of Muslims.[59]

Shuhrur believes that efforts to ground legislation in the Arab Islamic state on the *shari'a* has created many difficulties. Instead of the *shari'a* being the basis for such legislation, he maintains that it must be based on God's limits. The significance of this point is that he is saying that the Muslim jurists, whose consensus opinions over the centuries have constituted the *shari'a*, have misunderstood God's limits.[60] Those limits, as we have already seen, must be understood dynamically, and not be bound to any historical period. In such a state, legislation that is based on previous enactments that failed to abide by God's limits will be null and void. Moreover, only God can promulgate fixed laws. All positive laws, being not divine in origin, are subject to change and amendment. For that reason, all positive laws must specify the time period for which they are intended to apply.[61]

For Shuhrur, Arabs must learn that methods of knowledge evolve. Of course, important parts of the revelation that inspired the Prophet are fixed. One of its miracles, however, is that God formulated it in such a way as to suit the development of all tools of knowledge, no matter how elemental or advanced. Arab Muslims must not fear the application of all systems of knowledge and methodologies to the revelation. This is because God precisely wanted successive generations to come to ever fuller understandings of the miracle of the scripture.

The lesson, accordingly, is that Arab Muslims must enter into a new stage of their history, having at hand new tools of knowledge to provide a new perspective on the problems of their world. If they do not do this, they will be condemned to repeat the "defeats and backwardness" that they have suffered as a result of the continued insistence upon holding on to the systems and tools of knowledge of the early Islamic period and trying to comprehend Islam through those obsolete mechanisms.[62]

Ayubi's thesis of the overstated Arab state

Before examining the Shi'i Muslim reformist conceptualization of the state, it is fitting to refer to a work by the Egyptian expatriate scholar Nazih Ayubi, entitled *Overstating the Arab State*.[63] Ayubi received his Ph.D. at the University of Oxford, and taught for a few years in the 1970s at Cairo University. From 1979 to 1983 he held a position in the Department of Political Science at UCLA. Thereafter, from 1983 to 1995, he was Reader and eventually became the director of the Middle East Program at the University of Exeter. He died in December 1995, the year of the publication of the volume mentioned above. As with Shuhrur, Ayubi uses Marxist formulations, but unlike the Syrian engineer, Ayubi, as a trained political scientist, seeks to integrate these categories theoretically into his overall analysis of the Arab state, or states, rather, since he examines no fewer than twelve of these. Moreover, Ayubi devotes several hundred pages to the subject of the state, whereas Shuhrur's inquiry is of chapter length. Also, while Shuhrur was committed to an Islamic framework, Ayubi is not interested in vindicating Islamic principles but rather wishes to attempt a political sociology of the state that takes him into theories of corporatism, mode-of-production analysis, and Gramscian perspectives.

Despite the length of Ayubi's work, the thesis and theory may be summarized rather succinctly. The thesis is that whereas the Arab state is the legatee of hundreds of years of authoritarian rule, it is not a strong state. Because it relies on coercion, it is better characterized as "fierce," rather than strong. The Arab state is known for its large bureaucracies, especially the military security and administrative apparatuses. But that hardly makes it "strong." The theory of the book is grounded in an eclectic mix of corporatist and neo-Marxist analysis. The Arab state suppresses but does a rather poor job of extracting resources from its own population. The latter refuse it legitimacy (unless the state comes under attack from abroad), but the people are too fragmented to be able to challenge its rule.

In many respects, the contemporary Arab state in Ayubi's assessment is patterned along a "tributary mode of production," in which tribal elements continue to carry over in importance, even though the bureaucracies with which it is endowed and the civil society institutions with which it deals place it well beyond the elementary forms of political life bespoken by the concept of tribalism. In more recent decades, however, capitalism has evolved in the societies governed by these states, either through the growth of the private sector or under the aegis of the state itself in the form known as state capitalism. Ayubi utilizes the concept of articulation to maintain that the older tributary and the new capitalist modes of production have come to mutually influence one another on the terrain of state behavior. In this situation, the ruling elite – for several decades after independence consisting of the military, but later also civilians – is able to sit atop the power pyramid with little threat from social classes. It is true that regimes would be challenged in military coups, but this was rarely due to the opposition of broadly based social classes in the society. The state thus becomes oppressive, and social forces become its clients.

Exploitation is the hallmark of the contemporary Arab state. What it lacks is the resources Gramsci had in mind when he talked about the hegemonic bloc. In Gramscian theory, hegemony has to do with the fact that the standard Marxist explanation of states as executive committees of the ruling class is too simplistic. It is not that states are not class-based, nor that ruling classes do not say much more about the direction of state policies than other classes. It is that coercion by itself cannot explain satisfactorily how it is that the state can endure for such a long time, if the only tool available to it is the resources of the social class that rules the economy and the society. Something else needs to be added to the mix, and that is the ability of the state to orchestrate a coalition in society through cultural mechanisms, including religion and nationalism, to maintain the unity required of the various population groups residing within its territory. The bloc that exercises the hegemony is made up of varying class interests that, despite their differences, are amalgamated and held together through a combination of persuasion and compulsion. The construction of the hegemonic bloc occurs through the efforts of intellectuals, bureaucrats, administrators, and the military. Although Gramsci wrote that such hegemonic blocs will be contested with the creation of counter-blocs, Ayubi pays less attention to this factor because his interest is in showing the staying power of brittle authoritarian states in the Arab world. Although they are good at arresting and imprisoning the opposition, these states can be challenged, in his opinion, but it will be a long and bitter struggle, necessarily waged by civil society's institutions and leaders.

Despite the sophistication with which Ayubi invests his theory of the Arab state (or perhaps precisely because of it), it is not likely to attract the attention of a broad array of social groups in society. This is mainly due to his unwillingness to factor Islam into the picture (except by way of showing the abiding influence of traditional mentalities and practices on the operation of the contemporary Arab state). If anything, Ayubi wishes to avoid falling into the Orientalist trap of essentializing the Arab state. The failures of the Arab Islamic state that Shuhrur, for example, has highlighted, cannot be explained by Islam itself, despite the desire of many politicians and even some scholars to make this accusation. Perhaps in his rightful desire to avoid essentializing, Ayubi avoids analyzing how the solution to the coerciveness and low levels of legitimacy of the Arab state may be addressed by reference to concepts endemic to the Islamic perspective on politics. By contrast, of course, Shuhrur wants to foreground the Islamic factor, and for that reason, despite the denseness of his writing, his chances of being read by a broader range of groups in the Arab world are greater.

A Shi'i reformist rejoinder to Khomeini's theory of the mandate of the jurist

A final theoretical position on the state that will be reviewed here is that taken by the Shi'i Muslim reformist Muhsin Kadivar. He is a member of the reformist clergy in the Islamic Republic of Iran and has authored two works on the state and rule, both of which were permitted publication inside his native country. One of these is entitled *Theories of the State in Shi'ite Law* (1997);[64] and the other is called *The Government of Vilayat* (1998).[65] He also participated in a debate with Abdol Karim Soroush that was published by the reformist newspaper, *Salam*, under the title of *Religious Pluralism* (1999).[66] Kadivar is highly critical of Khomeini's doctrine of the mandate of the jurist, so it is somewhat surprising that he was allowed to publish his work within Iran, albeit by a small publisher with a modest print run.

In the preceding chapter, social contract theories were reviewed, including the thought of Ayatollah Mahdi Ha'iri Yazdi (d. 1999). Kadivar's thought is close to Ha'iri's, especially in regard to the rejection of Khomeini's thought, and to Soroush's in reference to the need to end the ideologization of religion by the state and the replacement of this exploitation by a search for spiritual authenticity. As one observer of Kadivar has put it, "rather than remaking society on the basis of religion, [Kadivar and Soroush] ... typically strive to renovate and reconstruct religion ... in response to certain newly found challenges and exigencies."[67]

Kadivar summarizes nine different theories of the state in Shi'ism: (1) monarchy legitimated by the *shari'a* (*saltanat-i marshu'ah*); (2) the general appointed *wilaya* of the jurists (*vilayat- intisabi-yi 'ammah-yi faqihan*); (3) the general appointed *wilaya* of the council of the highest ranking jurists (*vilayat-i intisabi-yi 'ammah-yi shura-yi maraji'-yi taqlid*); (4) the absolute appointed *wilaya* of the jurists (*vilayat-i intisabi-yi mutlaqah-yi faqihan*); (5) constitutional state with the oversight of the jurists (*dawlat-i mashrutah ba idhn va nizarat-i faqihan*); (6) rule of the people, with the oversight of the highest ranking jurists (khilafat-i mardum ba nizarat-i marja'iyyat); (7) the restricted elected wilaya of the jurist (vilayat-i intikhabi-yi muqayyidah-yi faqih); (8) the elected Islamic state (dawlat-i intikhabi-yi islami); (9) the vicegerency of the joint private property owners (vikalat-i malikan-i shakhsi-yi musha').

Although he did not specifically align himself with any of these models at the time he was writing about them, and because afterward his interests led him beyond such models, it is not easy to identify him with any of these. But since we know that he has sought to move away from the ideologization of religion and toward a spiritual Shi'ism, it seems warranted to suggest that he would endorse any of them that permitted this transition. Two of these (1 and 5) endorse monarchy, which rules them out, given Kadivar's opposition to monarchy. Number 2 is also excluded from his preferences since it permits the clergy to exercise wilaya beyond the limited scope of community morals; 3 and 4 are variations of Khomeinism, which are unacceptable to Kadivar. Number 6 comes closer to Kadivar's preferences, since, according to this model, wilaya is vested in the people, who are masters of their own future. At the same time, the top jurists exercise some oversight, which is troubling to him in view of his criticism of how the jurists have misused their power in the Islamic Republic of Iran. The seventh model is too close for comfort to the fifth and features the role of the top jurist. Kadivar's unwillingness to allow a single person to be the source of authority puts this model out of bounds. The ninth model is too eccentric and does not appear to represent Kadivar's thinking. It is the eighth model – the elected Islamic state – that represents Kadivar's position best, because it rejects the concept that the jurists are entitled to wield the substantive authority of the Imams and because it views freedom as the "sacred right" of every individual as a result of God's endowing him with such an attribute. It also sees the only difference between clergymen and laymen as lying in the clergy's prerogative to issue opinions on religious matters, to enjoin moral behavior and to reprobate evil conduct.[68]

Conclusion

As mentioned at the start of this chapter, the sociology-of-knowledge perspective is well suited to treatments of the state in contemporary Middle Eastern political theories. The applicability of the perspective is independent of the particular theoretical or ideological perspectives adopted by the authors who take up the state in their writings, whether they be Islamist, corporatist, liberal or Marxist. Contact with the West, which brought the region wars, losses of territory, nationalist secessions, economic exploitation, and cultural imperialism, as well as concepts of constitutionalism and citizenship, was the key to the dynamic driving the diverse interpretations of the role of the state in these theories.

Historically, Middle Eastern states were dominated by personalities rather than by the institutionalization of offices and jurisdictions. In contemporary Sunni writings on the state, Islamist perspectives have been advanced by Abu al-A'la Mawdudi and Sayyid Qutb, who believe that existing states are anti-Islamic because they have rejected the sovereignty of God and arrogated such sovereignty to themselves – despite claiming that it is the people who are sovereign. The solution is the restoration of the caliphate, albeit purified of the corruption that had come to be attached to that office over the centuries. Shi'i Islamist writings, such as those of Khomeini, agree that contemporary Middle Eastern states are apostate, but their solution is not the restoration of the despised caliphate that persecuted the Shi'a for all those centuries; instead, it is emulation of the practice of the Islamic Republic of Iran.

The Sunni views of the state themselves are not monolithic. They range from rejection of the caliphate as a necessary model of state formation, leaving it open to Muslims to devise any model that they believe is best suited to advance their interests, to the conservative hope for the restoration of the caliphate, but mediating its restoration by at least rhetorical claims of allegiance also to democracy, an institution asserted to have been anticipated by the classic model of the caliphate. As this chapter has shown, these claims do not emerge through a systematic, immanent critique of earlier theories of the state but as *ex post facto* assertions, which are made on account of the undeniable attractiveness of democratic values for the Muslim masses – however, they may actually conceptualize democracy. The conservative Sunni views of the state tend to point to such features in the early caliphate as the oath of allegiance that leading members of the community would swear to the ruler as evidence of Islam's penchant for democracy. But such oaths of allegiance, rather than legitimating the rule of the caliphs on the part of the people, in fact seemed to suggest the acquiescence by elites to the ruler, who appropriated his own investiture by means of force. Moreover, such conservative theories of the state by scholars such as Muhammad 'Imara or Muhammad Salim al-'Awwa, even though motivated in their articulation by political theories from outside the Middle East region, are thoroughly ahistorical because of their total disregard of the empirical record of Muslim states from the early Islamic period to the twentieth and twenty-first centuries.

By contrast to Islamist and conservative Sunni theories are theories evolved by scholars such as Muhammad Shuhrur, Nazih Ayubi, and Muhsin Kadivar. Though these theories differ from one another in important respects, they have in common the interest in showing how states evolve in response to interactions with their environment. Shuhrur does this by suggesting that the Middle Eastern state is at its most resilient in advancing the interests of its people by understanding God to be laying down limits, rather than categorical commandments. Ayubi shows that contemporary Arab states are essentially fierce, rather than strong, because they have tried to weld together a tribal and a sultanistic mode of production, a combination that has reduced the people to cynicism and passivity. Kadivar, a strong critic of Khomeini's theory of the mandate of the jurist, notes that Shi'ism in fact has produced as many as nine different models of state and is not particularly happy with any of them because of their elitist foundations.

SEVEN

Conclusions

My purpose in this book has been to examine the nature of the intellectual debates in contemporary Middle Eastern political theories about such issues as the nature of society, the role of the individual, and the conceptualization of the state. At the same time, I have also sought to critique aspects of these theories, in the hope of contributing to the dialogue that their authors deserve in writing them in the first place. Although this book is not meant to be a sustained engagement with the secondary literature on Middle Eastern political theories, it hopes to add to that literature through a sociology-of-knowledge approach, acknowledging the merits of comparative political theory, and of an insistence on theories that historicize explanations of politics.

If politics involve cooperation and contention to promote interests in public arenas, political theory is the study of what human beings think are the key issues of those politics and their efforts to solve the central questions germane to those issues. Major concepts of political theory, accordingly, include – but are not limited to – justice, authority, responsibility, obedience and freedom and how these values are related to the people's well-being, the common good, happiness, and a virtuous life.

I have emphasized that Middle Eastern political theories across most historical eras since the rise of Islam have been impacted by political theories from abroad. The interactions between autochthonous Middle Eastern political theories and political theories from other regions bring us into the realm of comparative political theory, a subfield of political theory that stresses that explanations of how politics work in one global region might be quite specific but maintains as well that immanent critiques of those explanations often bring to light general concepts and general theories that can provide persuasive alternatives to those same explanations. Theory, being by its nature comparative, its practitioners in various global settings may be able to enlighten one another, as Dallmyr put it, through "mutual interrogation, contestation, and engagement" across cultures.

At the same time, one must not overdo the specificity of global political theories for their regions. Theories involve questions, the analytical processes involved in trying to answer those questions, and the responses that are outcomes from those processes. Put this way, many questions that seem relevant for Middle Eastern political theories are also relevant for the political theories of other world regions. For example, all societies are faced with what forms of rule and representation of interests are best suited to achieve the maximum benefit for the people as a whole. They may or may not invoke "traditional" modes of answering this question. However, an immanent critique could reveal that those traditional modes can only go so far and not provide the logically and empirically most persuasive answers to it.

Returning to the question of what is particularly Middle Eastern about Middle Eastern political theories, the only logical reply is that these theories relate to such generic building blocks of political theory as justice, equality, freedom, reason, obligation, representation, and the like, as these are relevant for people living in the Middle East region. Middle Easterners have established frameworks for an understanding of how these concepts "played out" from either an outlook deeply embedded in religious perspectives or a non-religious perspective.

Whether Middle Eastern political theories are more the product of insular efforts or more influenced by external factors, they have emerged as a result of the actual realities through which Middle Easterners themselves have passed. According to the sociology-of-knowledge approach, concrete social conditions lead people to think the way they do about politics. This does not mean that ideas are always epiphenomenal, and material conditions always causally generate our theories about the world. For this approach also considers how knowledge, once produced, is utilized by individuals and groups to shape outcomes in their social structures, dynamics, institutions, organizations, and movements.

In Chapter 1, I brought out these themes, and I also reviewed the classic, medieval, and modern eras in terms of the mutual impact of historical trends upon theorizing and of ideas upon historical developments. In each of these periods – early Islam, Umayyad Kingship, 'Abbasid imperial rule, the late Ottoman period, and the twentieth-century Middle East, Muslims argued about how to proceed. Many differences separated them, but for all of their differences, their outlooks arose in response to concrete historical circumstances that were themselves in part a product of the ideal interests of the actors in those eras.

Chapter 2 focused upon the sacred and the secular in Muslim political thought in the period from about 800 to 1400, with an emphasis on the Sunni and Shi'i juristic theories of authority, the work of the Muslim philosophers, and the thought of ibn Khaldun. When al-Mawardi began to write on the constitutional theory of the state, the 'Abbasid caliphate was in serious trouble. A Shi'ite dynasty, the Buyids (ruled 945–1055) held power, although it permitted the caliphate to remain in Sunni hands. Such circumstances moved al-Mawardi to uphold an accommodationist theory – that is, one that maintained the necessity to accept the realities of power politics as the only way to preserve caliphal rule. By the fourteenth century, the noble principles upon which the caliphate was believed to have rested had become reduced to the crude doctrine of "might makes right." For the constitutional theorists to insist otherwise would have been to jeopardize the viability of the *umma*, which was under major threat of extinction, and that in turn would have put into question the chances of the believers to find redemption. Historical conditions were adverse enough to force the theorists to accept the "doctrine of necessity." Ibn Taymiyya, however, came to believe that these developments were so obnoxious that he dismissed the need for the caliphate. Yet it is far from clear what he had in mind as a substitute, since matters of rule have an immediacy that requires addressing. It seems his solution was some kind of concrescent force immanent in the religious community that would deal with the requirements of leadership and authority in ways that remained unarticulated in his works.

Adverse historical circumstances also beset the Shi'a. So bad did this situation become that they were counseled by their leaders to disguise their beliefs by engaging in pious dissimulation (*taqiya*).

Sunni constitutional ideals, despite being undermined by actual historical events, remained as points of reference upon which later political systems could draw. Thus the Ottomans interpreted the earlier writings of the Sunni jurists in a manner befitting their own grasp of state interests. The Iranian Safavids, in establishing Shi'ism as the state religion in the sixteenth century, harked back in their practice to earlier ideas about the Imams, and how the absence from the scene by the Hidden Imam legitimated their own rule as his deputies. It thus seems that juristic theories of authority generated in an earlier time, which had themselves been devised by actors constrained by the force of events, do not vanish from history but in fact become important forces that significantly shape this history's evolution.

Chapter 2 also analyzed the contributions of Muslim philosophers, including al-Farabi and ibn Rushd. Though they were interested in politics as an autonomous sphere of study, their intent was not to generate a secular theory. Instead, their ideas were shaped especially by Plato, the Neoplatonists and Aristotle, and they tried to reconcile revealed and philosophical truth. They too lived in periods of upheaval and could not have been oblivious to the rapid flow of events, as symptomized by the "amirate by seizure." Al-Farabi's thought thus combined the upholding of religious faith with commitment to philosophical ethics to produce the ideal type of the "virtuous city." Ibn Rushd, who witnessed less turmoil in his lifetime, felt that an integration of religious and non-religious knowledge was not only possible but necessary. Such a fusion would be a requisite for the ability of the human being to live a life of political virtue. To him, the intent of both religious and philosophical thought was the same: to establish the truth. But his attack on al-Ghazali's critique of philosophy and philosophers portended a break with the traditional skepticism among the 'ulama' concerning these. And, as we know, ibn Rushd's vindication of Plato and Aristotle was far from abstract. His writings on their thought were to a large extent commentaries on the state of the history and politics of his own time and place.

Chapter 2 also turned attention to Islam's outstanding social thinker, ibn Khaldun. He had less concern with the ideal typification of politics, his preference being rather for showing their dynamics: social solidarity, the circulation of elites, the rise and fall of civilizations. Ibn Khaldun was not a secularist but rather a realist whose attention was drawn to social structures, economic trends, political patterns. Recognizing that the idealized caliphate of the constitutional jurists had for centuries become perverted into kingship, he tried to explain this historical development through empirical inquiry, with particular attention to politics as an arena of change, struggle, and power.

As was the case with others (al-Farabi and ibn Rushd, to take only two examples), ibn Khaldun personally experienced disgrace and the falling out of favor. Accordingly, his model of the "power state," as Rosenthal has called it, was influenced by the environmental circumstances of his times. It would be wrong, however, to limit the influence upon his thought to what befell him only. The concrete historical conditions through which his part of the Muslim world was passing were central in the shaping of his ideas. It is true that the further impact of those ideas on historical developments are less clear, since his pioneering theories suffered oblivion for centuries until they were invoked by generations of writers in the twentieth century.

Chapter 3 concentrated on the need to problematize Middle Eastern political theories by stressing the theme of historicization. A chief characteristic of these theories over the centuries is their ahistorical nature, with perhaps the exception of expatriate scholars. Even scholars who show sensitivity to this shortcoming by wondering "why has history been absent," as Hasan Hanafi put it, do not seem to go beyond recognizing it as a problem. The response to this weakness in theorizing about politics, one must iterate, is that if the sociology-of-knowledge approach is valid, then historicization in analysis is the *sine qua non* of adequate explanation.

Innovative expatriates like 'Abd al-Ilah Balqaziz, Burhan Ghalyun, and Mohamed Arkoun have invited Middle Eastern theorists to break with ahistorical theorizing, but their efforts appear to have fallen on deaf ears. Sunni writers Hasan Hanafi and Muhammad 'Imara, probably responding to expatriate influence, have directed our attention to this issue, but did not follow through. Hanafi preferred to compartmentalize his call for historicization and kept it separate from his own basically ahistorical framework. As for 'Imara, his one statement about history's importance for analysis was overshadowed by his commitment to the Islamization of knowledge, an approach full of hypostatization traps.

Among Shi'i writers, Khomeini's demands that Muslims follow religious mandates totally ignore the historical record. 'Ali Shari'ati tantalizingly wrote of the relevance of historical dialectics, but he shied away from the bolder analysis that a commitment to the dialectics of history requires. The work of Abdol Karim Soroush, far more grounded in the disciplines of philosophical and social theory, probably holds greater promise for historicization. An integration of his explanations with some of the more programmatic writings of reformist non-'ulama' pietists could lead to breakthroughs in this area.

In Chapter 4, my attention shifted to the role of the individual. Middle Eastern political theories across all historical periods since the rise of Islam accord more attention to the rights of society than they do to the rights of the individual. One effect of British and French imperialism in the Middle East in the nineteenth and twentieth centuries was the spread of liberal thought. Some Middle Eastern thinkers were attracted to liberalism's preoccupation with individual rights, but collectivist theories dominated. After achieving independence most regimes further reinforced this tendency toward communitarianism by adopting socialist theories. Since the late 1980s, these regimes have moved away from socialism under the influence of "structural adjustment" policies mandated by the World Bank and the IMF, but by and large intellectuals in the Middle East have retained their skepticism about liberalism.

Still, liberalism's pull has apparently been so strong that writers feel they must at least address its central ideas. Cast in an apologic vein, such writings maintain that the Islamic heritage upholds individual rights. They do this not by critical inquiry but by the citation of scripture. More nuanced presentations, such as that of 'Abd al-Hamid Mursi, end by dismissing liberalism's individualist focus, stating that "Islam is displeased with it." For Mursi, as soon as one professes belief in God, one must yield to community interests. This position may be logically established, of course, but this cannot be done without an immanent critique of both individualism and communitarianism, which neither Mursi nor any other thinker appears ready to undertake.

Populist writer Muhammad 'Imara is among the most well known of Islamist intellectuals theorizing about politics. Though some regard him as an "Islamic liberal," one must wonder to what degree this is the case. According to him, recognition of individual rights risks defiance of God's sovereignty. Because the West worships the intellect, he writes, recognizing the primacy of such rights may be acceptable for them. Note that he does not conceive that many Westerners would not recognize this characterization of liberalism and the intellect. He admits he has called Islam a liberal religion, but he never analytically examines this characterization, contenting himself instead with the bland generalization that a liberalism deriving from non-religious sources – as in the United Kingdom – is inferior by far to one that derives from religious sources. But 'Imara seems totally heedless of the role of religion in the thinking of some of the most important theorists of liberalism in the West, such as Locke and Rousseau.

'Imara is not alone among Muslim thinkers in his simplistic characterization of liberalism as a body of thought resting on an edifice of selfishness, greed, hostility to the rights of others, and the like. Now, liberalism may be guilty of these unsavory values, but it is wrong to dismiss it in the manner of reifications that underscore the qualities above. The reason is that reification obviously disguises variation. As noted in Chapter 4, there is much ferment in the field over whether "justice as fairness" (Rawls) or utilitarianism (Gauthier) is the most advantageous version of liberal thought. Regrettably, however, such discussions seem beyond the purview of liberalism's Islamist critics. They seem content to allege that Islam is a revealed religion that is also liberal. Because it is a revealed religion, the individual must grant sovereignty to God, even though we are free to act. 'Imara and his allies, such as al-'Awwa, have forced us into a vicious circle. God's religion grants us the freedom to act. Our freedom to act opens the door to a life of prosperity and the pursuit of happiness. How do we know this? Because the freedom that we have is circumscribed by God's scripting our actions for us.

However, let us also recall colonialism's association with liberal pluralist thought. The colonialists cynically prevented the colonized Muslims from applying the lessons of liberal thought – a fact that greatly undermined its value and appeal in their minds. Macpherson's characterization of a rampant individualism is relevant in this context, as we saw in Chapter 4.

The approach to human nature by Islam and liberalism may assist in clarifying the relationship between individual and group rights. God invites human beings to accept Islam, in part as a means to return them to their own good natures. Liberalism stresses freedom as the natural condition of the human being. Perhaps these two positions are not ultimately compatible, although the Syrian thinker Muhammad Shuhrur seems to feel that viewing God as advising human beings to make choices rather than passively obeying commands may be an opening toward resolution of the problem.

The question is whether Shuhrur's theory of limits, and similar notions on the part of Abdol Karim Soroush, can reconcile Middle Eastern political theories with aspects of liberal individualism. They suggest that historical conditions shape the way we think – and so the way we conceptualize matters of politics. We are, therefore, again made aware that our reality counts for a great deal in regard to what we think about the major problems of the human being, society, and social transformation.

Chapter 5 took up the concept of society in Middle Eastern political theories. These theories over historical time have privileged the rights of the group over those of the individual. Only in the nineteenth century did Middle East thinkers begin to consider an alternative perspective.

In Western social contract theory, autonomous human beings join society because the state of nature is not fulfilling, at best, and dangerous, at worst. The main dynamic of this movement from the state of nature into society was not religious. The contract in Muslim social theory – at least before the nineteenth century – was different, devised and offered by God. If the contract was accepted, believers could look forward to a life fulfilled. But in accepting, they would not be able to reappropriate any "rights" in the event of dissatisfaction, because they did not have any. The rights are God's. Revealed law and natural law compete on this terrain, because natural law rests on the principle of the autonomous human being, an embodiment of reason and hence entitled to certain rights. Divine law, even under the most liberal interpretation, will not envision the human being's welfare, prosperity, and access to the good life without obedience in the first instance to God's commands. Such commands may not be self-evident, which could necessitate intermediaries – guardians of the law – who would offer their services to tell believers what they are. But *quis custodiet ipsos custodes?*

Chapter 5 closely examined two Sunni modernist theorists of social contract, Muhammad Khalaf Allah and Tariq al-Bishri, against the backdrop of late-nineteenth- and early-twentieth-century reformist/modernist Islam, known as the *salafiyya* movement. The members of this movement were interested in contractarian thought, so Khalaf Allah's and Bishri's "modernism" should not be surprising. They do take different perspectives, though both ultimately uphold the rights of the nation. In doing so, though, they see no conflict with upholding those of individuals, Khalaf Allah more explicitly and Bishri more implicitly.

Shi'ism, as classically understood, cannot easily reconcile individualism and collectivism. Its discursive narrative places sovereignty in God's hands and in the hands of the Prophet and those of the Imams. In medieval Shi'ism the clergy claimed to be the deputies of the Hidden Imam, and in the twentieth century, Khomeini claimed the right of jurists to rule (heretofore considered an infringement on the authority of the Imams, who alone were entitled to do so). Ha'iri, by contrast, separates religion from politics, viewing the latter as a purely practical realm requiring therefore the operation only of practical reason. Such reason has, in his view, nothing to do with God's revelation. Each, though for different reasons, rejects contractarian thought.

This chapter bears out the thesis that historical circumstances critically influence modes of thought. Khalaf Allah and Bishri were closely associated with the politics of Nasserism and therefore with that system's emphasis upon socialism. Khomeini before the mid-

1940s used to advocate that secular rulers were entitled to rule if they consulted the clergy. But he changed his views in 1970 in the light of dramatic changes brought about in Iran in the period after 1953. In Ha'iri's case, the picture is less clear, but no doubt Khomeini's radical innovation of the doctrine known as the mandate of the jurist, and his further radicalization of it shortly before his death into the absolute mandate of the jurist, deeply offended Ha'iri. It likely shaped his thinking on the relationship between religion and politics that he already had concluded was next to nonexistent.

The final substantive chapter of this book examined Middle Eastern political theories of the state. Whether writers on the state are non-Islamist Muslims, Islamists, or influenced by any of the Western bodies of thought, such as Marxism, liberalism, or corporatism, the thesis that historical contingencies have a way of influencing social theories is vindicated here. It could hardly be different, given the momentous changes the Middle East region has witnessed since the French Revolution – changes brought about by wars and loss of territory, occupation, ethnic and sectarian conflicts, nationalist secessions, economic exploitation, and attacks upon Islamic traditions and the cultural heritage of the Muslims as "backward" and even worse.

States in the Middle East have historically been organized as patrimonial polities, rather than political systems embedded in differentiated institutional structures and operating on the basis of abstract, impersonal rules and regulations. As such, they were dominated by personalities. Twentieth-century Sunni writers such as Abu al-A'la Mawdudi and Sayyid Qutb adopted Islamist positions. This led them to reject as un-Islamic, indeed as apostate, contemporary "Muslim" states because in their opinion they have not really applied Islamic law, and, moreover, their rulers have appropriated sovereign power, which is God's alone. If the caliphate – in its "original and pristine" form – were restored, this would solve the problem, as they saw it. Shi'i Islamist theorists agree that contemporary states in the region are apostate, but the answer is

CONCLUSIONS 245

not the restoration of the caliphate, since it persecuted the Shi'a throughout the Islamic period. Instead, the solution lies in imitating the model established by the Islamic Republic of Iran.

Sunni theories of the caliphate vary significantly. A very few reject the caliphate altogether. Among these are 'Ali 'Abd al-Raziq and, perhaps surprisingly to many, the medieval thinker ibn Taymiyya. In their view (especially more recent writers) Muslims can devise any model of state they want. Others ardently look to the recovery of the caliphate. They materialize "democracy" out of the oath of allegiance sworn to the Prophet and the first four caliphs by community leaders. However, it is obvious that this practice cannot be conflated with democracy, since a handful of community notables affirming their loyalty to a leader is not the same as mass participation in the expression of one's beliefs about power and representation of interests.

Contrast these views with those of theorists such as Muhammad Shuhrur, Nazih Ayubi, and Muhsin Kadivar, all of whom began contributing their perspectives at the start of the 1990s. Of course, their theories differ in regard to methodology, the social basis of politics and the state, and the consequences of social stratification and legal stipulations for state formation, consolidation, and practice. They concern themselves with historical contingency. For Shuhrur, a state founded on a cultural ethos that understands God's role to be to lay down limits and thresholds rather than mandate categorical behavior is likely to be flexible and responsive to major social transformations. Ayubi sees the resilience of the state in an altered mode of production, moving away from what he called a "tributary mode" to one that captures Gramsci's notion of a "people's state." Kadivar, who is less explicitly interested in social theories of the state per se (as opposed to Shi'i theories), advocates further inquiry and research, as almost all of the nine models he examines are rooted in reprehensible authoritarianism.

Contemporary Middle Eastern political theories cannot be easily summarized. Perhaps the major generalization that emerges has to do with a dialectic of discourses. Those writers whom one might consider advocates of "traditional" ends (such as salvation through belief in the unity of God and the Prophecy of Muhammad and the need to construct the political system after the example of the Prophet's own polity model) nevertheless are drawn to use modern concepts to vindicate those ends: for example, the public interest, or social justice, or political pluralism, or democracy. On the other hand, those writers whom one might deem supporters of "non-traditional" or "modern" ends (such as political pluralism, a classless society, or democracy) feel compelled to utilize historical concepts from the heritage of Islam: for example, "commanding the good and prohibiting evil," or hisba, or shura. Advocates of the former appeal for the Islamization of knowledge, while adherents of the latter support conceptual generalization based on universalism of analytical constructs. Among many examples that might be given are the differences between Muhammad 'Imara, Muhammad Salim al-'Awwa, and Ayatollah Khomeini, on the one hand, and Fu'ad Zakariya, Muhammad Shuhrur, and Abdol Karim Soroush, on the other.

The fact of this dialectic holds at least a theoretical promise for conceptual breakthroughs in the articulation of these contemporary political theories in the Middle East. But the reality, despite some preliminary achievements,[1] suggests that such breakthroughs are rather far in the future.

Contemporary Islamists, who are pressing for the full and immediate implementation of Islamic law in all areas of life, seem to ignore the empirical record established by those polities whose leaders believe they have been doing precisely that: for example, Iran under Khomeini and his successors, or Afghanistan under the Taliban. Instead, they have in mind an idealized model which they believe to have existed in the early Islamic period. But, as Zakariya suggests, it is always going to be human beings who apply the shari'a (or fail to apply it, for that matter). That being the case, simply calling for the implementation of the shari'a cannot protect the umma from the evils of an invalid application.[2]

Ultimately, Islamist theorists of politics have been so taken with the compelling nature of the sacred texts of Islam that this has led them to "the total neglect of history" and "shutting their eyes to the lessons provided by actual reality."

> These Islamic movements describe for us a picture of Islamic history that derives solely from the religious texts. For example, if they speak about Islam's position on social justice, their statements are full of verses and *hadiths* of the Prophet that call for such justice ... and they stop at that. They consider that with that, they have confirmed ... that Islam calls for social justice, and that this justice is materialized in Islam better than in any other system. But is pointing to texts alone sufficient to confirm this matter? ... the principal error into which fall those calling for the implementation of the *shari'a* ... is when they make the texts alone a basis for judging ... Islam's position on the major problems faced by the human being [today], ignoring what in fact has happened historically.[3]

One might press the point with the Islamists that they must pay attention to what has actually happened over the centuries under the aegis of these lofty principles that the scriptures have enunciated. But the Islamists will likely state their belief (as we saw with Muhammad 'Awwa in chapters 5 and 6) that iniquitous rule and failure to abide by the noble principles of the revelation and the Prophet's Sunna amount to abusive behavior and do not nullify the essence of Islam. Yet, does this not create great doubt in one's mind about the ability of this essence of Islam to influence the Muslims, if their conduct has been to isolate themselves and deviate from that essence for all these centuries?[4] If the principles are so noble (which they are), then why has their implementation been so elusive over all these historical epochs? It cannot be that the Arabs and the Muslims are, by nature, incapable of following noble principles.

However, these arguments appear to fall on deaf ears. Muhammad 'Imara, who by 1995 had moved away from his earlier sympathetic understandings of some aspects of Marxism, and then from his sympathetic understandings of some aspects of liberalism, to embrace positions identified with the movement called the "Islamization of knowledge," has this to say: the East prevailed in earliest times; then the Greeks and Romans took the initiative from the East on behalf of the West. However, then the Muslims prevailed. Yet, eventually, the Muslims fell into their long slumber, and the star of the West waxed for centuries. Nevertheless, the West became exploitative and authoritarian, and this is the current pass into which the world has fallen. Under such circumstances, there is nothing for it but "for the hand of the East to raise Allah's standard." Then he adds: this is no empty wish. "Rather, this is the true rule of history," which he validates by reference to Qur'an 5:54. Note what is going on here. 'Imara sees in a passage from the Qur'an a "rule of history."[5] This is from the pen of the same author who in 1981 wrote a collection of essays entitled *Islam and Historical Consciousness*.

On the other hand, the secularists (who, it bears stressing, are not anti-religious) have not worked out accommodations between Mu'tazilite rationalism and Ash'arite occasionalism. Such an accommodation needs to be achieved because the directly political issues – for example, social justice, public interest, and democratization – derive from ontological and epistemological foundations. Soroush, who warmly endorses Mu'tazilism, nonetheless criticizes rationalistic overdeterminism.

> Of course, I disagree with the Mu'tazilites on some issues. I find the Ash'arites experience-oriented or empirical, whereas I find the Mu'tazilites more Aristotelian. Of course, I'm not an empiricist in the sense that I think that human knowledge can be summed up in experience, but I'm very empirical in the sense that I'm not prepared to sacrifice science on the altar of First Philosophy [i.e. *a priori* deduction]. I think that the Ash'arites are stronger than the Mu'tazilites when it comes to empiricism. For example on ... the question of whether an act is good or bad, the rationality of good and bad acts doesn't mean that we derive everything from evident, *a priori* rationality; basing things on experience is rational too. This is a mistake that some writers make.[6]

It may be that Ash'arism and Mu'tazilism are not reconcilable. But dialogue among their respective adherents has not seriously begun. Studies based on the historicization of change will not succeed without such reconciliation, because Ash'arite ontological assumptions are hostile to historically grounded analysis. The reason for historicity is clear. Ahistorical arguments become apologias and essentially involve tautologies because at bottom they rest upon the effort to explain a variable with a constant, whereas a variable can only be explained by another variable. If the sociology-of-knowledge approach is correct, and ideas do emanate from the concrete experiences of human beings as this volume has been arguing, then ahistoricity is all the more problematical. And assuredly more is required than rhetorical appeals for historicization, which is not to underestimate the magnitude of the job ahead. At any rate, it is surely worth the effort, since without it all kinds of problems arise, from straw-man arguments to unconvincing assertions that history does not matter.

Notes

ONE

1. Sheldon Wolin, "Political Theory: Trends and Goals," *International Encyclopedia of the Social Sciences*, Vol. XII (New York: Macmillan and The Free Press, 1968), p. 318.
2. Sheldon Wolin, "Political Theory as a Vocation," *American Political Science Review* 63:4 (December 1969), p. 1076. He continues as follows: "Perforce, a political theory is, among many other things, a sum of judgments, shaped by the theorist's notion of what matters, and embodying a series of discriminations about where one province begins and another leaves off. The discriminations may have to do with what is private and what is public, or they may be about what will be endangered or encouraged if affairs move one way rather then another, or about what practices, occurrences, and conditions are likely to produce what states of affairs. The difficulty is the same regardless of whether the theoretical intention is to provide a descriptive explanation, a critical appraisal, or a prescriptive solution. By virtue of their location in a whole, one province shades off from and merges into others: where, for example, does the cure of souls end and the authority of the political order over religion begin? Where do the effects of technical education merge into questions about ethics and character? Where does the autonomy of administrative and judicial practices start and the 'mysteries of state' stop? How much of the impetus for the Crusades is to be assigned to religious motives and how much to political or economic considerations?"
3. Fred Dallmayr, "Introduction: Toward a Comparative Political Theory," *The Review of Politics* 59:3 (Summer 1997), p. 421.
4. Ibid., p. 422.
5. W. Montgomery Watt says that Twelver Shi'ism "took definite shape" between 874 and 920. "The Significance of the Early Stages of Imami Shi'ism," in

Religion and Politics in Iran: From Quietism to Revolution, ed. Nikki R. Keddie (New Haven: Yale University Press, 1983), p. 21.
6. Ira Lapidus, *A History of Islamic Societies* (New York: Cambridge University Press, 2002), pp. 99–100.
7. Islam arose in Western Arabia in the early seventh century, when the Prophet, Muhammad, first began to receive revelations in the year 610. The story of its development as a civilization cannot be summarized here, although much of this story is synoptically told later on in this book. The Middle East has been defined in various ways by different sources. For the purposes of this volume, when contemporary Middle Eastern political theories are discussed, the Middle East region is that area lying between and including Morocco in the West to Afghanistan in the East and Turkey in the North and the Sudan in the South. Islamic civilization is not congruent with the Middle East, since this civilization eventually spread as far East as Indonesia and to the south of the Sahara to countries such as Senegal, Cameroon, Nigeria, not to mention enclaves in Europe, North, Central and Latin America. At the time of the rise of Islam in Western Arabia, the central area of the Middle East was dominated by the Persian, Byzantine, and Ethiopian Empires and tribal systems in the areas lying between those empires.
8. That is, classical, medieval, early modern, modern and post-modern writers in the Islamic period, from the seventh century AD until today.
9. Marshall Hodgson, *The Venture of Islam: Conscience and History in a World Civilization*, 3 vols (Chicago: University of Chicago Press, 1974); Ira Lapidus, *A History of Islamic Societies*, 2nd edn (New York: Cambridge University Press, 2002).
10. Alfred Guillaume, *Islam* (London: Penguin Books, 1955). It would be wrong, however, to say Guillaume explains Islam's rise as a function of only the Prophet's personality.
11. W. Montgomery Watt, *Muhammad: Prophet and Statesman* (London: Oxford University Press, 1961).
12. Patricia Crone and Michael Cook, *Hagarism: The Making of the Islamic World* (New York: Cambridge University Press, 1977).
13. Patricia Crone, *God's Rule* (New York: Columbia University Press, 2004), p. 4.
14. H.A.R. Gibb, "The Evolution of Government in Early Islam," *Studia Islamica* 4 (1954), pp. 5–17, at p. 5.
15. Ibid.
16. Ira Lapidus, "The Golden Age: The Political Concepts of Islam," *Annals of the American Academy of Political and Social Science* 524 (November 1992), pp. 13–25, at p. 15.
17. The Hadith pertains to advice that Muslim cultivators sought from the Prophet as to how better to grow their date palm trees. Although reluctant to give it, the Prophet nevertheless provided it when pressed to do so. But instead of improving the yield, the Prophet's advice led to the trees dying. He thereupon said: "In matters of religion, come to me, but in matters pertaining to your world, you know better about them than I do" (*wa in kana min umur dinikum, fa ilayya; amma umur dunyakum, fa antum a'lam minni*). See the canonical works

of Hadith by Muslim, *Fada'il*, Hadith number 141, Ibn Maja, *Ruhun*, ch. 15; Ahmad ibn Hanbal, *al-Musnad*, Vol. III, p. 153; Vol. V, pp. 16, 398; Vol. VI, pp. 123, 128.

18. Lapidus, "Golden Age," p. 16.
19. It is, however, an oversimplification to allege that the supporters of the 'Abbasids were Iranians, as the claims advanced on behalf of the 'Abbasids enjoyed support among certain Arabs, most notably among those of Yemeni provenance.
20. Khalid Y. Blankinship, *The End of the Jihad State: The Reign of Hisham 'Abd al-Malik and the Collapse of the Umayyads* (Albany: State University of New York Press, 1994).
21. Guenther Roth, "Personal Rulership, Patrimonialism and Empire-Building in the New States," *World Politics* 20:2 (January 1968), pp. 194–206, at p. 195.
22. Bernard Lewis, "'Abbasids," *Encyclopaedia of Islam*, 2nd edn, vol. 1 (Leiden: E.J. Brill, 1960), p. 115
23. Lapidus, "Golden Age," p. 15.
24. For example, ibn Taymiyya lived in Syria at the time when that territory was governed from Cairo by the Mamluks. He was incarcerated several times in the citadel in Cairo for opposing ideas favored by the Mamluks. When the Mongols, who had overthrown the 'Abbasid caliphate at Baghdad in 1258, invaded Syria, he and his family fled from Harran, where he was born, to Damascus. Despite his disagreements with the Mamluks and his incarceration at their hands, he never called for their overthrow, since that might have caused anomie, which would have rendered it impossible for the Muslims of the area to carry out their religious obligations. However, when the Mongols began to violate some of the core principles of Islam, he could not refrain from publicly repudiating them, even if that meant a period of great instability.
25. Abu Yusuf Ishaq ibn Ya'qub al-Kindi, *On First Philosophy*, cited in "Al-Kindi," *Stanford Encyclopedia of Philosophy*, http://plato.stanford.edu/entries/al-kindi/. Incidentally, many centuries later, the leader of the Syrian Muslim Brotherhood, Yusuf al-Siba'i (d. 1959), was to say almost exactly the same thing regarding European socialism as a system of beliefs and practices from which the Muslims of the mid-twentieth century ought to learn.
26. Josef Van Ess, "Kadariyya," *Encyclopaedia of Islam*, 2nd edn, Vol. IV (Leiden: E.J. Brill, 1990).
27. The influence of Mu'tazili ideas remained strong well beyond the mid-ninth century, especially in the eastern provinces of the caliphate, where they were patronized by the Buyids (945–1055), and in Iran. And they remained closely tied to the theology of Shi'ism as a general rule. In the Sunni world, expressions of preference for Mu'tazilism became known in the twentieth century in the writing of non-theologians. Thus, in his work, *Duhat al-Islam*, 10th edn, Vol. III (Cairo: Matba'a al-Nahda al-Misriya, 2000), p. 207. Ahmad Amin lamented as a tragedy and even a crime the suppression of the Mu'tazila at the hands of the Ash'ari and Maturidi orthodoxy (this work was originally published in 1934–35). Later, the Egyptian philosopher Hasan Hanafi made

similar comments, and the Moroccan intellectual Muhammad 'Abid al-Jabiri has done the same.
28. Marshall G.S. Hodgson, *The Venture of Islam*, Vol. III: *The Gunpowder Empires and Modern Times* (Chicago: University of Chicago Press, 1974), pp. 25–7.
29. Ibid., p. 99.
30. Halil Inalcik, "Empire and Population," in *An Economic and Social History of the Ottoman Empire, 1300–1914*, ed. Halil Inalcik and Donald Quataert (Cambridge: Cambridge University Press, 1994), p. 11. Expounding further on this theme, he writes: "the general principle was adhered to that each individual should remain in his own status group, so that equilibrium in the state and society could be maintained. It seems that the Ottoman system found its logic in the fact that the state had been established through the efforts of a small professional military group... gathered around its military leader, Osman Ghazi. The dynasty preserved this central position as a keystone of the entire socio-political structure." Ibid., p. 17.
31. Hodgson, *Gunpowder Empires*, pp. 106–7.
32. Bernard Lewis, *The Political Language of Islam* (Chicago: University of Chicago Press, 1988), p. 27.
33. Serif Mardin, *The Genesis of Young Ottoman Thought* (Princeton: Princeton University Press, 1962), p. 8.
34. This is not to suggest that there were no differences among these jurists. For example, for al-Baghdadi and al-Mawardi, there was no doubting that the caliphate "conferred authority," whereas for al-Ghazali and ibn Jama'a the caliphate was seen as "legitimating rights acquired by force, provided that the holder of military power, by giving allegiance to the caliph, recognized the supremacy of the Sharia." H.A.R. Gibb, *Studies on the Civilization of Islam* (London: Routledge & Kegan Paul, 1962), p. 143.
35. Majid Khadduri, *War and Peace in the Law of Islam* (Baltimore: Johns Hopkins University Press, 1955), p. 16, as cited by Mardin, *The Genesis*, p. 83.
36. The concept of integral nationalism is associated with the ideas of Charles Maurras in France and Gottfried Treitschke in Germany. Peter Alter, in his study, has distinguished between "Rissorgiomento Nationalism," according to which a group such as the Greeks and Serbs seek to establish their state; and "Integral Nationalism," whereby the establishment of the state is the basis for further efforts to extend the boundaries of that state across a wider range of territory, often through militarism and chauvinism. On integral nationalism, see Carlton J.H. Hayes, *A Generation of Materialism* (New York: Harper, 1941); and Peter Arnold, *Nationalism* (London: Edward Arnold, 1994).
37. Fauzi Najjar, on the other hand, extends the crisis affecting Egyptian intellectuals back to the 1950s, when, as he puts it, they suffered a "crisis of confidence" in the relations between the intellectuals and the regime owing to the failure of the military to return to barracks after the July 1952 coup but instead continuing to interfere in the running of affairs. See his "State and University in Egypt in the Period of Socialist Transformation, 1961–1967," *The Review of Politics* 38:1 (January 1976), pp. 57–87, at p. 62. See also the series

published under the title *Azmat al-Muthaqqafin* (The Crisis of the Intellectuals) by the editor of *al-Ahram* in the 1960s.
38. Such charges have been made by university professors, such as 'Abd al-Sabur Shahin, who not only opposed the promotion of the secular-minded scholar of comparative literature at Cairo University, Nasr Hamid Abu Zayd, to professor but also instigated a court case against the latter that led to the decision by that body, upheld by a higher court, that Abu Zayd was an apostate and must therefore be forced to divorce his wife on grounds that a Muslim woman may not be married to an apostate.
39. Secularism is a contested concept. Without emptying it of all significance, it nevertheless seems important to point out that it means much more than separating religion from politics. It is a process of displacing religious factors from public life more generally, which Weber characterized as "the disenchantment of the world." Asad avers that "the notion that … experiences [of modernity] constitute 'disenchantment' – implying a direct access to reality, a stripping away of myth, magic, and the sacred – is a salient feature of the modern epoch." But, as Asad notes, secularism is also a process by which the contemporary state, in a self-justifying and triumphal manner, seeks to veil forms of community other than its own form. I take him to mean by this that not only states with a laic tradition, such as France, but even so-called "religious states," such as the Islamic Republic of Iran, are engaged in this process. The result is the production of citizens whose identities are molded by allegiance to the state's programs, even if that means that those programs (as happened in Iran in 1987–1988) call for the supervention of the state's interests over those of religion. I am referring to the famous *fatwa* (authoritative opinion) issued by Ayatollah Khomeini on the suspension of secondary principles of the faith (such as prayer, fasting, pilgrimage to Mecca, and rendering alms) should the state leadership determine that this was necessary to maintaining the state's integrity. It would be hard to find more direct evidence than this for the conception of *raison d'état*. See Talal Asad, *Formations of the Secular: Christianity, Islam, Modernity* (Stanford: Stanford University Press, 2003), pp. 13, 191. These points are made by Michael Lambek in his review of Asad's book in *American Anthropologist* 107:2 (June 2005), pp. 276–7.

TWO

1. Robert N. Bellah, "Civil Religion in America," *Daedalus* 96:1 (Winter 1967), pp. 1–21.
2. H.A.R. Gibb, "Al-Mawardi's Theory of the Caliphate," in *Studies in the Civilization of Islam*, ed. Stanford J. Shaw and William R, Polk (London: Routledge & Kegan Paul, 1962), pp. 162–4.
3. Cited by Ingrid Mattson, review of *Al-Ahkam al-Sultaniya: The Laws of Islamic Governance*, trans. Asadullah Yate, and of *The Ordinances of Government*, trans. Wafaa H. Wahba, *Journal of Law and Religion* 15:1/2 (2000–2001), pp. 399–403, at 401.

4. A.K.S. Lambton, "Khilafa: In Political Theory," *Encyclopedia of Islam*, 2nd edn, Vol. IV (Leiden: E.J. Brill, 1990), p. 949.
5. Malcolm Kerr, *Islamic Reform* (Berkeley: University of California Press, 1966).
6. Albert Hourani, *A History of the Arab Peoples* (London: Faber & Faber, 1991), p. 143.
7. E.I.J. Rosenthal, *Political Thought in Medieval Islam* (Cambridge: Cambridge University Press, 1958), p. 39.
8. Ibid., p. 24.
9. Gibb, "Some Considerations on the Sunni Theory of the Caliphate," in *Studies in the Civilization of Islam*, pp. 143–5.
10. Dominique Sourdel, "Khilafa: The History of the Institution," *Encyclopedia of Islam*, 2nd edn, Vol. IV, p. 939.
11. Rosenthal, *Political Thought*, p. 53.
12. H. Laoust, "Ibn Taymiyya," *Encyclopedia of Islam*, 2nd edn, Vol. III (Leiden: E.J. Brill, 1986), p. 954.
13. Rosenthal, *Political Thought*, p. 54.
14. Ibid., p. 115.
15. Charles E. Butterworth, "Political Islam: The Origins," *Annals of the American Academy of Political and Social Science* 524 (November 1992), p. 29.
16. Ibid., p. 32.
17. Rosenthal, *Political Thought*, p. 115.
18. Charles E. Butterworth, "Rhetoric and Islamic Political Philosophy," *International Journal of Middle East Studies* 3:2 (April 1972), p. 188.
19. Mohamed. Talbi, "Ibd Khaldun," *Encyclopedia of Islam*, 2nd edn, Vol. III, p. 828.
20. Ibid., p. 829.
21. Rosenthal, *Political Thought*, pp. 84 ff.

THREE

1. Robert A. Nisbet, "Introduction: The Problem of Social Change," in *Social Change*, ed. R.A. Nisbet (Oxford: Basil Blackwell, 1972), p. 1.
2. 'Abd al-Ilah Balqaziz, *Ishkaliyat al-Marji' fi al-Fikr al-'Arabi al-Mu'asir*. (Beirut: Dar al-Muntakhab al-'Arabi, 1992), pp. 10–11.
3. Basam Tibi, *The Challenge of Fundamentalism: Political Islam and the New World Disorder*. Berkeley: University of California Press, 1998), p. 161.
4. Muhammad Salim al-'Awwa, *Fi al-Nizam al-Dawla al-Islamiya*, 7th edn (Cairo: Dar al-Shuruq, 1989), pp. 133–4.
5. Abdallah Laroui, *La crise des intellectuels arabes: traditionalisme ou historicisme* (Paris: Maspero, 1974); English trans. *The Crisis of the Arab Intellectual: Traditionalism or Historicism* (Berkeley: University of California Press, 1976).
6. Laroui, *Crisis*, p. 84.
7. Ibid.
8. Ibid., p. 156.
9. Ibid., p. 157. Laroui's radical historicism, which is based on Marxism, is

not without its problems. For the moment, however, I am referring to him because he is among the first to emphasize the need for the historicization of social change in contemporary Arabo-Muslim thought.

10. Mohamed Arkoun (Muhammad Arkun), *al-Fikr al-Islami: Qira'a 'Ilmiya*, 2nd edn, trans. Hashim Salih (Casablanca and Beirut: Markaz al-Anma' al-Qawmi and al-Markaz al-Thaqafi al-'Arabi, 1996), p. 114. Although Arkoun writes in French, he personally has reviewed the translations into Arabic of his works, especially those by Hashim Salih.

11. Burhan Ghalyun, *Ightiyal al-'Aql: Mihna al-Thaqafa al-'Arabiya Bayna al-Salafiya wa al-Tab'iya*, 2nd edn (Cairo: Madbuli, 1990), pp. 157–61.

12. Nasr Hamid Abu Zayd, *Al-Nass, al-Sulta al-Haqiqa: al-Fikr al-Dini bayna Irada al-Ma'rifa wa Irada al-Haymana*, 3rd edn (Casablanca and Beirut: al-Markaz al-Thaqafi al-'Arabi, 1997), p. 12.

13. Fu'ad Zakariya, *al-Haqiqa wa al-Wahm fi al-Haraka al-Islamiya al-Mu'asira* (Cairo: Dar Qaba' li al-Taba'a wa al-Nashr, 1998), pp. 166–8.

14. Hasan Hanafi, "al-Liberaliya: Lam Tanjah fi Misr al-Ash'ariya," in *Hiwar al-Mashriq wa al-Maghrib*, ed. Jalul Faysal (Cairo: Madbuli, 1990), pp. 58–62.

15. As warrant for this, consider the following assertions by Hanafi in *Min al-'Aqida ila al-Thawra*, Vol. I (Cairo: Maktaba Madbuli, 1988): "The truth is that only individual consciousness and mass mobilization protect the contemporary human being and preserve the interests of the community. And those two things will come about only by an effective revolution ... led by a conscious vanguard of intellectuals, through which the individual's consciousness is transformed into the expression of the community's consciousness" (p. 9); "we believe in linking the tendencies [*janah*] of the nation. It is through such linkage that our [cultural] heritage can confront the major issues of our epoch, just as the progressive secularist (whether liberal, socialist, or nationalist) can achieve his goals by starting with the [cultural] heritage and spirit of his nation" (p. 39).

16. The first article was published as "Limadha Ghaba Mabhath al-Insan min Turathina al-Qadim?" in the journal, *al-Mustaqbal al-'Arabi* (Beirut), October 1979; reprinted in Hanafi, *Dirasat Islamiya* (Cairo: Maktaba Anglo-Misriya, 1981), pp. 393–415; and again in *Dirasat Islamiya* (Beirut: Dar al-Tanwir, 1982), pp. 299–315. And the second article was published as "Limadha Ghaba Mabhath al-Tarikh min Turathina al-Qadim," and was written originally for *Dirasat Islamiya* (Cairo: Maktaba Anglo-Misriya, 1981), pp. 416–56; and reprinted in *Dirasat Islamiya* (Beirut: Dar al-Tanwir, 1982), pp. 317–46.

17. "Limadha Ghaba Mabhath al-Insan," p. 229. Elsewhere, he ironically noted that although the word *insan* appears sixty-five times in the Qur'an, this expression "has not entered into the structure of systematic theology as an independent subject." See Hanafi, *Min al-'Aqida*, Vol. I, p. 226.

18. Hanafi was acutely aware of the fate of earlier thinkers who were attacked in this manner, including 'Ali 'Abd al-Raziq (d. 1966) and Taha Husayn (d. 1973), both of whom ran afoul of accusations of unbelief directed against them by conservative Muslims offended by their efforts to renovate Islamic thought and practices.

NOTES 257

19. Hanafi, "Limadha Ghaba Mabhath al-Insan," pp. 299–300.
20. The term "heritage" is a translation of the word *turath*. This word has been central to a wide array of seminars, symposiums, conferences, and debates in the Arab world over the last several decades. While it cannot be translated by a single term without the risk of loss of the rich overlay of connotations and associations attached to it, it is perhaps not amiss to render it in English as the ensemble of concepts, ideas, and propositions associated with the full range of subjects central to Islamic thought, including systematic theology, jurisprudence, philosophy, mysticism, theosophy, rhetoric, elocution, grammar, syntax, morphology, linguistics, etc.
21. Hanafi, "Limadha Ghaba Mabhath al-Insan," p. 300.
22. Ibid. Hanafi's remarkable decentering of God seems to open the door to precisely the sorts of accusations of unbelief from which he wishes to remain immune.
23. Hanafi, "Limadha Ghaba Mabhath al-Tarikh fi Turathina al-Qadim," p. 317.
24. Ibid., p. 319.
25. Curiously, for a thinker influenced by Marxism, Hanafi talks about *linear* movement and dynamics as indispensable for historicization. He does not mention dialectical movement at all – at least, not in this essay.
26. Ibid., p. 321.
27. Ibid.
28. Ibid., p. 322.
29. Hanafi, *Min al-'Aqida*, Vol. I, p. 9.
30. Ibid., p. 12.
31. Ibid., p. 17.
32. Ibid., p. 35.
33. Ibid., p. 38.
34. Hanafi, "Limadha Ghaba Mabhath al-Tar'ikh?" p. 322.
35. Hanafi, *Min al-'Aqida*, II, p. 126.
36. Hanafi, "Limadha Ghaba Mabhath al-Tarikh," p. 325.
37. Hanafi, "al-Judhur al-Tarikhiyyah li Azmat al-Hurriyyah wa al-Dimuqratiyyah fi Wijdanina al-Mu'asir," *al-Mustaqbal al-'Arabi*, no. 5 (January 1979), pp. 130–39, at 130.
38. Nasr Hamid Abu Zayd, *Naqd al-Khitab al-Dini* (Cairo: Sina' li al-Nashr, 1992), pp. 138–139.
39. Muhammad 'Imara, "al-Wa'y bi al-Tarikh wa al-Mustaqbal al-'Arabi," in 'Imara, *Dirasat fi al-Wa'y bi al-Tarikh* (Beirut: Dar al-Wahda li al-Taba'ah wa al-Nashr, 1981). In fact, only this third chapter deals explicitly with the concept of historical consciousness.
40. Ibid., p. 17.
41. Ibid., p. 21. When 'Imara says "everybody," I take him to mean his countryman Hasan Hanafi, but no doubt also 'Abdallah Laroui.
42. Ibid., p. 16.
43. Ibid.
44. Ibid., p. 17.
45. Ibid., p. 22.

46. Ibid., pp. 21–23.
47. Ibid., p. 23. Exactly what he means by the "non-dialectical, non-social method" is open to conjecture. Perhaps he means that it is a method opposed to that utilized by Marxists?
48. 'Ali's opponents were al-Zubayr b. al-'Awwam, Talhah b. 'Ubayd Allah, 'Abd Allah b. 'Umar, Zayd b. Thabit, Sa'id b. al-'As, Mu'awiyah b. Abi Sufyan, and 'Amru b. al-'As.
49. 'Imara, "al-Wa'y bi al-Tarikh," pp. 23–5. According to 'Imara, Iskafi underscored four points about the first great schism (fitna) in Islam: (1) the social struggle against economic oppression was the motive force behind the rebellion against the caliph, 'Uthman (d. 656) – 'Ali's predecessor; (2) the oath of allegiance to 'Ali was at the initiative of the rebels, who occupied Medina at that time; (3) the Quraysh, the tribe of the Prophet, and their wealthy supporters gave 'Ali their oath of allegiance under the influence of these rebels and did so in the hope that their political, social, and economic stature would be enhanced under the new dispensation; (4) the resulting dispute between 'Ali and his opponents was over wealth, since the day following his investiture 'Ali is said to have undertaken a social revolution to end distinctions of ethnicity, tribe, or chronology of conversion. The dominant historical tradition in looking at this period, according to 'Imara, has ignored these arguments based on material vested interests in favor of idealized or idiosyncratic explanations stressing cultural variables.
50. Ibid., p. 21.
51. Ibid., p. 22.
52. Ibid., p. 27.
53. Muhammad 'Imara, *Ma'alim al-Manhaj al-Islami* (Cairo: Dar al-Shuruq, 1991).
54. The International Institute for Islamic Thought has its headquarters in Cairo and Kuala Lumpur, and its publications in English are published in Herndon, Virginia – a suburb of Washington DC. As noted later in this volume, its objective is to facilitate the Islamization of knowledge, a goal that was established as early as 1971 by a group of Muslim scholars living in North America, who held their first international conference on this topic at Illinois State University.
55. 'Imara, *Ma'alim al-Manhaj*, p. 8. *Ijtihad*, or the resort to independent reasoning in order to adduce a legal rule in the event that the scripture (Qur'an and Sunna of the Prophet) were silent on the issue, had long been marginalized in Sunni Islamic thought until Muhammad 'Abduh (d. 1905) tried to rescue it from oblivion. 'Imara has seen himself as an exponent of 'Abduh's thought, and in this book he tries to explain the Muslims' reluctance to resort to *ijtihad* by reference to "fear and emotionalism."
56. Note his reification of "Western thought."
57. Presumably, he is here referring to Western ideas and political/economic domination.
58. 'Imara, *Ma'alim al-Manhaj*, p. 14.
59. See, for example, Hasan Hanafi, "al-Judhur al-Tarikhiya li Azmat al-Hurriyah wa

al-Dimuqratiyah fi Wijdanina al-Muʿasir, al-Mustaqbal al-ʿArabi 5 (January 1979), pp. 130–39.
60. On the importance of ibn Rushd for the project of the "Islamic left," a movement established by Hanafi in Egypt in the late 1970s, see Abu Zayd, Naqd al-Khitab al-Dini, p. 120. See also Hanafi's praise for ibn Rushd as a lonely voice against Ashʿarism's inimical influences in Hanafi, "al-Judhur al-Tarikhiya," p. 136. On Hanafi's problems with al-Ghazali, especially the latter's vindication of personal experience and perceptivity, discovery and instinct as against reason and science, see ibid., p. 138.
61. ʿImara, Maʿalim, pp. 44–6.
62. Ibid., p. 46.
63. As Hanafi put it: "We have inherited the position of the Ashʿaris. God is the creator of acts and responsible for their absence. Human capability was denied prior to and after the act. It was allowed only for the duration of the action, bereft of the ability to bring about [subsequent] action. Human action was a mere occasion for God to intervene and produce the real action. The human being had no past, nor a future history to come. The human being's act became suspended in the present, without time nor history. He was not responsible for his past actions nor for the future consequences of his [present] actions. Unhappily, the Muʿtazila did not endure long enough to confirm human capability in our consciousness as far as what comes before and after an action is concerned, and to confirm human responsibility for past and future actions. What can three centuries of Muʿtazilism do as against fourteen centuries [sic] of Ashʿarism?" Hanafi, "Limadha Ghaba Mabhath al-Tarikh," p. 325.
64. Abu Zayd, Naqd al-Khitab, pp. 39–40. Abu Zayd maintains that al-Ghazali was falling into linguistic formalism and suggested that his use of words such as fiʿl (act/action), faʿil saniʿ (fabricating producer) and sabab (cause) were highly idiosyncratic.
65. Hanafi, al-Judhur al-Tarikhiya, p. 136.
66. ʿImara, Maʿalim al-Manhaj, p. 124.
67. Ibid.
68. Ibid., pp. 101–2.
69. ʿImara has been advocating recourse to ijtihad from the very beginning of his career. His doctoral dissertation, entitled "The Theory of the Imamate and the Philosophy of Rule among the Muʿtazila (Nazariya al-Imama wa Falsafat al-Hukm ʿinda al-Muʿtazila), already anticipated this emphasis, which was to become further articulated in at least his earlier works. That dissertation became the basis for his book Islam wa Falsafat al-Hukm (1977). In his preface to its fourth edition, ʿImara wrote that he hoped that that edition would be the beginning of "a great project" to bring together contending viewpoints on state, religion, and authority so as to promote ijtihad in the face of the Arabs' contemporary problems. See his Al-Islam wa Falsafat al-Hukm (Cairo: Dar al-Shuruq, 1989), p. 6.
70. Indeed, ʿImara himself takes note of this "crisis" in his book, Azmat al-Fikr al-Islami (Cairo: Dar al-Sharq al-Awsat li al-Nashr, 1990).

71. Hanafi holds that the traditional starting point of the science of the foundations of religion ('ilm usul al-din) is praise of God and His prophet, rooted in pure belief, expressing a purely subjective faith. The trouble is, for Hanafi, that the "early fundamentalist learned person" (al-'alim al-usuli al-qadim) declares this endears him to pure belief as though his point of departure were his conclusions, and that there is nothing between the point of departure and the conclusions he reaches except fun and games and filling a gap. The problem is that this traditional scholar lacked methods of proof, failed to propose problems for solution. We need such methods, to make problematic what traditional scholars took for granted, argues Hanafi. For the mere expression of belief in the faith is the antithesis of proof and means the forfeiture of science. It is precisely this forfeiture that Hanafi claims he will reverse in his magnum opus, "the possibility of reconstructing the heritage in order to give the current age a new push toward progress." See Hanafi, Min al-'Aqida ila al-Thawra, Vol. I (Cairo: Maktaba Madbuli, 1988), p. 5.
72. Ibid., p. 33.
73. Ibid., p. 243.
74. 'Imara, al-Islam wa Falsafat al-Hukm, pp. 18–19, where he ringingly endorses the Mu'tazila, "this oppressed group," to which he wishes "to see justice done."
75. Abu Zayd, Naqd al-Khitab al-Dini, p. 121.
76. 'Imara, Islam wa Huquq al-Insan: Darurat, La Huquq (Cairo: Dar al-Shuruq, 1989), p. 18. Later he writes: "Islam's sanctification of human freedom reached the point that made human reason the path to grasping the existence of the divine presence." (p. 23).
77. Ibid., pp. 9–10.
78. For example, ibid., p. 17, where he says that Sunni Islam enshrines human reason, and that "the human being's attainment of maturity means the exercise of ijtihad in matters of religion and worldly affairs."
79. 'Imara, Ma'alim, p. 14.
80. 'Imara, al-Turath fi Daw' al-'Aql (Beirut: Dar al-Wahdah, 1980). The ten individuals in question were Abu Bakr, 'Umar, 'Uthman, 'Ali, Talhah b. 'Ubayd Allah, Zubayr b. 'Awwam, Sa'b b. Abi Waqqas, 'Abd al-Rahman 'Awf, Sa'd b. Zayd, and 'Amru b. Nufayl.
81. 'Imara, al-Islam wa Huquq al-Insan, p. 33.
82. Muhammad 'Abid al-Jabiri, al-Turath wa al-Hadatha (Beirut: Markaz Dirasat al-Wahda al-'Arabiya, 1991), pp. 31–2.
83. Such inconsistencies are brought out lucidly by Fu'ad Zakariya, al-Haqiqa wa al-Wahm fi al-Haraka al-Islamiya al-Mu'asira (Cairo: Dar Qaba' li al-Taba'a wa al-Nashr, 1998), pp. 18 ff.
84. See Shahrough Akhavi, "Islam, Politics and Society in the Thought of Ayatullah Khomeini, Ayatullah Taliqani, and 'Ali Shari'ati," Middle Eastern Studies, 24:4 (October 1988), pp. 404–31.
85. See Shahrough Akhavi, "Shari'ati's Social Thought," in Religion and Politics in Iran: From Quietism to Revolution, ed. Nikki R. Keddie (New Haven: Yale University Press, 1983), pp. 125–44.

86. Ruhullah Khomeini, *Islam and Revolution*, ed. and trans. Hamid Algar (Berkeley: Mizan Press, 1981), pp. 357–8, 406.
87. Ibid., pp. 368, 406, 424.
88. Ibid., pp. 370–96.
89. Ibid., pp. 356, 351, 409–10. Here we see Khomeini's predilection for Sufism, for which the individual's merging with the divinity is the ultimate goal in the human being's search for meaning.
90. Ibid., p. 376.
91. Khomeini, *Hukumat-i Islami*, 3rd edn (Najaf: n.p., 1391 HQ/1971), pp. 7–8.
92. 'Ali Shari'ati, *Islamshinasi* (Tehran: Husayniya-yi Irshad, n.d.), p. 53.
93. Ibid., pp. 69–70.
94. 'Ali Shari'ati, *Jabr-i Tarikh* (Tehran: n.p. 1354 HSh/1975), pp. 56–9.
95. Shari'ati, *Islamshinasi*, pp. 69–70.
96. Ibid., pp. 451–4.
97. Ibid., pp. 453–4.
98. Ibid.
99. Ibid.
100. Shari'ati, *Jabr-i Tarikh*, pp. 47–9.
101. Ibid., pp. 51–2.
102. Ibid., pp. 53–4.
103. Ibid., pp. 61, 65.
104. Ibid., p. 64.
105. Shari'ati, *Insan, Marksizm, Islam*. 2nd edn (Qum: n. p. 1355 HSh/1976), p. 26.
106. Cf. his comments in *Intizar: Mazhab-i I'tiraz* (Tehran: Husayniya-yi Irshad, 1355 HSh/1976), pp. 41–2: "Intizar is a historical determinism. Here am I, waiting in this corner of the world and this moment of history – it is possible that tomorrow or at any other moment a revolution will occur over the surface of the globe on behalf of truth, justice, and the oppressed masses in which I, too, must play a role. This revolution will not be [through] praying and dying but instead by the flag, sword, armor, and true *jihad* ... thus I believe in historical determinism, not chance historical occurrence. ... I here believe that history is moving deterministically toward the victory of justice, the decisive salvation of the oppressed masses, and the inevitable annihilation of oppression and oppressors." With this formulation of historical change, Shari'ati draws a contrast with Marxism, for which – he claims – "history, itself, like a living society, is independent of individuals." Ibid., p. 42. In his view, if Marxism may be said to have accorded any agency to the human being in historical change, it was really with Lenin and Mao that a break was made with the "dogmatic and dry" scientism and "sociologism" of the nineteenth century. For this notion, see Shari'ati, *Khud Sazi-yi Inqilabi* (Tehran: Husayniya-yi Irshad, n.d.), pp. 131–2.
107. On Soroush's intellectual positions, see *Reason, Freedom, and Democracy in Islam: Essential Writings of Abdolkarim Soroush*, trans. Mahmoud Sadri and Ahmad Sadri (New York: Oxford University Press, 2000); for secondary literary, consult, inter alia, Mehrzad Boroujerdi, *Iranian Intellectuals and the West: The Tormented Triumph of Nativism* (Syracuse: Syracuse University Press, 1996).

108. Soroush, *Reason, Freedom and Democracy*, p. 190.
109. The concept of the "Islamization of Knowledge" was coined by a group of Muslim scholars resident in the West who, in the aftermath of the June War of 1967 in the Middle East – a war that Egypt, Syria, and Jordan badly lost to Israel – established an organization in 1971 to "modernize" contemporary Muslims' understandings of the social world. Its founders held their convening conference in 1971 on the campus of Illinois State University. The ambitious task of these scholars and their supporters has been to Islamize all the disciplines. The main centers of research activity on the part of this group are in Herndon VA, Cairo, and Kuala Lumpur. Although Shi'ites are not excluded from participating, the Islamization of Knowledge movement is dominated by Sunni scholars and writers.
110. For Muntaziri's thought, see Shahrough Akhavi, "The Thought and Role of Ayatollah Hossein'ali Montazeri in the Politics of Post-1979 Iran," *Iranian Studies* 41:5 (December 2008), pp. 645–66.

FOUR

1. A.K.S. Lambton, *State and Government in Medieval Islam* (New York: Oxford University Press, 1988), p. xv.
2. I.R. Netton and Mawil Y. Izzi Dien, "Shakhs," *Encyclopaedia of Islam*, 2nd edn, Vol. IX (Leiden: E.J. Brill 1997), p. 217.
3. 'Abd al-Karim Zaydan, *al-Fard wa al-Dawla fi al-Shari'a al-Islamiya* (Baghdad: Matba'a Salman al-'Azmi, 1965). A later edition was published in Kuwait in 1978, but I could not secure a copy
4. Ibid., p. 13.
5. Ibid.
6. Mahmud al-Sharqawi, *al-Fard wa al-Mujtama' fi al-Islam* (Cairo: Maktaba Anglo-Misriya, 1960).
7. Ibid., p. 11.
8. Ibid., p. 138. He does not specify the title or any of the details of Hocking's book, including the page from which he found this citation. But one assumes that he is referring to Hocking's *The Spirit of World Politics with Special Studies of the Near East* (New York: Macmillan, 1932). Hocking allegedly continues: "At times, some people ask whether the Islamic system can produce new thoughts and promulgate independent laws appropriate for the demands of contemporary life. The answer to this question is that it has within itself all the wherewithal for growth; and as for its capacity for development, it surpasses many comparable systems and laws. The difficulty is not the *shari'a*'s lack of means for growth and resurgence, but rather the lack of inclination to utilize them."
9. Sayyid 'Abd al-Hamid Mursi, *al-Fard wa al-Mujtama' fi al-Islam* (Cairo: Maktaba Wahba, 1989).
10. Ibid., pp. 108–13.
11. Ibid., pp. 113–14.

NOTES 263

12. Leonard Binder, *Islamic Liberalism* (Chicago: University of Chicago Press, 1988).
13. Muhammad 'Imara, *Hal al-Islam Huwa al-Hall?* 2nd edn (Cairo: Dar al-Shuruq, 1998), p. 84.
14. Ibid., *passim*.
15. Ibid., p. 84.
16. Fu'ad Zakariya, *al-Haqiqa wa al-Wahm fi al-Haraka al-Islamiya al-Mu'asira* (Cairo: Dar Qaba' li al-Taba'a wa al-Nashr, 1998), pp. 14–16.
17. Hasan Hanafi, "Limadha Ghaba al-Insan min Turathina al-Qadim?" *Dirasat Islamiya* (Cairo: Maktaba Anglo-Misriya, 1981), pp. 393–415.
18. Ibid., p. 393.
19. Ahmad Amin, *Duhat al-Islam*, Vol. III (Cairo: Matba'a al-Nahda al-Misriya, 2000), p. 207.
20. I do not mean regnant in the Middle East, of course, even though liberalism has been one of the competing, non-Islamic models of politics in that region.
21. Especially in his revised version of *A Theory of Justice* (Cambridge: Harvard University Press, 1999).
22. David Gauthier, *Morals by Agreement* (New York: Oxford University Press, 1986).
23. Muhammad 'Imara, *Hal al-Islam Huwa al-Hall?* (Cairo: Dar al-Shuruq, 1995), p. 130.
24. Ibid., p. 132.
25. Ibid., p. 71.
26. Ibid., p. 200.
27. Ibid., p. 201.
28. C.B. Macpherson, *The Political Theory of Possessive Individualism: Hobbes to Locke* (New York: Oxford University Press, 1964), p. 3.
29. Elizabeth A. Mayer, *Islam and Human Rights*, 3rd edn (Boulder: Westview Press, 1999).
30. Wajih Kawtharani, "al-Mujtama' al-Madani wa al-Dawla fi al-Tarikh al-'Arabi," in *al-Mujtama'al-Madani fi al-Watan al-'Arabi wa Dawruhu fi Tahqiq al-Dimuqratiya* (Beirut: Markaz Dirasat al-Wahda al-'Arabiya, 1992), pp. 119–131, at p. 119.
31. Ibid., pp. 119–120. Kawtharani notes that sometimes the first word in the modern concept of civil society is rendered in contemporary Arabic by the expression *ahli*, rather than *madani*. But he notes that *ahl* (people, members, folk, kin) and its adjectival form, *ahli*, refer to groups whose basic characteristic is membership in Islam and allegiance to its *umma*. Rather than discard the phrase *al-mujtama' al-ahli*, however, Kawtharani in fact prefers it to the more commonly utilized *al-mujtama' al-madani*. The ground upon which he does so is that the former term better characterizes "the relations between Arab society in history – seen as a vessel within which is produced politics, culture, commodities, relationships of exchange – on the one hand, and the state as a ruling body that organizes and regulates the relationships of these people, on the other hand." Ibid., p. 120.
32. Ahmd 'Abd al-Mu'ti Hijazi, "Taqdim," in Haytham Mana', *Huquq al-Insan fi*

al-Thaqafa al-'Arabiya al-Islamiya (Cairo: Markaz al-Qahira li Dirasat Huquq al-Insan, 1995), p. 6.
33. Haytham Mana', Huquq al-Insan fi al-Thaqafa al-'Arabiya al-Islamiya (Cairo: Markaz al-Qahira li Dirasat Huquq al-Insan, 1995), p. 23.
34. Ibid., p. 22.
35. Ibid., p. 65. Mana' puts it this way: "One of the greatest contemporary tragedies is the consideration that the fundamental freedoms [vouchsafed by human rights schemes, such as the Declaration of the Rights of Man of 1789 or the Universal Declaration of Human Rights of 1948] contradict Islam and force it into battle with human rights... The central concept of punishment has been linked [in Islam] to the divine essence, rather than that of the human being."
36. Wael Hallaq, *A History of Islamic Legal Theories: An Introduction to Sunni Usul al-Fiqh* (New York: Cambridge University Press, 1997), p. 245. See pp. 245–54 for an excellent review of Shuhrur's theory of limits.
37. *Al-Kitab wa al-Qur'an: Qira'a Mu'asira* (Damascus: al-Ahali li al-Taba'a wa al-Nashr wa al-Tawzi', 1990; and Cairo: Sina' li al-Nashr, 1992)
38. *Direasat Islamiya Mu'asira fi al-Dawla wa al-Mujtama'* (Damascus: al-Ahali li al-Taba'a wa al-Nashr wa al-Tawzi', 1994).
39. *Nahwa Usul Jadida li al-Fiqh al-Islami* (Damascus: al-Ahali li al-Taba'a wa al-Nashr wa al-Tawzi', 2000).
40. *Mashru' Mithaq al-'Amal al-Islami* (Damascus: al-Ahali li al-Taba'a wa al-Nashr wa al-Tawzi', 1999); trans. into English by Dale Eickelman and Ismail S. Abu Shehadeh and published by the same press, 2000.
41. Shuhrur, al-Kitab wa al-Qur'an: Qira'a Mu'asira (Cairo: Sina' li al-Nashr, 1992), pp. 453 ff.
42. Soroush, "Some of Our Religious Intellectuals Are Still Afraid of Being Called Liberal or Secular," www.drsoroush.com/English/News_Archive/E-News-20061027.html.
43. Soroush, "We Should Pursue Shari'ati's Path, But We Should Not Be Mere Followers," www.drsoroush.com/English/Interviews/E=Int-Shariati_June2008.html.
44. "Interview Soroush: Enlightenment and Philosophy in Islam," *ISIM Review* 20 (Autumn 2007), pp. 36–7.

FIVE

1. Eric Wolf, "Inventing Society," *American Ethnologist* 15:4 (November 1988), pp. 752–61, at p. 752.
2. Ibid., p. 754.
3. W. Montgomery Watt has distinguished between what he terms Sunni Islam's "constitutionalism" and Shi'ism's "autocracy" – by which he means that Sunnis choose the leader (caliph), whereas in Shi'ism leadership inheres in the imam as a matter of his divinely bestowed charisma. Clifford Geertz has substituted "contractualism" for "constitutionalism" and "intrinsicality" for "autocracy," terminology endorsed by Frederick Denny. This seems to

suggest contactarian themes. But Watt's point relates to political legitimacy, not to social contract principles, which are thoroughly suffused with ideas of natural law and natural rights. See W. Montgomery Watt, *Islamic Philosophy and Theology* (Edinburgh: Edinburgh University Press, 1962), pp. 52–3. Frederick M. Denny, *An Introduction to Islam*, 2nd edn (London: Macmillan 1994), pp. 92–3, 104. One might hold that Ibadi Muslims, a more moderate branch of the puritanical Kharijites – the first schismatics of Islam – and now mainly located in Oman, eastern Africa, northwestern Libya, and southern Algeria, have a "contractualist" interpretation of their leaders' rule, whereby unjust rulers may be removed by the 'ulama' who appointed them. But such obligation is rooted not in natural law and natural rights but, rather, in divine law and Allah's rights. Ibadi doctrine requires just rule by leaders because politics is ordained by God and not an artifact of independent human action. At any rate, the Ibadi views are not relevant for Sunnism.
4. As an imported idea, it would be considered *bid'a* or *ibtikar* (unwarranted innovation) by Muslim traditionalists. On Tahtawi's and Kemal's interest in social contract and natural law, see respectively Albert Hourani, *Arabic Thought in the Liberal Age, 1798–1937* (London: Oxford University Press, 1962), pp. 69–70, 75; and Serif Mardin, *The Genesis of Young Ottoman Thought* (Princeton: Princeton University Press, 1962), pp. 289–36.
5. Barker argues that St Thomas Aquinas was an important precursor of social contract theory because he reflected a liberalism rooted in a blend of the Bible, Roman law and Aristotelian concepts of politics. See Ernest Barker, "Introduction," in *Social Contract: Essays by Locke, Hume and Rousseau*, ed. and trans. E. Barker (New York: Oxford, 1960).
6. *'Ahd* appears twenty-nine times in the Qur'an and means "covenant" or "promise." In verbal forms, it appears seventeen times, meaning "to stipulate, to make a covenant." Most references are to God's covenants with prophets and peoples, but some are to agreements among people.
7. *'Aqd* appears only once as a noun, in Qur'an 5:1: "O believers, fulfill your contracts." In verbal form it appears twice, signifying "to make" or "to swear a compact" – once referring to a marriage contract and once to God's punishment of those who break their oaths or promises.
8. *Bay'* appears seven times in the Qur'an, meaning "commercial traffic, trafficking" or "bargain." The traffic/trafficking in question refers to trade, profits from which God warns will not avail at the time of reckoning. Once, in Qur'an 9:111, the reference is to believers' rejoicing in the bargain they have made with God. The word also appears seven times in verbal form to connote "making a bargain" or "contract," "swearing fealty," "swearing an oath;" "to sell;" "to traffick with one another." Almost always these refer to exchanges between believers and the Prophet. *Bay'a* (swearing allegiance to the leader) does not appear in the Qur'an, although it was shortly to become an important concept in the Muslim theory of rule.
9. *Mawthiq* appears three times in the Qur'an, meaning "covenant," "agreement," "pledge." Each reference appears in Sura 12 in regard to the story of Joseph and his brothers.

10. In the Qur'an *mithaq* means "covenant," "compact," solemn agreement," "treaty. It appears twenty-five times, usually in reference to God's covenants with various prophets and peoples.
11. Murray Forsyth, "Hobbes's Contractarianism: A Comparative Analysis," in *The Social Contract from Hobbes to Rawls*, ed. David Boucher and Paul Kelly (New York: Routledge, 1994), p. 38.
12. Majid Khadduri, *War and Peace in the Law of Islam* (Baltimore: Johns Hopkins University Press, 1955), pp. 7–9; Mardin, *The Genesis*, 82–92.
13. Barker, "Introduction," p. x.
14. John Locke, "An Essay Concerning the True Original Extent and End of Civil Government," in Barker, ed. *Social Contract*, p. 87.
15. Jean-Jacques Rousseau, "The Social Contract," in ibid., p. 185.
16. Kevin E. Dodson, "Autonomy and Authority in Kant's *Rechtslehre*," *Political Theory* 25:1 (February 1997), pp. 93–111.
17. Malcolm H. Kerr, *Islamic Reform* (Berkeley: University of California Press, 1966), p. 162.
18. Ibid.
19. 'Abd al-Raziq, *al-Islam wa Usul al-Hukm* (Cairo: Matba'a Misr, 1925), *passim*.
20. I do not mean to imply by the expression "patronage by the regime" that writers were essentially acting at the behest of the state. Rather, I mean that prior to the June War neither the government nor most influential intellectuals were particularly interested in elaborating thought that was founded in Islamic traditions. Indeed, the most creative thought in the realm of political theory seemed to be based on secular leftist thought (whether non-Marxist or Marxist), the chief rival of which appeared to be some variant of pluralist approaches.
21. Suha Taji-Farouki, *Modern Muslim Intellectuals and the Qur'an* (New York: Oxford University Press, 2006), p. 179.
22. Muhammad Ahmad Khalaf Allah, *al-Qur'an wa al-Dawla* (Cairo: Maktaba Anglu-Misriya, 1973?), p. 31.
23. Ibid., pp. 9–10.
24. Khalaf Allah, *Dirasat fi al-Nuzum wa al-Tishri'a al-Islamiyya* (Cairo: Maktaba Anglu-Miriyya, 1977), pp. 9–12; also Khalaf Allah, *al-Qur'an*, pp. 138–9.
25. Khalaf Allah, *Mafahim Qur'aniyya* (Kuwait: Matabi' al-Risala li al-Majma' al-Watani li al-Thaqafa wa al-'Ulum wa al-Adab, 1984), p. 87.
26. Khalaf Allah, *al-Usus al-Qur'aniyya li al-Taqaddum* (Cairo: Kitab al-Ahali, 1984), p. 20.
27. Ibid., pp. 39–40.
28. Khalaf Allah, *Dirasat*, pp. 3–9, 49.
29. Ibid., p. 49. Of great interest are his use of the term "public opinion" and his anachronistic application of it to the earliest period of Islam.
30. Ibid., p. 50.
31. Khalaf Allah, *al-Qur'an*, pp. 48–9. *Maslaha* does not appear in the Qur'an. A few jurists in later centuries – notably, al-Juwayni (d. 1085), al-Ghazali, and al-Tawfi (d. 1316) – did address this concept. According to Khadduri, "Maslaha," *Encyclopedia of Islam*, 2nd edn, Vol. VI (Leiden: E.J. Brill, 1991), pp.

739–40, by al-Ghazali's time, *maslaha* was a "mature concept" that meant the furthering of the Muslims' *manfa'a* (benefit, utility), and averting *madarra* (that which is harmful), and more broadly signified the final purpose of the *shari'a*. That purpose included preserving Islam, preserving the life of the Muslim and his progeny and property, and maintaining human reason. Al-Ghazali classified *maslaha* into three categories. Two of these, namely "needs" (*hajjiyyat*) and "improvements" (*tahsinat*), could be the basis of a juridical opinion (*hukm*) only if the jurist could identify a relevant canonical text through the use of analogical reasoning (*qiyas*). But the third category, which he called "necessities" (*darurat*), needs no analogical reasoning and may simply be invoked directly as a source of law. For example, what are the believers' options against enemies who use captured Muslims as shields in a battle? May they attack their enemies, even though this might result in the deaths of these captives, given the proscription against taking the life of a devotee of the faith? Al-Ghazali's response is that necessity requires them to fight the enemy at the risk of the captives' death, because if the enemy triumphs, they would jeopardize the whole Muslim community. Al-Tawfi went beyond al-Ghazali by maintaining that the observance of the Muslims' interest always overrides even primary principles of the faith in the domain of social relations. Yet *maslaha* remained a marginal concept of jurisprudence for centuries because jurists frowned on resorting to independent judgment (*ijtihad*) to derive a legal ruling, stressing instead transmitted evidence (*naql*) and imitation (*taqlid*). In the late nineteenth and early twentieth centuries, due to the efforts of 'Abduh and Rida, "under the impact of Western legal thought the concept of *maslaha* has become the subject of an increasing interest among jurists." Khadduri, "Maslaha," p. 739. What made this development possible was 'Abduh's equation of *shari'a* with natural law. Rida in particular sought to vindicate the argument that the expression of the public interest – *maslaha* – was the basis for reinterpreting the *shari'a* to facilitate adaptation to modern circumstances. Under Rida's stewardship, al-Tawfi's elaboration of *maslaha* was resuscitated in the pages of the journal of the *salafiyya* movement, *al-Manar*, in 1905, the very year of 'Abduh's death.

32. Khalaf Allah, *al-Qur'an*, pp. 49–51.
33. Ibid., p. 55.
34. Khalaf Allah, *Dirasat*, pp. 3–4, 52–4; *al-Qur'an*, pp. 50–51.
35. Khalaf Allah, *al-Qur'an*, pp. 70–74.
36. Ibid., pp. 83–7.
37. Ibid., p. 120.
38. Ibid., pp. 115, 157, 172–3. As he puts it, "The state of the public good is the state that rules according to the principles revealed by God, that treats all the Muslims equally and achieves in the heart of the Islamic community extensive mutual responsibility at the expense of the wealthy and in favor of the needy and the poor."
39. Ibid., p. 106.
40. Ibid., p. 119; see also Khalaf Allah, *Mafahim*, pp. 27–8.
41. Khalaf Allah, *al-Qur'an*, pp. 175–6.

42. Ibid., p. 189.
43. Khalaf Allah, Mafahim, pp. 18–28.
44. Ibid., pp. 42–3.
45. Ibid., pp. 73–86.
46. Khalaf Allah, al-Usus, p. 7. This is a remarkable rendition, as it seems to place the Qur'an in the service of human beings, rather than considering human beings to be in the service of God and His book. We have earlier encountered a similar anthropocentric view in the writing of Hasan Hanafi.
47. Leonard Binder, Islamic Liberalism (Chicago: University of Chicago Press, 1988), p. 246.
48. Roel Meijer, "History, Authenticity and Politics: Tariq al-Bishri's Interpretation of Modern Egyptian History," Occasional Paper no. 4 (Amsterdam: Middle East Research Associates, 1989), p. 41.
49. Binder, Islamic Liberalism, p. 246.
50. Tariq al-Bishri, Bayna al-Islam wa 'Uruba (Cairo: Dar al-Shuruq, 1998), p. 27.
51. Bishri excludes the nineteenth-century Ottoman Tanzimat reforms (1830s–70s) and those of Muhammad 'Ali and his successors in Egypt (1805–79) from this list because he perceived them to have culturally surrendered to the West. Yet, he does admit that they sought to modernize the state "in the service of an Islamic political existence." Tariq al-Bishri, al-Hiwar al-Islami al-'Ilmani (Cairo: Dar al-Shuruq, 1996), pp. 10–12.
52. Tariq al-Bishri, Manhaj al-Nazar fi al-Nuzum al-Siyasiyya al-Mu'asira li Buldan al-'Alam al-Islami (Cairo: Dar al-Shuruq, 2005), pp. 46–7.
53. Ibid., p. 47.
54. Ibid., pp. 70, 72.
55. Tariq al-Bishri, al-Haraka al-Siyasiyya fi Misr, 1945–1952 (Cairo: n.pub., 1972), pp. 505–6.
56. Tariq al-Bishri, al-Muslimun wa al-Aqbat fi Itar al-Jama'a al-Wataniyya (Beirut: Dar al-Wahda, 1982).
57. Perhaps in keeping with his drift away from structuralist historical analysis and towards Islamic apologia, Bishri's most recent work on the Copts is much less forgiving of the role played by this religious minority. Now, he criticizes the Copts for their isolation, which he considers to be intentional and, apparently, unprovoked. See Tariq al-Bishri, al-Jama'a al-Islamiyya: al-'Uzla wa al-Indimaj (Cairo: Kitab al-Hilal, 2005).
58. Tariq al-Bishri, al-Malamih al-'Amma li al-Fikr al-Siyasi al-Islami fi al-Tarikh al-Mu'asir (Cairo: Dar al-Shuruq, 1996), pp. 5–6.
59. Tariq al-Bishri, Mahiya al-Mu'asira (Cairo: Dar al-Shuruq, 1996), p. 11.
60. Bishri, al-Malamih, pp. 75–6.
61. Ibid., p. 50.
62. Ibid., pp. 82–3.
63. Ibid., pp. 83–5.
64. Ibid., pp. 90–91.
65. Bishri, al-Hiwar, pp. 37–8.
66. Frank Griffel, "The Harmony of Natural Law and Shari'a in Islamist Theology," in Shari'a: Islamic Law in the Contemporary Context, ed. Abbas Amanat and Frank

Griffel (Stanford: Stanford University Press, 2007), p. 61.
67. Ibid., al-Malamih, p. 91.
68. Bishri, Bayna al-Islam, p. 26.
69. Ruhollah Khomeini, Kashf-i Asrar (Tehran? n.pub., 1363 HQ/1943/44).
70. On Khomeini's doctrine of wilayat al-faqih, see Joseph Eliash, "Misconceptions Concerning the Juridical Status of the Iranian 'Ulama'," *International Journal of Middle East Studies* 10:1 (February 1979), pp. 9–25; Shahrough Akhavi, "Contending Theories in Shi'ite Law on the Doctrine of Wilayat al-Faqih," *Iranian Studies*, 29:3–4 (Summer-Fall, 1996), pp. 228–68.
71. Ruhollah Khomeini, Hukumat-i Islami, 3rd edn (Najaf: n.p., 1971), p. 121.
72. Ibid., p. 112.
73. Ibid., p. 121.
74. Ruhollah Khomeini, Kitab al-Bay', 5 vols (Qom: Matba'a-yi Isma'iliyan, 1409 HQ/1988), 2: 478–82.
75. Said Arjomand, *The Turban for the Crown* (New York: Oxford University Press, 1988), pp. 177–8.
76. Ni'matullahi Salihi Najafabadi, Vilayat-i Faqih: Hukumat-i Salihan (Tehran: Mu'assasah-yi Khadamat-i Farhang-i Rasa', 1364 HSh/1984), pp. 45–6, 22–3.
77. Ibid., pp. 31–2.
78. Ibid., p. 36.
79. Ibid., p. 38.
80. Ibid., pp. 46–7.
81. Ibid., p. 50.
82. Ha'iri, Hikmat va Hukumat (London: Intisharat-i Shadi, 1995), p. 54.
83. Ibid., pp. 54–5.
84. Ibid., p. 55.
85. Ibid., p. 58.
86. Ibid., pp. 61–2.
87. Ibid., p. 62.
88. Ibid., pp. 63–4.
89. Ibid., p. 65.
90. Ibid., pp. 70–82.
91. Ibid., pp. 84–5.
92. Ibid., pp. 89–90.
93. Ibid., pp. 91–2.
94. Ibid., pp. 92–5.
95. Ibid., pp. 92–7.
96. Ibid., pp. 102–5.
97. Ibid., pp. 105–8.
98. Ibid., pp. 108–9.

SIX

1. Max Weber, "Politics as a Vocation," in *From Max Weber: Essays in Sociology*, ed. Hans. H. Gerth and C. Wright Mills (New York: Oxford University Press, 1958), pp. 77–128, at p. 78; emphasis in the original.

2. To take only one example, Muhammad Sa'id al-'Ashmawi, *al-Khilafa al-Islamiya* (Cairo: Sina li al-Nashr, 1990), p. 16.
3. Patricia Crone, *God's Rule: Government and Islam* (New York: Columbia University Press, 1994), p. 3.
4. Bernard Lewis, *The Political Language of Islam* (New York: Cambridge University Press, 1988), pp. 35–6.
5. Critics of Mawdudi, Qutb, and their followers have made two points about these verses and the uses to which they have been put by the Islamists. The first is that they have instituted a sudden change in the interpretation of words that were understood to connote judging and arbitrating with that which translates the meanings into ruling. In other words, this criticism regards Mawdudi's and Qutb's interpretations to be unacceptable heretical innovation (*bid'a*). The second criticism is that the context of the verses is that the references are not to Muslims but to "the people of the book," and more particularly to the Jewish people. Thus, even if the verses connote what Mawdudi and Qutb maintain they do, it is a moot point, because the referents are not the believers (Muslims).
6. For the effort by the leading Iraqi Shi'i jurist Muhammad Baqir al-Sadr (d. 1980) to legitimate the Islamic state through the Qur'an, in this case, Q. 5:44, see Chibli Mallat, *The Renewal of Islamic Law* (Cambridge: Cambridge University Press, 1993), pp. 62–7.
7. Ali 'Abd al-Raziq, *al-Islam wa Usul al-Hukm* (Cairo: Matba'a Misr, 1925).
8. Muhammad 'Imara, *al-Islam wa Usul al-Hukm: Dirasa wa Watha'iq bi Qalam Muhammad 'Imara* (Beirut: al-Mu'assasa al-'Arabiya li al-Taba'a wa al-Nashr, 1974), p. 44.
9. Ibid.; author's italics removed.
10. Ibid., pp. 49–50.
11. Even though he takes this position, 'Imara earlier in his career had maintained that the caliphate was not a divinely ordained institution but rather "civil" (*madani*) in nature. See *Al Dawla al-Islamiyya bayna al-'Almaniyya wa al-Sulta al-Diniyya* (Beirut: Dar al-Shuruq, 1988), p. 15.
12. Muhammad 'Imara, *Islamiyat al-Ma'rifa* (Cairo, Madinat al-Nasr: Dar al-Sharq al-Awsat, 1991).
13. Ironically, in claiming precedence for Islam, 'Awwa cites Qur'an 12:40 and Qur'an 5:45, 47 and 48, which we have already discussed earlier in this chapter as favorite verses of the Islamists, as evidence of Islamic revelation's preoccupation with a theory of the state. But these verses actually apply to the "people of the book," and more specifically to the people of the Jewish faith. See Muhammad Salim al-'Awwa, *Fi al-Nizam al-Siyasi li al-Dawla al-Islamiya*, 7th edn (Cairo: Dar al-Shuruq, 1989), p. 23.
14. Husayn Fawzi al-Najjar, *al-Islam wa al-Siyasah: Bahth fi Usul al-Nazariyah al-Siyasiyah wa Nizam al-Hukm fi al-Islam* (Cairo: Dar al-Sha'b, 1977).
15. 'Awwa, *Fi al-Nizam*, pp. 21 ff.
16. Democracy, of course, is a type of regime, and different states have different regimes. A regime is really a set of rules that regulate how political power is utilized. Democratic regimes have rules that seek to decentralize that

power and open up optimum access points to political constituencies for the purposes of influencing the use of power. States, as opposed to regimes, are political organizations that, as Weber stressed, claim the monopoly of the legitimate use of violence across an extent of territory.
17. 'Awwa, Fi al-Nizam, p. 24.
18. Ibid.
19. Ibid., p. 25.
20. Ibid., pp. 26–7.
21. Albert Hourani, *Arabic Thought in the Liberal Age* (New York: Oxford University Press, 1962), pp. 5–6.
22. Ibid., pp. 49–61.
23. Ibid., pp. 55–6.
24. Ibid., pp. 60–62.
25. Ibid., pp. 63–4.
26. Ibid., pp. 133–4.
27. Muhammad Sa'id al-'Ashmawi, *al-Khilafa al-Islamiya* (Cairo: Sina li al-Nashr, 1990), p. 235.
28. Muhammad Shuhrur, "al-Dawla," in Shrhrur, *Dirasat Islamiya Mu'asira fi al-Dawla wa al-Mujtama'* (Damascus: al-Ahali li al-Taba'a wa al-Nashr wa al-Tawzi', 1994), pp. 179–80.
29. Ibid., p. 180. It is true that Marx speculated about the possibility of that state as an actor autonomous from the base of society in his discussion of the French state under the rule of Louis Napoleon. See Marx's *Eighteenth Brumaire of Napoleon Bonaparte* (1851), where he wrote that occasionally a state may hover above its own society, without roots in any particular social class. But it is not clear whether Shuhrur is mindful of this, and he certainly does not invoke it.
30. Ibid.
31. Ibid., pp. 180–81.
32. Ibid., p. 182.
33. Ibid., pp. 184–5.
34. Ibid., p. 186.
35. Ibid.
36. Ibid., pp. 186–7.
37. Ibid., pp. 187–8.
38. The Prophet's consultation with his Companions, incidentally, had to do with issues of war, such as what to do with POWs and whether or not to meet the enemy head-on in an offensive charge or to maintain defensive positions and meet the foe when it attacked. Whether such a restricted practice can be rendered into the concept of "freedom of belief" and "freedom of expression," of course, is hardly self-evident.
39. Shuhrur, "al-Dawla," p. 188.
40. Ibid., pp. 188–9.
41. Ibid., pp. 189–90.
42. Ibid., pp. 190–91.
43. Ibid., pp. 191–2.

44. Ibid., p. 192.
45. Ibid., p. 193.
46. Ibid., pp. 193–4.
47. Of course, pro-Zionist Jews (or "righteous Gentile Christians," for that matter) would not be covered by his analysis and would presumably have to pay the poll tax, since they would be supporting a state that drove Muslims from their homes and aided in their exile.
48. Ibid., pp. 195–6.
49. Ibid., p. 196.
50. On these concepts, see the previous chapter's discussion of Shuhrur in the context of the role of the individual in society.
51. Shuhrur, "al-Dawla," pp. 196–7.
52. Ibid., pp. 198–9.
53. Ibid., p. 199.
54. Ibid., p. 200.
55. Ibid., pp. 201–2.
56. On this point, see Elizabeth A. Mayer, *Islam and Human Rights*, 3rd edn (Boulder: Westview Press, 1999), *passim*.
57. Shuhrur, "al-Dawla," pp. 202–3.
58. These famous phrases appear in Marx's *Contribution to the Critique of Hegel's Philosophy of Right* (1843) and *The Eighteenth of Brumaire of Napoleon Bonaparte* (1852).
59. Shuhrur, "al-Dawla," p. 203.
60. In certain respects, Shuhrur is echoing the laments of Jamal al-Din al-Afghani and Muhammad 'Abduh more about a century and a half earlier that the problems of the Muslims are to a great extent due to the negative influence of the 'ulama'.
61. Shuhrur, "al-Dawla," p. 203.
62. Ibid., pp. 204–6.
63. Published by I.B. Tauris in London in 1995.
64. *Nazariyah-ha yi Dawlat dar Fiqh-i Shi'a* (Tehran: Nashr-i Nay, 1376 H.Sh.).
65. *Hukumat-i Vila'i* (Tehran: Nashr-i Nay, 1377 H.Sh.).
66. *Pluralizm-i Dini* (Tehran: Ruznamah-yi Salam, 1378 H.Sh.).
67. Yasuyuki Matsunaga, "Mohsen Kadivar, An Advocate of Postrevivalist Islam in Iran," *British Journal of Middle Eastern Studies*, 34:3 (December 2007), p. 321.
68. Muhsin Kadivar, *Nazariyyaha-yi Dawlat dar Fiqh-i Shi'a*, pp. 57–188.

SEVEN

1. Michaelle Browers, *Democracy and Civil Society in Arab Political Thought: Transcultural Possibilities* (Syracuse: Syracuse University Press, 2006).
2. Zakariya, *al-Haqiqa wa al-Wahm*, pp. 7–11.
3. Ibid., pp. 12–13.
4. Ibid., p. 13.
5. Muhammad 'Imara, *Hal al-Islam Huwa al-Hall?* (Cairo: Dar al-Shuruq, 1995), p. 202.

6. See www.drsoroush.com/English/Interviews/E-INT-Neo-Mutazilite_July 2008.html. It is curious that he finds Aristotle to be non-empiricist. Certainly Aristotle is considered highly empirical in regard to his political theory (as opposed to Plato). But this does not detract from Soroush's general point that the Mu'tazilites are, in his view, overly formalistic.

Bibliography

Abaza, Mona. *Debates on Islam and Knowledge in Malaysia and Egypt.* London: Routledge, 2002.
'Abd al-Karim, Khalil. "Awjuh Manfiyah li al-Fikr al-'Arabi al-Islami al-Mu'asir: Dirasah Shamilah Naqdiyah 'an Kitab Yusuf al-Qaradawi, *al-Hall al-Islami Faridah Wajibah*," *Qadaya Fikriyah* 11 (July 1995), pp. 259–68.
'Abd al-Raziq, Ali. *al-Islam wa Usul al-Hukm.* Cairo: Matba'a Misr, 1925.
Abu-Rabi', Ibrahim M. *Intellectual Origins of Islamic Resurgence in the Modern Arab World.* Albany: SUNY Press, 1995.
Abu Zayd, Nasr Hamid. *Al-Nass, al-Sulta al-Haqiqa: al-Fikr al-Dini bayna Irada al-Ma'rifa wa Irada al-Haymana*, 3rd edn. Casablanca and Beirut: al-Markaz al-Thaqafi al-'Arabi, 1997.
Akhavi, Shahrough. "Contending Theories in Shi'ite Law on the Doctrine of *Wilayat al-Faqih,*" *Iranian Studies* 29:3–4 (Summer–Fall 1996), pp. 228–68.
———. "The Dialectics of Contemporary Egyptian Social Thought: The Traditionalist and Modernist Discourses of Sayyid Qutb and Hasan Hanafi," *International Journal of Middle East Studies* 29:3 (August 1997), pp. 377–401.
———. "Islam, Politics and Society in the Thought of Ayatullah Khomeini, Ayatullah Taliqani, and 'Ali Shari'ati," *Middle Eastern Studies* 24:4 (October 1988), pp. 404–31.
———. "Shari'ati's Social Thought," in *Religion and Politics in Iran: From Quietism to Revolution*, ed. Nikki R. Keddie, pp. 125–44. New Haven: Yale University Press, 1983.
———. "Shi'i Theories of Social Contract," in *Shari'a: Islamic Law in the Contemporary Context*, ed. Abbas Amanat and Frank Griffel, pp. 137–55. Stanford CA: Stanford University Press, 2007.
———. "Sunni Modernist Theories of Social Contract in Contemporary Egypt," *International Journal of Middle East Studies* 35:1 (February 2003), pp. 23–49.

———. "The Thought and Role of Ayatollah Hossein'ali Montazeri in the Politics of Post-1979 Iran," *Iranian Studies* 41:5 (December 2008), pp. 645–66.

Amin, Ahmad. *Duhat al-Islam*, 10th edn, Vol III. Cairo: Matba'a al-Nahda al-Misriya, 2000.

Arjomand, Said, ed. *Authority and Political Culture in Shi'ism*. Albany NY: SUNY Press, 1988.

———. *The Shadow of God and the Hidden Imam*. Chicago: University of Chicago Press, 1984.

———. *The Turban for the Crown*. New York: Oxford University Press, 1988.

Arkoun, Mohamed (Muhammad Arkun), *al-Fikr al-Islami: Qira'a 'Ilmiya*, 2nd edn, trans. Hashim Salih. Casablanca and Beirut: Markaz al-Anma' al-Qawmi and al-Markaz al-Thaqafi al-'Arabi, 1996.

Arnold, Peter. *Nationalism*. London: Edward Arnold, 1994.

Asad, Talal. *Formations of the Secular: Christianity, Islam, Modernity*. Stanford CA: Stanford University Press, 2003.

'Ashmawi, Muhammad Sa'id. *Al-Islam al-Siyasi*. 2nd edn. Cairo: Sina' li al-Nashr, 1989.

———. *Al-Khilafa al-Islamiya*. Cairo: Sina' li al-Nashr, 1990.

al-'Awwa, Muhammad Salim. *Fi al-Nizam al-Dawla al-Islamiya*, 7th edn, pp. 133–4. Cairo: Dar al-Shuruq, 1989.

Ayubi, Nazih. *Overstating the Arab State*. London: I.B. Tauris, 1995.

Azmeh, Aziz. *Islam and Modernities*. London: Verso, 1996.

———. *The Times of History: Universal Topics in Islamic Historiography*. Budapest: Central European University Press, 2007.

Barker, Ernest, ed. and trans. *Social Contract: Essays by Locke, Hume and Rousseau*. New York: Oxford University Press, 1960.

Balqaziz, 'Abd al-Ilah. *Ishkaliyat al-Marji' fi al-Fikr al-'Arabi al-Mu'asir*. Beirut: Dar al-Muntakhab al-'Arabi, 1992.

Bellah, Robert N. "Civil Religion in America," *Daedalus* 96:1 (Winter 1967), pp. 1–21.

Binder, Leonard. *Islamic Liberalism*. Chicago: University of Chicago Press, 1988.

al-Bishri, Tariq. *Bayna al-Islam wa 'Uruba*. Cairo: Dar al-Shuruq, 1998.

———. *Al-Haraka al-Siyasiyya fi Misr, 1945–1952*. Cairo: n.pub., 1972.

———. *Al-Hiwar al-Islami al-'Ilmani*. Cairo: Dar al-Shuruq, 1996.

———. *Al-Jama'a al-Wataniyya: al-'Uzla wa al-Indimaj*. Cairo: Kitab al-Hilal, 2005.

———. *Mahiya al-Mu'asira*. Cairo: Dar al-Shuruq, 1996.

———. *Al-Malamih al-'Ammah li al-Fikr al-Siyasi al-Islami fi al-Tarikh al-Mu'asir*. Cairo: Dar al-Shuruq, 1996.

———. *Manhaj al-Nazar fi al-Nuzum al-Siyasiyya al-Mu'asira li Buldan al-'Alam al-Islami*. Cairo: Dar al-Shuruq, 2005.

Blankinship, Khalid Y. *The End of the Jihad State: The Reign of Hisham 'Abd al-Malik and the Collapse of the Umayyads*. Albany NY: SUNY Press, 1994.

Boroujerdi, Mehrzad. *Iranian Intellectuals and the West: The Tormented Triumph of Nativism*. Syracuse NY: Syracuse University Press, 1996.

Browers, Michaelle. *Democracy and Civil Society in Arab Political Thought: Transcultural Possibilities*. Syracuse NY: Syracuse University Press, 2006.

Brumberg, Daniel. *Reinventing Khomeini: The Struggle for Reform in Iran.* Chicago: University of Chicago Press, 2001.
Butterworth, Charles. *Alfarabi: The Political Writings.* Ithaca NY: Cornell University Press, 2001.
———. *Philosophy, Ethics and Virtuous Rule: A Study of Averroes' Commentary on Plato's "The Republic."* Cairo: American University in Cairo Press, 1986.
———. "Political Islam: The Origins," *Annals of the American Academy of Political and Social Science* 524 (November 1992), pp. 26–37.
———. "Rhetoric and Islamic Political Philosophy," *International Journal of Middle East Studies* 3:2 (April 1972), pp. 187–98.
Butterworth, Charles, and I. William Zartman, eds, *Between the State and Islam.* New York: Cambridge University Press, 2001.
Chehabi, Hoochang. *Iranian Politics and Religious Modernism: The Liberation Movement of Iran.* Ithaca NY: Cornell University Press, 1990.
Crone, Patricia. *God's Rule.* New York: Columbia University Press, 2004.
———. *Medieval Islamic Political Thought.* Edinburgh: Edinburgh University Press, 2004.
Crone, Patricia, and Michael Cook, *Hagarism: The Making of the Islamic World.* New York: Cambridge University Press, 1977.
Dabashi, Hamid. *The Theology of Discontent: The Ideological Foundation of the Islamic Revolution in Iran.* New York: New York University Press, 1993.
Dallmayr, Fred. "Introduction: Toward a Comparative Political Theory," *Review of Politics* 59:3 (Summer 1997), pp. 421–7.
Denny, Frederick M. *An Introduction to Islam,* 2nd edn. London: Macmillan 1994.
Dodson, Kevin E. "Autonomy and Authority in Kant's Rechtslehre," *Political Theory* 25:1 (February 1997), pp. 93–111.
Eliash, Joseph. "Misconceptions Concerning the Juridical Status of the Iranian 'Ulama'," *International Journal of Middle East Studies* 10:1 (February 1979), pp. 9–25.
Enayat, Hamid, *Modern Islamic Political Thought.* Austin: University of Texas Press, 1980.
Esposito, John L. *Islam and Politics,* 3rd edn. Syracuse NY: Syracuse University Press, 1991.
Esposito, John L., and John J. Donohue, eds, *Islam in Transition: Muslim Perspectives.* 2nd edn. New York: Oxford University Press, 2007.
Euben, Roxanne. *Enemy in the Mirror: Islamic Fundamentalism and the Limits of Modern Rationalism.* Princeton NJ: Princeton University Press, 1999.
———. *Journeys to the Other Shore: Muslim and Western Travelers in Search of Knowledge.* Princeton NJ: Princeton University Press, 2006.
Fischer, Michael M.J. *Iran: From Religious Dispute to Revolution.* Cambridge MA: Harvard University Press, 1980.
Fischer, Michael, and Mehdi Abedi, *Debating Muslims.* Madison: University of Wisconsin Press, 1990.
Forsyth, Murray. "Hobbes's Contractarianism: A Comparative Analysis," in *The Social Contract from Hobbes to Rawls,* ed. David Boucher and Paul Kelly. New York: Routledge, 1994.

Gauthier, David. *Morals By Agreement*. New York: Oxford University Press, 1986.

Ghalyun, Burhan. *Ightiyal al-'Aql: Mihna al-Thaqafa al-'Arabiya Bayna al-Salafiya wa al-Tab'iya*, 2nd edn. Cairo: Madbuli, 1990.

Gibb, H.A.R. "Al-Mawardi's Theory of the Caliphate," in H.A.R. Gibb, *Studies on the Civilization of Islam*, ed. Stanford Shaw, pp. 151–65. London: Routledge & Kegan Paul, 1962.

———. "The Evolution of Government in Early Islam," *Studia Islamica* 4 (1954), pp. 5–17.

———. *Studies on the Civilization of Islam*. ed. Stanford Shaw. London: Routledge & Kegan Paul, 1962.

Griffel, Frank. "The Harmony of Natural Law and Shari'a in Islamist Theology," in *Shari'a: Islamic Law in the Contemporary Context*, ed. Abbas Amanat and Frank Griffel, pp. 38–61. Stanford: Stanford University Press, 2007.

Guillaume, Alfred. *Islam*. London: Penguin, 1955.

Haddad, Yvonne. Y. *Contemporary Islam and the Challenge of History*. Albany NY: SUNY Press, 1982.

Haim Sylvia, ed. *Arab Nationalism: An Anthology*. Berkeley: University of California Press, 1976.

Ha'iri, Mahdi. *Hikmat va Hukumat*. London: Intisharat-i Shadi, 1995.

Hallaq, Wael. *A History of Islamic Legal Theories: An Introduction to Sunni Usul al-Fiqh*. New York: Cambridge University Press, 1997.

Hanafi, Hasan. "al-Judhur al-Tarikhiya li Azmat al-Hurriyah wa al-Dimuqratiyah fi Wijdanina al-Mu'asir, al-Mustaqbal al-'Arabi 5 (January 1979), pp. 130–39.

———. "al-Liberaliya: Lam Tanjah fi Misr al-Ash'ariya," in *Hiwar al-Mashriq wa al-Maghrib*, ed. Jalul Faysal. Cairo: Madbuli, 1990.

———. "Limadha Ghaba Mabhath al-Insan min Turathina al-Qadim?" *al-Mustaqbal al-'Arabi* (Beirut), October 1979; reprinted in Hanafi, *Dirasat Islamiya*, pp. 393–415. Cairo: Maktaba Anglo-Misriya, 1981.

———. "Limadha Ghaba Mabhath al-Ta'rikh min Turathina al-Qadim?" in Hanafi, *Dirasat Islamiya*, pp. 416–56. Cairo: Maktaba Anglo-Misriya, 1981.

Hayes, Carlton J.H. *A Generation of Materialism*. New York: Harper, 1941.

Hijazi, Ahmad 'Abd al-Mu'ti. "Taqdim," in Haytham Mana', *Huquq al-Insan fi al-Thaqafa al-'Arabiya al-Islamiya*. Cairo: Markaz al-Qahira li Dirasat Huquq al-Insan, 1995.

Hodgson, Marshall. *The Venture of Islam: Conscience and History in a World Civilization*, 3 vols. Chicago: University of Chicago Press, 1974.

Hourani, Albert. *A History of the Arab Peoples*. London: Faber & Faber, 1991.

———. *Arabic Thought in the Liberal Age, 1798–1939*. London: Oxford University Press, 1962.

'Imara, Muhammad. *Al-Dawla al-Islamiyya bayna al-'Almana wa al-Sulta al-Diniyya*. Beirut: Dar al-Shuruq, 1988.

———. *Azmat al-Fikr al-Islami*. Cairo: Dar al-Sharq al-Awsat li al-Nashr, 1990.

———. *Dirasat fi al-Wa'y bi al-Tarikh*. Beirut: Dar al-Wahda li al-Taba'a wa al-Nashr, 1981.

———. *Hal al-Islam Huwa al-Hall?* Cairo: Dar al-Shuruq, 1998.

———. *Al-Islam wa Falsafat al-Hukm*, 4th edn. Cairo: Dar al-Shuruq, 1989.

----. *Islam wa Huquq al-Insan: Darurat, La Huquq.* Cairo: Dar al-Shuruq, 1989.
----. ed. *al-Islam wa Usul al-Hukm: Dirasc wa Watha'iq bi Qalam Muhammad 'Imara.* Beirut: al-Mu'assasa al-'Arabiya li al-Taba'a wa al-Nashr, 1974.
----. *Islamiyat al-Ma'rifa.* Cairo, Madinat al-Nasr: Dar al-Sharq al-Awsat, 1991.
----. *Ma'alim al-Manhaj al-Islami.* Cairo: Dar al-Shuruq, 1991.
Inalcik, Halil. "Empire and Population," in *An Economic and Social History of the Ottoman Empire, 1300–1914,* ed. Halil Inalcik and Donald Quataert. Cambridge: Cambridge University Press, 1994.
Jabiri, Muhammad 'Abid al-. *al-Turath wa al-Hadatha.* Beirut: Markaz Dirasat al-Wahda al-'Arabiya, 1991.
Kadivar, Muhsin. *Hukumat-i Vila'i.* Tehran: Nashr-i Nay, 1377 H.Sh.
----. *Nazariyah-ha yi Dawlat dar Fiqh-i Shi'a.* Tehran: Nashr-i Nay, 1376 H.Sh.
----. *Pluralizm-i Dini.* Tehran: Ruznamah-yi Salam, 1378 H.Sh.
Karpat, Kemal. ed. *Political and Social Thought in the Contemporary Middle East.* New York: Praeger, 1968.
Kawtharani, Wajih. "al-Mujtama' al-Madani wa al-Dawla fi al-Tarikh al-'Arabi," in *al-Mujtama'al-Madani fi al-Watan al-'Arabi wa Dawruhu fi Tahqiq al-Dimuqratiya,* pp. 119–31. Beirut: Markaz Dirasat al-Wahda al-'Arabiya, 1992.
Kerr, Malcolm. *Islamic Reform.* Berkeley: University of California Press, 1966.
Khadduri, Majid. "Maslaha," Encyclopedia of Islam, 2nd edn, Vol. VI, pp. 739–40. Leiden: E.J. Brill, 1991.
----. *War and Peace in the Law of Islam.* Baltimore MD: Johns Hopkins University Press, 1955.
Khalaf Allah, Muhammad Ahmad. *Dirasat fi al-Nuzum wa al-Tashri'a al-Islamiyya.* Cairo: Maktaba Anglu-Misriyya, 1977.
----. *Mafahim Qur'aniyya.* Kuwait: Matabi' al-Risala li al-Majam' al-Watani li al-Thaqafa wa al-'Ulum wa al-Adab, 1984.
----. *Al-Qur'an wa al-Dawla.* Cairo: Maktaba Anglu-Misriyya, 1973.
----. *Al-Usus al-Qur'aniyya li al-Taqaddum.* Cairo: Kitab al-Ahali, 1984.
Khomeini, Ruhollah Musavi. *Hukumat-i Islami,* Najaf: n.pub., 1391 HQ/1971.
----. *Islam and Revolution: Writings and Declarations of Imam Khomeini,* ed. and trans. Hamid Algar. Berekely: Mizan Press, 1981.
----. *Kashf-i Asrar.* Tehran: n.pub., 1363 HQ/1943–44.
----. *Kitab al-Bay'.* 5 vols. Qom: Matba'a-yi Isma'iliyan, 1409 HQ/1988.
"Al-Kindi," Stanford Encyclopedia of Philosophy, http://plato.stanford.edu/entries/al-kindi.
Kurzman, Charles. *The Unthinkable Revolution in Iran.* Cambridge MA: Harvard University Press, 2004.
Lambton, A.K.S. "Khilafa: In Political Theory," Encyclopedia of Islam, 2nd edn, Vol. IV. Leiden: E.J. Brill, 1990.
----. *State and Government in Medieval Islam.* New York: Oxford University Press, 1988.
Lapidus, Ira. *A History of Islamic Societies.* New York: Cambridge University Press, 2002.
----. "The Golden Age: The Political Concepts of Islam," *Annals of the American Academy of Political and Social Science* 524 (November 1992), pp. 13–25.

Laroui, 'Abdallah (al-'Arwi, 'Abdallah). *La crise des intellectuels arabes: traditionalisme ou historicisme*. Paris: Maspero, 1974. English translation, *The Crisis of the Arab Intellectual: Traditionalism or Historicism*. Berkeley: University of California Press, 1976.

Laoust, H. "Ibn Taymiyya," Encyclopedia of Islam, 2nd edn, Vol. III. Leiden: E.J. Brill, 1986.

Lewis, Bernard. "'Abbasids," Encyclopaedia of Islam, 2nd edn, Vol. 1. Leiden: E.J. Brill, 1960.

———. *The Political Language of Islam*. Chicago: University of Chicago Press 1988.

Macpherson, C.B. *The Political Theory of Possessive Individualism: Hobbes to Locke*. New York: Oxford University Press, 1964.

Mallat, Chibli. *The Renewal of Islamic Law*. Cambridge: Cambridge University Press, 1993.

Mana', Haytham. *Huquq al-Insan fi al-Thaqafa al-'Arabiya al-Islamiya*. Cairo: Markaz al-Qahira li Dirasat Huquq al-Insan, 1995.

Mardin, Serif. *The Genesis of Young Ottoman Thought*. Princeton NJ: Princeton University Press, 1962.

———. *Religion and Social Change in Modern Turkey*. Albany: SUNY Press, 1989.

———. *Religion, Modernity and Society in Turkey*. Syracuse NY: Syracuse University Press, 2006.

Matsunaga, Yasuyuki. "Mohsen Kadivar, An Advocate of Postrevivalist Islam in Iran," *British Journal of Middle Eastern Studies* 34:3 (December 2007), pp. 317–29.

Mawsilili, Ahmad. *Al-Fikr al-Islami al-Mu'asir: Dirasat wa Shakhsiyat. Sayyid Qutb: Bahth Muqaran li Mabadi' al-Usuliyin wa al-Islahiyin*. Beirut: Dar Khidr, 1990.

———. *The Islamic Quest for Democracy, Pluralism and Human Rights*. Gainesville: University Press of Florida, 2001.

———. *Qira'ah Nazariyah Ta'sisiyah fi al-Khitab al-Islami al-Usuli : Nazariyat al-Ma'rifa wa-al-Dawla wa-al-Mujtama'*. Beirut: al-Nashir li al-Taba'a wa al-Nashr wa al-Tawzi' wa al-I'lan, 1993.——— . *Radical and Moderate Islamic Fundamentalism: The Quest for an Islamic State*. Gainesville, University Press of Florida, 1999.

———. *Radical Islamic Fundamentalism: The Ideological and Political Discourse of Sayyid Qutb*. Beirut: AUB Press, 1992.

———. *Al-Usuliya al-Islamiya: Dirasa fi al-Khitab al-Aydiyulji wa al-Siyasi 'inda Sayyid Qutb*. Beirut: al-Nashir li al-Taba'a wa al-Nashr wa al-Tawzi' wa al-I'lan, 1993.

Mayer, Elizabeth A. *Islam and Human Rights*, 3rd edn. Boulder CO: Westview Press, 1999.

Meijer, Roel. *History, Authenticity and Politics: Tariq al-Bishri's Interpretation of Modern Egyptian History*, Occasional Paper no. 4. Amsterdam: Middle East Research Associates, 1989.

Moaddel, Mansoor, *Class, Politics and Ideology in the Iranian Revolution*. New York: Columbia University Press, 1993.

———. *Islamic Modernism, Nationalism and Fundamentalism: Episode and Discourse*. Chicago: University of Chicago Press, 2005.

Moaddel, Mansoor, and Kamran Talattof, eds. *Contemporary Debates in Islam*. London: Palgrave Macmillan, 2000.

Mosely, K.P. "East Wind, West Wind," *Theory and Society* 12:3 (May 1983), pp. 405–19.
Mursi, Sayyid 'Abd al-Hamid. *al-Fard wa al-Mujtama' fi al-Islam*. Cairo: Maktaba Wahba, 1989.
Musallam, Adnan. *From Secularism to Jihad: Sayyid Qutb and the Foundations of Radical Islamism*. Westport CT: Praeger, 2005.
Najafabadi, Ni'matullah Salihi. *Vilayat-i Faqih: Hukumat-i Salihan*. Tehran: Mu'assasah-yi Khadamat-i Farhang-i Rasa, 1363 HSh/1984.
Najjar, Fauzi. "Islamic Fundamentalism and the Intellectuals: The Case of Nasr Hamid Abu Zayd," *British Journal of Middle East Studies* 27:2 (2000), pp. 177–200.
———. "State and University in Egypt in the Period of Socialist Transformation, 1961–1967," *The Review of Politics* 38:1 (January 1976), pp. 57–87.
al-Najjar, Husayn Fawzi, *al-Islam wa al-Siyasah: Bahth fi Usul al-Nazariyah al-Siyasiyah wa Nizam al-Hukm fi al-Islam*. Cairo: Dar al-Sha'b, 1977.
al-Naqib, Khaldun Hasan. *Al-Dawla al-Tasalhutiya fi al-Mashriq al-'Arabi al-Mu'sir: Dirasa Bina'iya Muqarana*. Beirut: Markaz Dirasat al-Wahda al-'Arabiya, 1991.
Netton, I.R., and Mawil Y. Izzi Dien. "Shakhs," *Encyclopaedia of Islam*, 2nd edn, Vol. IX. Leiden: E.J. Brill, 1997.
Nisbet, Robert A. "Introduction: The Problem of Social Change," in *Social Change*, ed. R. Nisbet. Oxford: Basil Blackwell, 1972.
Piscatori, James, ed. *Islam in the Political Process*. New York: Cambridge University Press, 1983.
Rawls, John. *A Theory of Justice*, rev. edn. Cambridge MA: Harvard University Press, 1999.
Rodinson, Maxime. *Islam and Capitalism*. Austin: University of Texas Press, 1976.
Rosenthal, E.I.J. *Political Thought in Medieval Islam*. Cambridge: Cambridge University Press, 1958.
Roth, Guenther. "Personal Rulership, Patrimonialism and Empire-Building in the New States," *World Politics* 20:2 (January 1968), pp. 194–206.
Sachedina, Abdul Aziz. *Islamic Messianism*. Albany: SUNY Press, 1981.
———. *Islamic Roots of Democratic Pluralism*. New York: Oxford University Press, 2001.
———. *The Just Ruler*. New York: Oxford University Press, 1988.
Salvatore, Armando. *Islam and the Political Discourse of Modernity*. Reading: Ithaca Press, 1997.
Shari'ati, 'Ali. *Insan, Marksizm, Islam*. 2nd edn. Qum: n.pub., 1355 HSh/1976.
———. *Intizar: Mazhab-i I'tiraz*. Tehran: Husayniya-yi Irshad, 1355 HSh/1976.
———. *Islamshinasi*. Tehran: Husayniya-yi Irshad, n.d.
———. *Jabr-i Tarikh*. Tehran: n.pub., 1354 HSh/1975.
———. *Khud Sazi-yi Inqilabi*. Tehran: Husayniya-yi Irshad, n.d.
al-Sharqawi, Mahmud. *al-Fard wa al-Mujtama' fi al-Islam*. Cairo: Maktaba Anglo-Misriya, 1960.
Shepard, William E. *Sayyid Qutb and Islamic Activism*. Leiden: E.J. Brill, 1996.
Shuhrur, Muhammad. *Direasat Islamiya Mu'asira fi al-Dawla wa al-Mujtama'*. Damascus: al-Ahali li al-Taba'a wa al-Nashr wa al-Tawzi', 1994

———. *Al-Kitab wa al-Qur'an: Qira'a Mu'asira*. Damascus: al-Ahali li al-Taba'a wa al-Nashr wa al-Tawzi', 1990; and Cairo: Sina' li al-Nashr, 1992.

———. *Mashru' Mithaq al-'Amal al-Islami*. Damascus: al-Ahali li al-Taba'a wa al-Nashr wa al-Tawzi', 1999; trans. into English by Dale Eickelman and Ismail S. Abu Shehadeh and published by the same press, 2000.

———. *Nahwa Usul Jadida li al-Fiqh al-Islami*. Damascus: al-Ahali li al-Taba'a wa al-Nashr wa al-Tawzi', 2000.

Soroush, Abdolkarim (Surush, 'Abd al-Karim). *Reason, Freedom, and Democracy in Islam: Essential Writings of Abdolkarim Soroush*, trans. Mahmoud Sadri and Ahmad Sadri. New York: Oxford University Press, 2000.

Sourdel, Dominique "Khilafa: The History of the Institution," Encyclopaedia of Islam, 2nd edn, Vol. IV. Leiden: E.J. Brill, 1990.

Taji-Farouki, Suha. *Modern Muslim Intellectuals and the Qur'an*. New York: Oxford University Press, 2006.

Talbi, Mohamed. "Ibd Khaldun," Encyclopedia of Islam, 2nd edn, Vol. III. Leiden: E.J. Brill, 1986.

Tarabishi, Jurj. *Al-'Aql al-Mustaqil fi al-Islam*. Beirut: Dar al-Saqi, 2004.

———. *Ishkaliyat al-'Aql al-'Arabi: Naqd 'Naqd al-'Aql al-'Arabi'*. Beirut: Dar al-Saqi, 1998.

———. *Madhbahah al-Turath fi al-Thaqafah al-'Arabiyah al-Mu'asirah*. Beirut: Dar al-Saqi, 1993.

Tibi, Bassam. *Arab Nationalism: Between Islam and the Nation-State*. New York: St. Martin's Press, 1997.

———. *The Challenge of Fundamentalism: Political Islam and the New World Disorder*. Berkeley: University of California Press, 2002.

Van Ess, Josef. "Kadariyya," Encyclopaedia of Islam, 2nd edn, Vol. IV. Leiden: E.J. Brill, 1990.

Watt, W. Montgomery. *Islamic Philosophy and Theology*. Edinburgh: Edinburgh University Press, 1962.

———. *Muhammad: Prophet and Statesman*. London: Oxford University Press, 1961.

———. "The Significance of the Early Stages of Imami Shi'ism," in *Religion and Politics in Iran: From Quietism to Revolution*. New Haven: Yale University Press, 1983.

Weber, Max. "Politics as a Vocation," in *From Max Weber: Essays in Sociology*, ed. Hans. H. Gerth and C. Wright Mills. New York: Oxford University Press, 1958.

Wensinck, A.J. *Concordance and Indexes of Muslim Traditions*, 4 vols. Leiden: E.J. Brill, 1992.

Wolf, Eric. "Inventing Society," *American Ethnologist* 15:4 (November 1988), pp. 752–61.

Wolin, Sheldon. "Political Theory as a Vocation," *American Political Science Review*, 63:4 (December 1969), pp. 1062–82.

———. "Political Theory: Trends and Goals," *International Encyclopedia of the Social Sciences*, Vol. XII. New York: Macmillan and Free Press, 1968.

Zakariya, Fu'ad. *Al-Haqiqah wa al-Wahm fi al-Harakah al-Islamiyah al-Mu'asirah*. Cairo: Dar Qaba' li al-Taba'a wa al-Nashr, 1998.

Zaydan, 'Abd al-Karim. *al-Fard wa al-Dawla fi al-Shari'a al-Islamiya*. Baghdad: Matba'a Salman al-'Azmi, 1965
Zubaida, Sami. *Islam, The People and the State*, 2nd edn. London: Zed Books, 1993.
———. *Law and Power in the Islamic World*. London: I.B. Tauris, 2003.

Index

'Abbasid dynasty, 17–19, 30, 52, 56, 236
'Abd al-Malik, Anwar (Anouar Abdel-Malek), 1, 88
'Abd al-Rahman III, 75
'Abd al-Raziq, 'Ali, 159, 162, 245; *Islam and the Foundations of Rule*, 200; theories of the state, 200–12
Abduh, Muhammad, 84, 101, 105, 144, 157, 158, 162, 165, 203
Abu Bakr, caliph, 54, 103, 207
Abu Hanifa, Nu'man ibn Thabit, 27
Abu al-Hudhayl al-'Allaf, 24
Abu Yusuf Ya'qub bin Ibrahim al-Ansari al-Kufi, 54
Abu Zayd, Nasr Hamid, 79, 82–3, 93, 102; prosecution of, 82
Afghanistan, 248
agrarian reform, 40, 106
ahl al-bayt (the people of the Prophet's house), 57
ahl al-shi'a (the Shi'a), 57
ahl al-sunna wa al-jama'a (the Sunnis), 57
Alexander the Great, 17

Algerian thinkers on historicization, 75–86
'Ali b. Abi Talib, 22, 57, 58, 96, 183
al-'Alim, Mahmud Amin, 88
American Constitution, 7
American revolution, 121
Amin, Samir, 88
'Amr b. 'Ubayd, 24
Anglo-Iranian Oil Company (AIOC), 45
'aql (reason-based knowledge), 62
Aquinas, St Thomas, 155
Arab nationalism, 41, 73, 78, 88
Aristotle, 3, 20, 52, 61, 63, 65, 98, 151, 185, 206, 238
Arkoun, Mohamed (Muhammad Arkun), 79–80, 117, 239
Arslan, Alp, 19
'asabiyya (social solidarity), 69–70, 170
al-Ash'ari, Abu Hasan, 25
Ash'ariyya school, 22, 25, 26, 27, 87, 92, 93, 94–105, 152, 153, 154, 156, 191, 248–9
al-'Ashmawi, Muhammad Sa'id, 211
Atatürk *see* Kemal, Mustafa

al-'Awwa, Muhammad Salim, 76–7, 206–12, 233, 246, 247
Ayubi, Nazih, 233, 245; *Overstating the Arab State*, 227–9
al-Azhar University, 36, 42

Badawi, Muhammad Taha, 209
al-Baghdadi, Abu al-Mansur, 20, 31, 52
ibn Bajja, Abu Bakr Muhammad ibn Yahya (Avempace), 66
Balqaziz, 'Abd al-Ilah, 75–6, 117, 239
al-Baqillani, Abu Bakr, 20
Ba'th Party (Syria), 124
ibn Battuta, Abu 'Abdullah Muhammad, 126
bay'a (oath of allegiance), 209–10
bayt al-mal (exchequer), 18
Berlin Wall, fall of, 125
Binder, Leonard, 2, 128, 168
al-Biruni, Abu Rayhan, 126
al-Bishri, Tariq, 49, 162, 168–76, 193, 243–4
Boullata, Issa J., 2
British colonialism, 39–40, 42, 43, 44, 45, 48, 240
Browers, Michaelle, 2
Burujirdi, Ayatollah Husayn, 106, 179
Buyid dynasty, 19, 53, 70, 236
Byzantium, 13

Cain and Abel story, 111
Cairo University, 36
caliphate, 13, 14, 16, 18, 20, 30, 159, 196, 201, 205, 218, 233, 238, 246; collapse of, 19, 164, 237; functions of, 53–4; in Cordoba, 75; Mongol destruction of, 71; re-establishment of, 199, 202, 208–9, 246; Sunni theory of, 52–6
Catholic Church, 132
causality, concepts of, 98, 100
Christianity, 12, 26, 137
Cicero, 70, 155
citizen, words for, 139

civil, etymology of, 138–9
civil rights, 192
civil society, 137–8, 139, 161, 228
classical period, 11–16
clergy, 181–2; rise of, 10
clientelism, 139
communism, 127; *see also* Marxism
Confucius, 3
Constantine Affair, 173
constitutionalism, 145, 240
contractualism, 159, 163, 170, 178
contradiction, 110, 112, 225
Copts, 173
Council of Experts, 184
Croce, Benedetto, 93
Crone, Patricia, 196
customs, changing of, 224

Dallmayr, Fred, 4–5
Dar al-'Ulum University, 36
date palms Hadith, 15
Dawisha, Adeed, 2
dawla (state), 196
Day of Judgment, 221, 225
democracy, 88, 103, 104, 145, 207, 217, 219, 224, 232, 233, 240, 246, 247; crisis of, 223
Democrat Party (Turkey), 38–9
de-sacralized model of politics, 71
Descartes, René, 131
determinism, historical, 113
din wa dawla (religion and state), 14, 200, 205
din wa dunya (religion and secular affairs), 14
divorce, 119, 143
diwan al-kharaj (land tax), 18
double contract, doctrine of, 170
Durkheim, Émile, *The Division of Labor in Society*, 127

Eastern Question, 34
Egypt, 39–43, 48–9, 124, 159–61, 168, 172; independence of, 40;

INDEX 285

legal system of, 173; national project of, 174–5; thinkers on historicization, 75–86, 75
Enayat, Hamid, 2
Erbakan, Necmettin, 39
exploitation, 228

al-Farabi, Abu Nasr, 21, 52, 65, 66, 71, 72, 126, 237, 237, 238
fard (individual), 121
farmanrava (ruler), 181
Fascism, 40
fatalism, 142, 223
Fatima, 8, 57
Fatimid dynasty, 19, 53, 58
fatwa (legal ruling), 109
fiqh (jurisprudence), 218
fiqh-i puya (dynamic jurisprudence), 106, 144
fitra (good nature), 137
free will, 113, 131
French imperialism, 240
French Revolution, 33, 121
Fu'ad, King, 202–3

Gabriel, archangel, 84
Gadamer, Hans-Georg, 8
Galen, 20
Gauthier, David, 134, 147, 241
General Will, 175
Ghalyun, Burhan, 79–82, 117, 239; *The Assassination of Reason*, 80
al-Ghazali, Abu Hamid, 20, 31, 54–5, 98, 99, 100, 126, 208, 238; *The Incoherence of the Philosophers*, 64, 105
Ghaznavid dynasty, 19
Gibb, H.A.R., 13
Gorbachev, Mikhail, 125
government, establishment of, 15
Gramsci, Antonio, 88, 228–9
Greece, 38; Ancient, 3
Greek philosophy, 4, 20, 61–70; translation of, 22, 61

Grotius, Hugo, 188–9

Hadith, 15, 28, 140, 180, 190, 208, 248
Haim, Sylvia, 1
Ha'iri Yazdi, Ayatollah Mahdi, 178, 179, 184–92, 193, 230, 244, 245; *Philosophical Wisdom and Government*, 184
hakim (judge; governor, ruler), 181
Hallaq, Wael, 141
Hamdanid dynasty, 19
Hammurabi, 3
Hanafi, Hasan, 86–94, 98, 99, 101, 102, 104, 105, 117, 130, 239; *From Belief to Revolution*, 93; "The Methods of Exegesis", 86; "Why Has the Study of History Been Absent in Our Old Heritage?", 89, 90; "Why Has the Study of the Human Being Been Absent in Our Old Heritage?", 89
Hanafi school, 28, 31, 54
hanifiyya (curvature), 222
ibn Hanzala, 'Umar, 180–81
Harun al-Rashid, 75
Hasan, son of Muhammad Ibn Hanafiyya, 23
ibn Haytham, Abu 'Ali al-Hasan, 126
ibn Hazm, Abu Muhammad 'Ali ibn Ahmad ibn Sa'id, 94, 126, 208
Hegel, G.W.F., 185, 212, 224, 225
hegemony, 228–9
hidden being, 114
Hidden Imam see Imam, twelfth
Hindu thought, 4
hisba (calling to moral account), 247
Hisham ibn 'Abd al-Malik, 13
historical determinism, 113, 115
historicity, 86, 90, 94–105, 107, 109–15, 115–16, 159, 168, 174, 218, 239, 240, 249; concept of, 79; of religious texts, 83
history, philosophy of, 95

Hizbullah, 199
Hobbes, Thomas, 131, 156, 191
Hocking, William Earnest, 125
Hourani, Albert, 1, 36, 210
al-hukm (judgment, rule), 167, 184, 198
hukuma (government), 197
human rights, 141, 225; concept of, 139
Husayn, 'Adil, 49
Husayn, Taha, 202
Husayn b. 'Ali, 23

ijma' (consensus), 43
ijtihad, 95, 97, 100–101, 102, 106, 109, 112, 115, 144, 145, 157, 159, 162, 173, 216
Imam, twelfth, 179, 237; occultation of, 59–60
imamate, 201, 206–7, 240, 245; theory of, 56–61, 176, 237
'Imara, Muhammad, 49, 86–94, 94–105, 117, 128, 134, 135, 136, 146, 202–6, 211, 233, 239, 241, 246, 247; *Islam and Historical Consciousness*, 248; *Studies in Historical Consciousness*, 94
imperial Islamic society, 14
independence of Middle Eastern countries, 35
individual, 1, 142, 172, 187, 192, 225, 241; accountability of, 206; freedom of, 219; in Western thought, 132; position of, 119–48; rights of, 123, 128, 243
individualism, 153; possessive, 136; theory of, 122
al-insan (human being), 140
intizar (awaiting, especially the return of the Hidden Imam in Shi'ism), 107, 115
Iran, 34, 43–7, 199, 230, 232, 246, 248; Constitutional Revolution, 46, 60, 177; Iranian Revolution,
10, 46, 87, 178
al-Iskafi, Abu Ja'far Muhammad b. 'Abd Allah, 96, 97
Islam: anthropocentric, 90; as liberal religion, 129; as religion and state, 74; as true religion, 80; crisis of, 130; historicity of, 218; political positions within, 222; resurgence of, 135, 170, 171; rise of, 11; seen as democratic, 103; seen as ennobling the individual, 114; system of rule, 85
Islamic left, 87
Islamism, 47, 88; militant, 161
Islamization of knowledge, 48, 116, 117, 130, 136, 206, 239, 245–7
Israel, 1967 war, 41, 47
istiqama (straightness), 222

al-Jabiri, Muhammad 'Abid, 87, 104, 99
jabr (determinism), 99
jabr-i tarikh (historical determinism), 113
jahiliya (age of ignorance), 149–50
al-Jahiz, Abu 'Uthman 'Amr ibn Bahr, 144
ibn Jama'a, Badr al-Din, 20, 31, 55, 56, 70, 158, 208
jama'a (group), 150
Jews, 26
jihad (exertion for the sake of God), 16, 66, 211
jizya (poll tax), 219, 221
Judaism, 12
justice: as fairness, 242; concept of, 61–2

Kadivar, Muhsin, 230–31, 233, 245; *The Government of Vilayat*, 230; *Theories of the State in Shi'ite Law*, 230
Kant, Immanuel, 131, 156, 157, 186
Karpat, Kamal, 1

ibn Kathir, Isma'il, 209
Kautilya, 3
Kawtharani, Wajih, 138
Kemal, Mustafa (Atatürk), 38, 44
Kemal, Namik, 152
Kerr, Malcolm, 1, 158–9
Khalaf Allah, Muhammad Ahmad, 162–8, 173, 193, 243–4
ibn Khaldun, Abu Zayd 'Abd al-Rahman b. Muhammad, 20, 52, 66–70, 72, 75, 91, 126, 138, 236, 238; *The Prolegomenon*, 67
Khalid, Shaykh Khalid Muhammad, 83–5, 157
Khatami, Muhammad, 47
Khawarij movement, 22
Khilafat Movement, 202
Khomeini, Ayatollah Ruhollah, 9, 46, 47, 59, 60–61, 105, 106–9, 116, 117, 179–81, 183, 193, 199, 230–31, 232, 239, 244, 245, 246, 247, 248; *Islamic Government*, 60, 178; *Revealing the Secrets*, 178; critique of, 233
al-Khuli, Shaykh Amin, 162
al-Kindi, Abu Yusuf Ya'qub ibn Ishaq, 21, 66
kingship *see* monarchy
al-Kirmani, Hamid al-Din, 58

Lambton, Ann, 119, 120
land reform *see* agrarian reform
Lapidus, Ira, 10, 14
Laroui, 'Abdallah ('Abdallah al-'Arwi), 77, 86, 239
law, natural, 151, 155, 172–3, 176, 191, 192, 244
leadership, 8–9, 56, 153, 155, 181, 204; of umma, 56–61, 103, 201
Lenin, V.I., 36, 88
Lewis, Bernard, 31
liberalism, 8, 88, 128, 129–30, 146, 240, 241, 247; meaning of, 132–4, 147

Libya, 36
life chances, 129
limits, 226, 247; theory of, 143, 144, 212–26, 243
Locke, John, 131, 150, 156, 191
Luther, Martin, 131

Ma'bad al-Juhani, 23
Macpherson, C.B., 136, 147, 241–2
al-madina al-fadila (the virtuous city), 21
al-Mahdi, imam, 58, 59–60
Mahmud of Ghazna, 53
malik (king), 16
Malik Shah, 19
Maliki school, 68, 72
al-Ma'mun, 26
al-Mansur, caliph, 56
Mardin, Serif, 1
marriage, 119, 143; annulment of, 82
Marwan al-Dimashqi al-Qubti, 23
Marx, Karl, 212
Marxism, 7, 34, 40, 42, 47, 79, 88, 95, 96, 110, 111, 168, 213, 225, 227, 247; abandonment of, 49
al-Mas'udi, Abu al-Husayn 'Ali ibn al-Husayn, 126, 209
maslaha mursala (public interest), 43, 159
masses, faith in, 169
al-Maturidi, Abu Mansur Muhammad, 26
Maturidiyya thought, 22, 26–7
al-Mawardi, Abu al-Hasan, 31, 52, 70, 154, 158, 208, 236; *Al-Ahkam al-sultaniyya*, 3, 53–4
Mawdudi, Abu al-A'la, 197–8, 232, 244
Mayer, Elizabeth A., 137
medieval period, 11, 17–19
Medina, 12, 28, 50, 84, 141, 200, 220; Constitution of, 210; mosque of, 103
Mencius, 3

messengers, 215
milla (religious community; nation), 196
minorities, rights of, 221
ibn Miskawayh, Abu 'Ali Ahmad ibn Muhammad ibn Ya'qub, 75, 126
modernism, 169
modernization, 44, 171
monarchy, 9, 10, 48, 68, 177, 201, 204, 216, 230, 231, 238; incompatibility with Islam, 106
Mongols, 19; destruction of caliphate, 71; sack of Baghdad, 200
moral relativism, 225
Morocco, thinkers on historicization, 75–86
Mu'tazila thought, 22, 24, 75, 83, 94, 96, 102, 131, 144, 191, 248
Mubarak, Husni, 41, 125
Muhammad, Prophet, 8, 12, 14, 15–16, 28, 63, 84, 85, 103–4, 106, 109, 122, 135, 137, 138, 141, 142, 153, 163, 166, 200, 201, 202, 209, 215, 216, 217, 220, 222, 247, 248; authority of, 203–4; revelation of, 226
Muntaziri, Ayatollah Husayn 'Ali, 118
Murji'a thought, 22, 23
Mursi, Sayyid 'Abd al-Hamid, 146, 241; *The Humanism of Arab Socialism*, 125; *The Individual and Society in Islam*, 125
Musaddiq, Muhammad, 45, 178
Muslim Brotherhood, 40, 41, 76, 124, 206
Muslims, conception of the world, 89–90
Mutawakkil, caliph, 131

al-Nahda, 36
Najafabadi, Ayatollah Ni'matallah Salihi, 178, 182–4; *Guardianship of the Jurist: Government by the Righteous*, 179
Najjar, Fauzi, 206
naql (transmitted knowledge), 62
Naqshbandi order, 58
Naraqi, Mulla Ahmad, 179–80
Nasser, Gamal Abdel, 41, 42, 124, 160
Nasserism, 162, 245
National Front (Iran), 49
neo-Platonism, 71, 238
Nisbet, Robert, 74
Nizam al-Mulk, 31; *Siyasatnama*, 3
nomocracy, 31–2
nomos (law), 65
nubuwa (prophecy), 214

oath of allegiance, 209–10, 246
objective truth, 7
occultation of Imam, 59–60, 107, 112, 115 *see also* Imam, twelfth
organic intellectuals, 88
Ottoman Empire, 29–32, 50, 236, 237; collapse of, 37
ownership, 189–90

Pahlavi, Muhammad Reza, 44, 106, 178
pan-Arabism, 37, 160
particularization, 216
party politics: activity in the Middle East, 139 *see also* pluralism, political
patriarchy, 223
patrimonialism, 17, 50
people of the book, 219–20
People's Mujahidin of Iran (PMOI), 49
Persia, 13
Persian thought, 4
piety, 140, 222
pious dissimulation (taqiya), 9, 71, 237
Plato, 3, 20, 52, 61, 65, 71, 77, 185, 206, 238; *Republic*, 61, 65

pluralism, political, 219, 220, 247
political parties, Islamic, 219
political theory: comparative, 3, 4–5; conceptualization of, 2, 3–4; Middle Eastern, 5–7
Polybius, 70
popular election, 154
printing press, introduction of, 33
private property, 133, 189–90
prophets, 215
Ptahhotep, 3
public goods, 133
punishment, 141, 144

Qadariyya thought, 22, 23–4
Qur'an, 25, 26, 28, 53, 55, 58, 59, 77, 79, 80, 83, 103, 104, 108, 109, 112, 121, 122, 134, 135, 138, 142–3, 152, 162, 164, 167, 168, 172, 177, 180–81, 197–8, 220; as work of literature, 82; sacralization of, 143; temporality of, 83; verses of (2:247, 163; 2:256, 205, 207; 3:26, 163; 3:64, 124; 3:104, 166; 3:159, 205; 4:58, 120, 154, 167; 4:58–59, 180–81; 4:59, 165; 4:83, 165; 5:1, 184; 5:45–48, 198; 5:54, 248; 39:36–38, 124; 42:38, 186, 205; 49:13, 140, 202; 60:8–9, 220, 221; 60:9, 221; 9:29, 221; 12:40, 198; 12:67, 198; 109:6, 205)
Qutb, Sayyid, 124, 176, 197, 232, 244

rationalism, 81
Rawls, John, 134, 147, 241
Refah party (Turkey), 39
religion: civil, 51; sacred, 51
religious brotherhoods, 137, 171
religious perspective, divisibility of, 6
Republican People's Party (RPP) (Turkey), 38

Reza Khan, 43–4, 177
Rida, Shaykh Rashid, 101, 105, 158–9, 202
Rightly Guided Caliphs, 13, 15, 17, 20, 103, 204, 209, 211, 218, 223
rights, civil and political, 243
risala (message), 214
Rosenthal, E.I.J., 55, 62, 73
Rousseau, Jean-Jacques, 131, 156–7, 185–6, 188, 189, 191, 212
ibn Rushd, Abu al-Walid Muhammad ibn Ahmad (Averroes), 21, 52, 64, 65, 66, 71, 72, 94, 98, 99, 100, 212, 237, 238; *The Incoherence of the Incoherence*, 64–5
Russian Revolution, 43

sacred: definition of, 51; in relation to the secular, 51–73
al-Sadat, Anwar, 22, 41, 125, 160; assassination of, 87
al-Sadiq, Ja'far, 9, 176, 180
Safavid dynasty, 58, 71, 237
Saffarid dynasty, 19
Sakarya River, battle of, 38
Salafiya movement, 101–2, 203
Saljuq dynasty, 19, 31
salvation, doctrine of, 15
Samanid dynasty, 19
secular, in relation to the sacred, 51–73
secularism, 47, 48, 72, 130, 145, 175, 205, 221–2; eclipse of, 159
Selim I, 30
separation of powers, 85, 211
al-Shafi'i, Muhammad ibn Idris, 27, 28, 53
shah (king), 16
shahadat (attesting to), 107
shakhs (individual), 121–2
Shalabi, Muhammad Mustafa, 209
shari'a (Islamic law), 22, 30, 32, 42, 43, 53, 55, 56, 65, 76, 107, 119, 120, 123, 129, 165, 176, 177, 197,

206, 208, 226, 246
Shari'ati, 'Ali, 9, 49, 105, 107, 117–18, 143, 144, 240; and historicization, 109–15
al-Sharqawi, Mahmud, *The Individual and Society in Islam*, 124–5
Shi'ism, 8–9, 14, 19, 21, 45, 53, 110, 236, 239, 244, 246, 247; clergy of, 176–7; Isma'ili, 57–8; Ithna'ashari, 57–8; suppression of, 71; theories of (on social contract, 176–92, 193; on historicization, 105–7; on the imamate, 56–61; on the state, 199, 230–31, 232, 233); Zaydi, 57–8
Shuhrur, Muhammad, 148, 229, 233, 242, 245, 246; *The Book and the Qur'an*, 141–5; theory of limits, 212–26
shura (consultation), 103, 205, 217, 219, 247; concept of, 83, 85–6
al-Siba'i, Mustafa, 124
ibn Sina, Husayn, ibn 'Abdullah ibn Hasan ibn 'Ali (Avicenna), 63, 64, 65, 66, 126
al-siyasa al-'aqliyya (rational politics), 138
al-siyasa al-madaniya (civic politics), 21, 138
social contract, theories of, 243 (Shi'ite, 176–92, 193; Sunni, 151–7, 157–62, 193, 244)
socialism, 34, 42, 47, 48, 49, 88, 124, 145
society, 149–94; concept of, 243 (evolution of, 150); nature of, 1
sociology-of-knowledge approach, 7–11
sociology, Islamic science of, 126
Socrates, 3
Soroush, 'Abdol Karim ('Abd al-Karim Surush), 105, 107, 117–18, 142, 145, 148, 230, 240, 242, 246; and historicization, 115–16

sovereignty, 61, 128–9, 159, 167, 213; of God, 121, 129, 130, 146, 147, 197, 199, 232, 241, 246; of the people, 129; of *umma*, 158
state: apostate, 199, 232, 246; Arab (Ayubi's theory of, 227–9; fierceness of, 227); Arab Islamic, 212–26; conceptualization of, 1; founded on religion, 216; in Weber's definition, 196; Islamic, 109, 205, 221–2; Marxist view of, 213; model of, 39; personalization of, 196, 232, 245; power state, 238; role of, 133, 166; theories of, 195–233, 245 (in 'Abd al-Raziq al-Raziq, 200–2; Shi'ite, 199, 233; Sunni, 197–8, 232–3, 246)
Suez Canal, 40; nationalization of, 41
Sufism, 14, 18, 58, 171, 223, 224
Sulayman the Magnificent, 30
sultan (sultan), 16, 55
Sunna, 122, 138, 166, 247
Sunni Islam, 9, 21, 57, 70, 71, 108, 144, 181, 199, 236, 239; crisis in thought of, 104; theories of (on caliphate, 52–6; on constitution, 237; on social contracts, 151–7, 157–62, 193, 244; on state, 197–8, 232–3, 246)
al-Suyuti, Jalal al-Din, 208
Syria, thinkers on historicization, 75–86

al-Tabari, Muhammad ibn Jarir, 209
Taba'taba'i, Muhayyn Husayn, 182
Tahtawi, Rifa'a Rafi', 152
tajdid (renewal), 98
Talbi, Mohamed, 67, 68
Taliban, 248
tawhid (unicity), 109–10, 134, 226
taxation, 15, 17, 54, 66, 133, 219; land tax, 18
Taylor, Charles, 8
ibn Taymiyya, Taqi al-Din, 20, 31,

52, 56, 61, 70, 237, 245
Tibi, Basam, 76
de Tocqueville, Alexis, 172
tolerance, 140, 141
tribalism, 12, 13, 14, 149, 170, 228, 247
trigonometry, 33
trusts, kinds of, 167
Turkey, 37–9, 40

'ulama' (Muslim clergy), 30, 36, 44, 46, 59, 60, 61, 65, 106, 143, 177, 222, 237, 238
'Umar ibn al-Khattab, caliph, 54, 103
Umayyad dynasty, 13, 17, 30, 154, 236
umma (Muslim community), 17, 53, 54, 55, 67, 68, 150, 158, 167, 172, 196; creation of, 15; leadership of, 56–61; umma islamiyya, 167; umma qawmiyya, 168; umma wasat, 28
'umran (prosperousness), 69
Union of Soviet Socialist Republics (USSR), 125
Unitary National Progressive Bloc (Egypt), 163
United States of America (USA), 45, 106, 160
'Uthman, caliph, 54
utilitarianism, 134

velayat-i faqih [Ar. wilayat al-faqih] (guardianship of the jurist), 46, 59, 178, 179–80, 182–3, 199, 230–31, 233, 247
vocations, 62

Wafd Party (Egypt), 40
warrior ethic, 29, 30
wars of apostasy, 207
Wasil ibn 'Ata', 24
Weber, Max, 8, 11, 129
West: encounter with, 195; imitation of, 171–2
Westernization, 78, 97, 177
wizara (ministerial system), 18
Wolf, Eric, 150
Wolin, Sheldon, 4
women: rights of, 120; role of, 2, 39; votes of, 106

Yazdi, Shaykh 'Abd al-Karim, 179
Young Turks movement, 37

Zakariya, Fu'ad, 84, 85, 86, 130, 246; *Reality and Fantasy in Regard to the Contemporary Islamic Movement*, 83
zakat (alms), 54
Zaydan, 'Abd al-Karim, *The Individual and the State in Islamic Law*, 123–4